Designing a Digital Portfolio

Contents at a Glance

DESIGNING A DIGITAL PORTFOLIO

Cynthia L. Baron

New Riders

1249 Eighth Street, Berkleley, California 94710
An Imprint of Peachpit, A Division of Pearson Education

DESIGNING A DIGITAL PORTFOLIO

International Standard Book Number: 0-7357-1394-4

Library of Congress Catalog Card Number: 2003104257

Printed in the United States of America

First printing: January 2004

07   7

Trademarks

All terms mentioned in this book that are known to be trademarks or service marks have been appropriately capitalized. New Riders Publishing cannot attest to the accuracy of this information. Use of a term in this book should not be regarded as affecting the validity of any trademark or service mark.

The KODAK logo is a registered trademark of Eastman Kodak. The Kodak logo is reproduced with permission of Eastman Kodak company.

Warning and Disclaimer

Every effort has been made to make this book as complete and as accurate as possible, but no warranty of fitness is implied. The information is provided on an as-is basis. The authors and New Riders Publishing shall have neither liability nor responsibility to any person or entity with respect to any loss or damages arising from the information contained in this book or from the use of the programs that may accompany it.

Publisher
Stephanie Wall

Executive Acquisitions and Development Editor
Marjorie Baer

Production Manager
Gina Kanouse

Senior Development Editor
Jennifer Eberhardt

Senior Project Editor
Sarah Kearns

Copy Editor
Chrissy Andry

Senior Indexer
Cheryl Lenser

Proofreader
Beth Trudell

Composition
Kim Scott
Amy Hassos

Manufacturing Coordinator
Dan Uhrig

Interior Designer
Cynthia L. Baron

Cover Designer
Aren Howell

Marketing
Scott Cowlin
Tammy Detrich
Hannah Onstad Latham

Publicity Manager
Susan Nixon

DEDICATION

To my dear friend and colleague, Nancy Bernard. This book would have been a lesser thing without your generous spirit.

Table of Contents

ABOUT THE AUTHOR

 **Cynthia L. Baron** is Technical Director at Northeastern University (Boston), a lecturer in the Department of Visual Arts, and one of the founding members of the Multimedia Studies program. She also holds an MBA with a concentration in Marketing. Cynthia has been active in the creative community for most of her professional life. She has consulted for corporations and non-profits, and has published several articles in newspapers and periodicals. Cynthia is the editor of the *DesignWhys* series for Rockport Publishers and the former contributing editor to *Critique Magazine*, one of the most important design publications of the '90s. She is the author or co-author of a number of books, most recently *The Little Digital Camera Book* for Peachpit Press. Her 1996 book, *Creating a Digital Portfolio*, was the first title ever published on the topic. In her free time, she creates computer-based art, merging her poetry with illustration and photography.

About the Reviewers

These reviewers contributed their considerable hands-on expertise to the entire development process for *Designing a Digital Portfolio*. As the book was being written, these dedicated professionals reviewed all the material for technical content, organization, and flow. Their feedback was critical to ensuring that *Designing a Digital Portfolio* fits our readers' need for the highest-quality technical information.

Rita Armstrong has been a Design Recruiter for Roz Goldfarb Associates since 1988. Over the years, she has sought out and placed talented designers and design managers in packaging, digital, and industrial design. She is passionate about encouraging designers to gain the business tools they need to promote their talent. She has spoken at conferences, given seminars at design schools, and contributed to articles and books, including a chapter in Roz's own, *Careers by Design*. Before toiling in Theater, Advertising, and Non-Profit Communications, she graduated from Fordham University with a BA in Communications with a concentration in Journalism and Film.

Nancy Bernard has worked in visual communications for 25 years. With a BA from Clark University in Fine Arts and Art History, she became an illustrator and lettering designer and then a packaging project manager with Fossella Associates in Boston, Massachusetts. In 1991, she moved to California and joined Neumeier Design team as a packaging designer. When Neumeier launched the magazine, *Critique*, Nancy served as the managing editor. Since the closure of *Critique* in 2001, Neumeier Design has re-formed in San Francisco as Neutron, LLC. As Director of Collaboration, Nancy helps such organizations as Apple, HP, Kodak, Sun, and Symantec build the best brands they've ever had through facilitation, seminars, workshops, and an extensive network of terrific designers. In her free time, she continues to write critical essays for the design press.

Jennifer Fuchel studied Fine Arts and Graphic Design for her Bachelor's degree at Binghamton University and continued her studies at Boston University, where she received her Masters of Fine Arts in Graphic Design. Her thesis included a three-dimensional modeled animation that received awards from the New England Film Festival (1989) and was exhibited at the Smithsonian American History Museum in Washington, D.C. Jennifer has worked on many professional projects including graphics and interactivity for *What's New, New England* (1988), one of the first laser disc-driven, touch–screen-based, public-access information kiosks; graphics and animation for WGBH's television show *Where In The World Is Carmen San Diego*; and interface design for Lotus Development Corporation.

Jennifer is an Associate Professor in Graphic Design at The New England School of Art & Design at Suffolk University and is an adjunct professor at Harvard Summer School. Jennifer is also an active visual artist who works in acrylic paint and ceramic bas-relief.

ACKNOWLEDGMENTS

I was blessed with an embarrassment of riches in writing and producing this book. Although I can never say enough in thanks to all the people who helped me along the way, I can at least let them know in print how much I appreciate their help.

First, to my reviewer "dream team": Rita Armstrong of Roz Goldfarb + Associates, Professor Jennifer Fuchel of the New England School of Art and Design, and Nancy Bernard of Neutron, Inc. Thank you all for your insightful comments and suggestions. Your feedback was invaluable, and permeates every chapter.

A quick read of Appendix B will reveal what a talented, savvy, and articulate group of creatives I interviewed. I am very aware of the time each of you was willing to grant, and continue to treasure our conversations. From established stars to talents on the verge, you were all unstintingly open with your ideas, your opinions, and your time.

In a book like this one, a lot depends on who you know, and who they know in turn. Nancy Bernard knows how much in her debt I am. Among others, she led me to Nancy Hoefig, who stands out as being the first branch of a particularly fruitful tree. In addition, I owe a big thank you to my dear friend and frequent co-author Dan Peck for playing yenta. I owe another to Roz Goldfarb for her introduction, and for making time in Rita's schedule for chapter review. My network of friends wouldn't be complete without mentioning Shayne Bowman, among many things my gateway to iView Media Pro, a terrific piece of software I rely on for organizing my own work.

I relied heavily on artwork by Russ Apotheker—particularly for graphics in Chapter 10 on pages 192, 193, and 194; Chapter 12 on page 246; and Chapter 13 on page 259—and the programming that some of them required. Thank you, Russ, for being available, and for working so hard.

And it would hardly be an adequate acknowledgments section without high praise to the supportive professionals at Pearson Education. My New Riders team of Stephanie Wall and Jennifer Eberhardt went well beyond their roles, especially when life crises arose and deadlines had to shift. It's been a privilege to work with them, and to count them as friends. Then there's the design and production side of things. Cover designer Aren Howell was gracious, and I thank her for her forbearance in working with me to meld my concept with her talent. Sarah Kearns was always on top of production (which seemed to happen blindingly fast) and never complained, even when I occasionally got nit-picky.

A special thank you to Marjorie Baer, for supporting my book idea, blessing it with her eagle eye, and keeping the project on her busy radar screen.

And, as usual, thank you Shai. No matter how little you saw me during the months I worked on this book, you never complained, or were anything less than totally supportive. I am a very, very lucky woman.

TELL US WHAT YOU THINK

As the reader of this book, you are the most important critic and commentator. We value your opinion and want to know what we're doing right, what we could do better, what areas you'd like to see us publish in, and any other words of wisdom you're willing to pass our way.

When you contact us, please be sure to include this book's title, ISBN, and author, as well as your name and email address. We will carefully review your comments and share them with the author and editors who worked on the book.

Email: **errata@newriders.com**

FOREWORD

In the course of my work, I often speak to student or professional groups about career, marketplace, and workplace issues. An overwhelming number of questions relate to the structure and content of portfolios. "What should the format be? How to demonstrate different forms of work: two-dimensional and three-dimensional? How should the work be viewed? How should it be delivered? How much work should be shown? What samples should be included?" There is no other topic of such significance, for all recognize the role portfolios play in securing a position.

Developing a portfolio, and especially a digital portfolio, is without question the most critical and mandatory vehicle to demonstrate an individual's skill and accomplishment. It is the first introduction to a future employer, the first foot in the proverbial door. The portfolio is also a repository of past work, a personal archive to be maintained and treasured. Although professionals have strong opinions about how to develop the portfolio and what they feel is the "correct" method, ultimately the portfolio is a marketing tool. To successfully function as a marketing instrument, the portfolio should be as unique as its owner.

Our design and interactive media culture moves forward at a lightning pace and, as always, the pressure is to keep up. However, I would suggest that sometimes it is also valuable to look back, for otherwise we lose perspective. Bells and whistles are not a substitute for substance. We need to make sure, in our fixation on the latest, newest, hottest, that the fundamentals of the traditional portfolio are not lost. Portfolios were once presented on 35-millimeter slides—an interesting precursor to the digital portfolio. A slide was a 35-millimeter representation of the real thing and, at the end of the day, the real object was still important. There is still a need, and a place, to experience the quality of a final printed piece.

This book is unique as it offers, with clarity and logic, the process of developing a portfolio—along with personal experiences that add first-hand information. It respects the traditional portfolio, while it successfully tackles the digital challenge on all issues relating to the choices of structure, content, and delivery. I believe you will agree that it fulfills a tremendous need. And, hopefully, it will aid you in fulfilling *your* future potential.

Roz Goldfarb
President, Roz Goldfarb Associates
August 2003

Why you need a portfolio now

For most people, a portfolio describes their collection of financial investments. For those of us who make our living as artists or designers, "portfolio" refers to a collection of material we've created. The two types of portfolios are not actually so different. Both represent the fruits of hard labor. Both are the result of choices made to maximize potential. And both can spell the difference between long-term success or failure.

Unfortunately, when not actively job- or client-hunting, we tend to ignore our portfolios. This nasty habit starts when we're students. Although the portfolio looms as the single most important factor in their future, students often are so caught up in class projects that they don't prepare their portfolio until after graduation—too late to take advantage of a portfolio seminar or faculty review.

There's really no excuse for not being digital in some form. You're always looking for ways to market, but the fluidity of being online enables people to get at your work in a way that they just can't otherwise.

—Jamey Stilling

Procrastination continues into our careers. In a busy office—or a bad economy—client deadlines take precedence, sometimes for months or even years. "Why spend the time on a portfolio? I have a job already," is the argument. But anyone who has been out in the marketplace long enough to have experienced an economic bust knows that you can have a job on Monday and a pink slip without a parachute on Friday. On the following Monday, not having a portfolio becomes a strategic error.

If you're a freelancer, you don't need just any digital portfolio. You need one filled with recent work and wrapped in a current approach. But when every billable hour counts, it's hard to justify the upkeep. Unfortunately, if a prospect finds your site and sees the dust practically shake off the page, they won't call you with a useful critique. You will never know you lost a job. When you're trying to remain competitive, a vintage portfolio can be as useful as none at all.

No question about it—creating and maintaining your portfolio is a serious and complex self-marketing issue. It deserves your best effort: creativity, attention to detail, planning, and time-consuming production. Knowing that a good portfolio doesn't happen overnight, you should be working on it long before your need becomes critical. No excuses! If you have time to do freelance or personal projects for fun or extra cash, you can make time for your portfolio.

With the recognition that a portfolio project is overdue, it's time to figure out what that means for you and whether a digital portfolio is your answer.

WHAT IS A DIGITAL PORTFOLIO?

A *digital portfolio* is a collection of creative assets distributed via computer-based media. This broad definition covers a range of forms: PDF attachments, CD presentations, DVD demo reels, work housed on laptops, and websites. A digital portfolio can include text, photography, illustration, graphic design, interactivity, animation, audio material, and video.

SHOULD YOUR PORTFOLIO BE DIGITAL?

More and more, the answer to this question is a resounding "yes," no matter what stage of your career you're in. Students and others just breaking into their profession need a way to communicate with potential employers and clients at long distances. Bulk-mailing printed samples in the Internet age is just plain silly.

Looking for a new job? A digital portfolio makes it easier to get an interview and harder to be rejected. In large companies, the first person to consider your application is probably someone in Human Resources who knows they aren't qualified to judge creative work. It's easier for them to forward you up to the next level than to review your samples. Besides, the act of sending a digital sample telegraphs your status as an experienced candidate.

Established professionals almost always have a traditional portfolio, and some resist developing another. "I don't need a new book because the one I have is full of current work, and my client list is stable—and I'm not a Web designer!" But companies fail, and clients change studios. Beyond that, these days everyone wants an online taste test before they pick up the phone. One potential client that calls someone else because they can't look at a URL before they call you is one lost client too many.

The last three people I placed all had some sort of digital presentation. Candidates triple their chances of getting an interview if their resume is accompanied by digital samples.

—Rita Armstrong

It's also not as hard as it might seem. Graphic design, video, and animation are already produced digitally, and the files can be modified for online use; some 2D traditional work can be scanned; and large 2D and 3D work can be photographed with digital cameras. If properly built, the digital portfolio is modular and flexible, so it's relatively easy to update.

Finally, digital portfolios are very convenient. If you maintain a website, almost anyone in the world can view your work, and you can access it for a presentation at a moment's notice. On CD or DVD, your portfolio is highly portable—and great backup insurance. You don't have to worry about leaving it behind for evaluation or making multiple expensive copies of it.

If they send a traditional book by, then I have to remember to send the book back. Digital form is great. I can just put the entire book into an electronic file.

—Cynthia Rabun

All these plusses make a digital portfolio an obvious and usually superior portfolio format. But its plusses are not universally appreciated. Portfolio expectations vary, depending on the nature of the work you intend on showing and who you want to see it. Even in professions where digital portfolios are a completely accepted mode of presentation, there are some employers or clients who will insist on seeing printed work—instead of or in addition to the digital version. While some creative individuals can move everything to digital media, others must continue to maintain a traditional portfolio—as their only portfolio or as their primary form—because their profession demands it.

Traditional portfolios are still required for:

- **Galleries**. Although the number of galleries able to view digital work is growing, many curators still want to see slides or transparencies. And of course, before showing your work, they'll want to see the originals.
- **Environmental or product-based design**. Industrial designers, graphic designers specializing in packaging, architects, and interior designers(whether or not they also decide to create a digital portfolio) almost always maintain a traditional portfolio as well. Three-dimensional design is never as effective when forced into a 2D format.
- **Video, animation, and performing artists**. VHS tapes continue as the format for the standard demo reel, although DVD use is quickly gaining ground.

Architects are more interested in seeing hand-drawing, model-making, and even digital skills on paper rather than on the screen. It is much easier to evaluate someone's portfolio by flipping through it.

—Chris Grimley

- **Print designers**. A digital portfolio has become a must for making the first cut, but a traditional portfolio of printed samples can still be important to examine decisions you've made on typography and texture.
- **School applications**. Educators, although they may be perfectly comfortable with computers, frequently require slides, not CDs or websites for an admissions portfolio.
- **Security**. In some specialized cases, your agreement with a client may prevent you from putting a project into a digital portfolio. If you want to show it, you might have to present it in person. See Chapter 12, "Copyright & portfolio," for a detailed discussion of this topic.

In almost all of these situations, a digital portfolio is still a useful adjunct for self-promotion and marketing, as well as an excellent "calling card" before a personal presentation. The more ways you have to interest a prospective client or employer, the more confident they are in your abilities and the more likely you will be seriously considered for the position you want.

WHY THIS BOOK IS FOR YOU

This book was conceived as a source for a creative who needs to develop any form of digital portfolio. It examines the portfolio process from beginning to end with a fresh eye, in the context of the increasingly virtual world most art and design professionals now inhabit.

For an established professional, I offer some critical how-tos of digital portfolio development and creation. Perhaps you have been presenting yourself and your work for years and have a very good sense of your profession, skills, and talents, and your local market. But making your work accessible in digital form demands new criteria, technical skills, and maybe a fresh look at the work you've done and your assumptions about it.

For the technically adept who might be less well-versed in self-marketing and professional presentation, I present the digital portfolio process as part of a larger scheme. This book will give you a good overview of the portfolio process, lead you through the concepts and issues from basic to complex, and help you develop a digital portfolio that is right for you.

Either way, this book should make the process of developing your new portfolio a little less painful.

ASSUMPTIONS

Although this book has plenty of useful hints and very specific technical how-tos, its focus is on process and results. You're free to use your favorite tools. If you don't have any favorites yet, I've suggested some good step-by-step books in Appendix A, "Resources," to help you learn the software basics. Throughout the book, I recommend specific software programs for different types of presentations, offer guidelines on how to use them most effectively for different stages of your portfolio project, and help you assess what you should choose to meet your goals efficiently.

I do assume that you have some artistic talent within your chosen medium of expression and that you don't need definitions for basic art terms such as scale, proportion, figure, and ground. If you do, you should consider reading the discussion on partnering in Chapter 6, "Digitizing traditional work," before you do anything else.

I admit that I've tilted the topics in this book toward graphic designers because their portfolios generally require the most complex preparation. Design portfolios also carry the most demanding expectations because the people who judge them look at the thinking behind the portfolio as much as the highlighted work within it.

But to a less strenuous degree, the same holds true for portfolios in other disciplines. Today, almost every creative professional is expected to have his work on CD or online—or both. With so many portfolios online or on disk, a portfolio that follows classic design principles does a better job of showcasing the work within it.

A well-designed portfolio is a way for an illustrator or photographer to boost his or her work out of the excruciatingly competitive world of clip art and stock images. It's a way for an animator or other moving image artist to present his work more accessibly and with finesse. It raises the visibility and the stock of fine and performing artists. Most importantly, it allows you to show the world that you value and respect your work—the first step in making sure that others do too.

Part I

Planning

CHAPTER 1

Professions

Portfolios are bound together by the personality and goals of those who create them. When you define the type of work you want to do and identify yourself within it, you lay the first building block for your unique portfolio.

Defining yourself to the world is more difficult than it used to be. One job description can have dozens of different titles, each of which puts a slightly different spin on how much experience and what talents and skills the position demands.

If you want to work on electronic media projects, what do you call yourself? A graphic designer? For some people graphic design equals print design. An interface designer? You need to know something about interface design to do justice to a website. But interface design—the human factors part of design—is often handled by a person with an engineering or industrial design background. Then there's the interactive designer—the person who designs the look and feel of a project. That's usually a very different person from a Flash developer, who might also have a design role in the interface but will be expected to do production and scripting. There's an elegant term favored by some people who design for various media—experience designer. Someone in a design studio should recognize the term, but it will completely stump most potential clients.

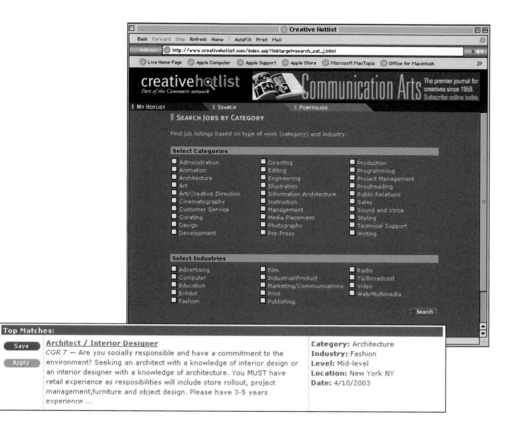

www.creativehotlist.com
The Communication Arts portfolio and job website has finely tuned its subject list. But many of the jobs and portfolios cross-list in a variety of categories, like this one looking for an interior designer for the fashion industry.

Does this seem like splitting hairs? Maybe. But if you make the wrong choice as you develop your portfolio, you could end up doing work you don't like or not getting a job in your area at all. This first chapter helps you figure out who you are and where you fit. You should emerge from this chapter identifying yourself with one of these professions and preparing to create a portfolio that meets its mix of expectations.

PORTFOLIO INGREDIENTS

It's obvious that a portfolio isn't worth much unless it contains good work. But good work alone isn't always enough. Every profession has a different definition of what "good" is. What works magnificently when you present to an art director who needs an illustration will fall flat when she needs a freelance designer—and vice versa. For each role and audience, your portfolio must contain the right kind of work, in the right format. Meet the unspoken assumptions, and you send the message that you know who you are and what you want to do.

The ingredients of a successful portfolio, appearing in different proportions in the portfolio cases that follow. Like a great chef, you use the recipe as a guideline, not a law, finding the uniquely right proportion for your work.

That's good advice, you may be thinking, but somewhat useless. How do you know what's needed when? It's hard to answer that in any specific case because every hiring situation has unique requirements, and every portfolio is individually created. But there is a short list of underlying elements that, when combined in appropriate proportions, can help to craft a portfolio that speaks effectively to its intended eyes and ears.

Variety

You might think that variety would be a plus because it shows the full range of your work and capabilities. Sometimes it is, but you'd be surprised how often it works against you. If your pieces are too diverse, in medium, look, subject, or clientele, they can imply that you haven't yet figured out what you do best—and that you have yet to find your creative voice.

Style

As artists and designers mature, their work frequently develops a creative signature. For some professions, an identifiable style is nothing short of a requirement. For others, it's intrusive, like an out-of-tune voice in a chorus, because it gets in the way of a client's message.

Technology and craft

Bad craft and inappropriate technology are always negative, but for some professions, they're a much bigger issue than in others. Many fine artists create personal websites that use text or navigation badly. These lacks can be painful to those in the know, but a potential curator will just go straight to the work without noticing. Weak craft in a design portfolio is, on the other hand, never forgiven.

Process

Work in process, or work about your process, can explain how you evolve your ideas and what it would be like to work with you. In many professional situations, how you think and problem-solve can be as important as your aesthetic decisions. For professions where production is expensive or time-consuming, process work and prototypes are so important that not showing them is suspect.

Concept | creativity

There is a difference between creativity in your individual projects and creativity in your presentation of those projects. Your portfolio presentation can be anything from a naked PDF file to an interactive DVD in a specially designed jewel case. Expectations for your presentation vary tremendously by profession. In some cases, like for print-centric corporate identity designers, a Flash presentation is a big waste of time.

PURPOSE

The portfolio elements are basic, but their mix is affected by your immediate need— the life change that is prompting you to create or update your portfolio. Are you developing and presenting it…

- For professional growth and discovery?
- For acceptance into an academic program?
- To curators or gallery owners?
- To provide elements for a larger project?
- For a full-time job?
- To gain or retain clients?

Your purpose will color the type of work you include, its format, and your presentation. It will interact with the other elements to create a framework that is specific to your industry.

YOUR PORTFOLIO MIX

How you approach your portfolio—digital or traditional—should depend on the category of creative professional you are and your purpose. The following descriptions define these categories. They're followed by examples of how your category interacts with a likely purpose. These templates will help you determine your ideal mix of portfolio elements, unify your portfolio, and emphasize your strengths in the context of your professional needs. Hopefully, they'll also make it clear how important it is to have a portfolio that is organized and modular, so you can reconfigure it as your situation and needs change.

As you read the following descriptions, concentrate on the one that fits you best. You're required by the way people evaluate your work to choose a category and stay consistent within it. Does your work, your chosen market, and your current portfolio seem to work within the framework of one of the descriptions below? If it works within more than one, you may be a highly versatile person, but you'll either have to make a choice, or you'll need more than one portfolio. (Check out Chapter 4, "Format," for more on multiple portfolios.)

Art

This category is comprised of people who have considerable control over the subject, message, media, and presentation of their creative work. That freedom usually extends to the digital portfolio. If you want to make a commercial living from your art, you should look at the other categories instead of or in addition to this section. The two types of portfolios, although sometimes created by the same people, really shouldn't mix.

STUDENT

Students belong in the art category because their primary focus isn't (or shouldn't be) making a living from their artwork—although every student would much prefer to freelance for spending money than waiting tables. Being a student is a transitional state. Because you're still on the road to your goal and able to change focus as you experience new options, you can create a portfolio that includes many facets of your creative life.

PURPOSE: ADMISSION   Admission portfolios are special: the people judging your work tell you exactly what they want to see. Don't take this gift for granted. Meet the requirements as closely as you can. If digital portfolios aren't mentioned as a submission medium, don't send one, even if all your artwork is computer-based. Some academic institutions are just old-fashioned, and the admission committee isn't comfortable handling technology. Others are perfectly adept with computers but have very good reasons (see Chapter 4) why they may not welcome disks.

In general, an admission committee is looking for variety to assess your strengths, weaknesses, and level of preparation. In undergraduate portfolios, craft is seen as less important than potential because technique and good habits can be taught. Graduate portfolios take craft issues much more seriously, particularly if the applicant has already majored in art or design.

Variety will drive most undergraduate admissions choices. Don't attempt a high-concept presentation unless you are applying to graduate school, and even then, only if you are certain it is one of your strengths.

While you're in school

Student portfolios should evolve constantly as you learn and complete more projects. Weed out the older work as quickly as you can. It's the rare high school project that can hold its own after a year or two of higher education.

Start a digital portfolio early, but maintain a small-format print portfolio to show samples quickly. Many students get their first experiences in their field in internships, co-ops, or as part-time or summer freelancers. You meet people at parties, events, and even on the street. You never know when an opportunity to design a logo or shoot a CD cover might depend on your being able to show your ideas away from a computer.

Keep your student portfolio as wide-ranging as possible. Even if you plan on becoming a designer, continue to include good examples of your illustration or photography work. You'll have most of your life to carry a focussed portfolio, so enjoy a range of media while you can.

Surprisingly, a fair number of artists who contact me do not have their own websites to refer me to and are looking for Web representation. Most can send image files as attachments, and this is generally how I receive images from artists to review.

—Mary Ann Kearns

Fine artist

A fine artist is someone who views his or her work solely as a means of creative or philosophical expression. An artist doesn't need a digital portfolio, but many find it a useful way to expand their audience and market their work. Although you'll seldom get a show or a commission on your digital portfolio alone, if you're lucky it could open the door to a studio visit or an invitation to a competition.

Purpose: Exhibition or commission

The art world was slow to accept any merger of art and technology, including that of traditional art forms and a digital portfolio. Many artists still operate exclusively by sending out 35mm slide sheets—an expensive way to promote themselves and their work. Curators who are sticklers for tradition still consider slides de rigeur, but fortunately, their numbers are shrinking. An artist should at least have a small space on one of the many group or art catalog sites for prospective clients or curators.

Even if you have wide interests and the ability to work effectively in different media, your digital portfolio should emphasize style above all other elements. A creative presentation is less important than a clean, unfussy one that showcases your work.

www.911gallery.org
Fine arts is defined by its intent, not by its media. The variety of materials in the shows curated by Mary Ann Kearns for the Boston Cyberarts festival demonstrates this fact.

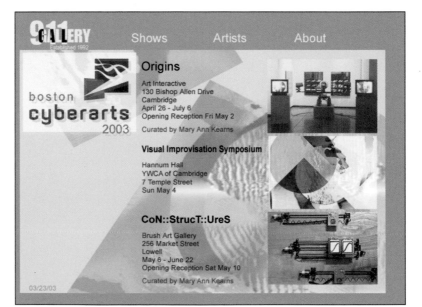

As a fine artist, variety works against you. The art world looks for a unique, consistent style. Only after developing a track record of successful shows can multiple interests and media be combined in one portfolio. Unless your artwork involves technology, craft is only relevant in that bad craft can push people away. The fine art digital portfolio should keep its focus on the work, minimizing presentation concept.

2D graphics

Three groups of image-makers belong here: people who compose and/or shoot live images, those who create images through multiple forms of image capture and digital compositing, and those who draw or paint pictures—either in traditional media or on the computer. The groups can be fluid, although photographers and their clients tend to view most computer image compositing (as opposed to image enhancement) as a form of illustration. For convenience sake, I've combined compositors and illustrators into the Graphic Artist category.

PHOTOGRAPHER

Photographers capture images, either digitally or on film. They were among the first artists to use digital media to archive, display, and sell their work. Ironically, despite the increased audience the Web offers, it has become harder for an individual photographer's work to stand out. With the growing interest in image-making, digital cameras, and Photoshop, there are more images available than ever before. The competition makes it more important than ever that a professional photographer present a unique Web-based portfolio.

www.jameystillings.com
Jamey Stillings is a prime example of a photographer whose site enhances his work and highlights his strengths.

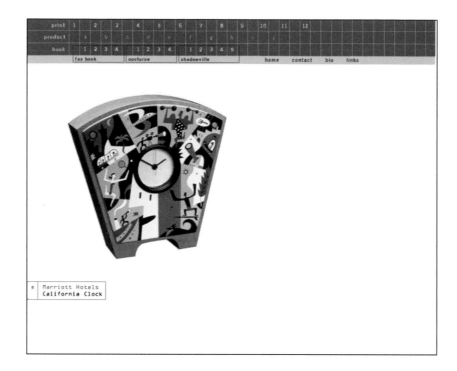

www.bartalos.com
Illustrator Michael Bartalos' website makes it easy for a prospective client to see examples of his work in different categories.

Graphic artist

Illustrators and fine artists often use the same tools and effects, but to different purposes. Unlike fine artists, illustrators create artwork on assignment. They must not only be talented and skilled in their media, but also good at interpreting and executing the creative concepts of others. Graphic artists absolutely need a digital portfolio.

2D artist digital portfolios must project a unique way of approaching an assignment as well as stylistic identity. The portfolio presentation should have a concept that highlights both of these strengths.

Purpose: License or freelance   Like for fine artists, style is the most important element in this type of portfolio. But the bar is much higher in the concept and execution of a graphic artist's Web portfolio than it is for a fine artist. Market forces require most 2D professionals to create sites with a large database of work. To avoid turning the site into a numbing catalog, a good freelance portfolio should complement the artist's style the way a good matte and frame enhance a 2D graphic. The concept is very important. Technology and craft must be very good but largely invisible.

Design

The design professions share a common ground in their roles as interpreters, integrators, and collaborators. Although there is little fluidity across the spectrum of design professions (architects don't usually design annual reports, any more than designers create elevations) there is quite a lot of crossover at the edges. An exhibit or experience designer might have been trained in architecture, industrial design, or graphic design.

ARCHITECT

An architect designs buildings, interior spaces, and landscapes—the interactive space of the real world. Because of the stakes involved, the architectural profession has a strong commitment to apprenticeship. A new architect can expect to spend time in a CAD support role before they are trusted to actually take part in the design process, so their technical skills must be strong.

Although many young architects and most architectural firms now have some form of digital portfolio, it remains supplemental to the traditional print-based archive of models, elevations, plans, renderings, and photographs.

www.marckesano.com
Although not required, an elegant site such as U.C. Berkeley graduate Patrick Marckesano's harks back to the elaborate, hand-bound cases architects used to create. It combines adept coding with high style.

www.rob.id.au
As these shots from Robert Shearing's portfolio attest, an industrial designer must have strong illustration and rendering skills.

maia

one two three four five six

maia

one two three four five six

INDUSTRIAL DESIGN

Industrial designers design products and systems. Excellent 3D visualization talent and sketching skills are important prerequisites and play a big role in their portfolio presentations. Their strengths in usability and navigation make them naturals for careers in multimedia design. Although industrial designers overlap architects in many of the technical tools of their trade, their portfolio requirements diverge. Unlike architects, ID portfolios are frequently digital, both in Web and CD form.

Process material is extremely useful. An industrial design digital portfolio should emphasize all stages of the development cycle, for example, from first sketches to the built project. Portfolio concept is seen as part of your design and usability skills and will play a major role as well.

Purpose: Freelance or full-time   Young 3D designers, even ones with great creative promise, will spend their first years exercising their modeling or drafting expertise. As a result, a portfolio that doesn't display the highest possible professional craft with the widest variety of tools will go to the bottom of the pile. Process is very effective as well. Unlike some other design professions, even established professionals often show projects that did not get built or produced in their portfolios. There are always more design ideas than there can be actual commissions.

Graphic designer

A graphic designer combines text, image, and sometimes sound to visually communicate ideas and solve strategic and marketing challenges. Graphic designers are more likely to deal with two-dimensional projects, but many also design packaging, signage, and, of course, interactive sites. A graphic designer with a good eye for space might design the interior of a store as part of a client's overall branding and marketing system.

Designers deal with many topics and clients, so a design portfolio should emphasize a variety of project briefs. Pieces that display good visual thinking will be more effective than pedestrian desktop publishing, even if one piece was a student project, and the desktop work was professionally printed.

Graphic designers need some form of digital portfolios at every point in their careers. Its format and design considerations will almost certainly be affected by the type of work in which the designer specializes. A package designer may have a portfolio that is formatted more like that of an industrial designer because so much of the work is 3D. Corporate identity designers will often show more process and speculative work.

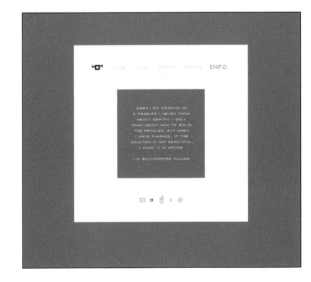

www.dialogbox.com
A graphic designer must have a good grounding in classic design practice. Britt Funderburk's portfolio immediately shows his understanding of visual space and typographic knowledge.

MULTIMEDIA DESIGNER

Unlike graphic designers, who also may do multimedia design as one medium among many, a multimedia designer is most comfortable designing for the computer screen. Multimedia designers are expected to be extremely technologically adept, and their portfolios should display these skills. A multimedia designer (or design firm) lacking a digital portfolio is a highly unusual multimedia designer.

PURPOSE: FREELANCE OR FULL-TIME   Technical presentation, flair, and attention to detail are particularly critical for the design portfolio. Variety in project and approach are encouraged. Because of the emphasis on how you think, a design portfolio is a great place for process and personal project work. Craft is also highly regarded.

The designer's digital portfolio requires a concept that not only presents the actual work well but is a design project in itself. This "wrapper" is frequently interactive, although the interaction for a print-based designer can be a simple linear slideshow instead of a complex multilayered experience.

A multimedia designer's digital portfolio is more technically demanding, and an elegantly designed and executed "wrapper" is often a plus. Considering you might have created sites that have been redesigned (or closed down) after you worked on them, showing prototypes or work in process is often a necessity. This portfolio is often a design object in its own right, but the portfolio should still not be allowed to overwhelm the projects.

www.cefaratti.com

Multimedia design combines sophisticated presentation with excellent digital craft. Mike Cefaratti's portfolio pages are not only attractively designed, they load blindingly fast.

Freelance or full-time: production

A production specialist is hired for one reason only—to implement—whether they are writing JavaScript, optimizing graphics, or creating Flash-based interaction. Creativity and a good eye are a bonus, not the main event. A professional developer knows this and prides herself on her speed, efficiency, and accuracy, even under pressure. This pride should be on display in a production portfolio by exquisite attention to craft and detail. Process and variety are still useful.

Many designers or graphic artists apply for production positions in a soft economy. If you fit this description, you need a different balance of work in your digital portfolio than the one you use when applying for a creative position.

Motion graphics

Designers and illustrators are beginning to add time and motion to their repertoire of tools and media. There is a difference, however, between incorporating interactive elements into a design and concentrating on movement and imagery. Motion graphics professionals add performance and storytelling to their visual skills, as well as a keen understanding of timing.

Although the "formal" portfolio presentation might still be a videotape, the digital portfolio is fast becoming as important for anyone dealing with film or video as it is for a designer because more and more motion work is being designed explicitly for the Internet.

ANIMATOR

Animation was once identified exclusively as hand-drawn cartoon entertainment. Today, most animation is computer-based or -assisted. Computer animators make it possible to "walk through" designed virtual spaces, visualize abstract scientific principles, and merge real and imaginary elements seamlessly in film.

To maximize their visibility and options, animators' portfolios take two distinct forms: a highly compressed, low-bandwidth sampling on the Internet and a richer, deeper version on tape or on disk.

A video or animation portfolio is all about having a clever and creative way of looking at the world and the technical mastery to realize your vision. Process and variety are useful in supporting roles.

www.deluxepaint.net

An animator's imagination is as important as his or her technical skills. Humor, personality, and exaggeration are welcome, as shown in this collage of four animated expressions from Cemre Ozkurt's opening screen.

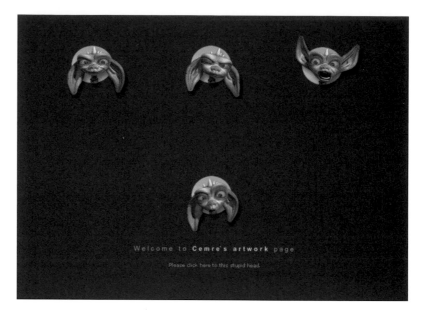

Welcome to **Cemre's artwork** page

Please click here to this stupid head.

VIDEOGRAPHER | DV PRODUCTION

In a quick and simplistic analogy, a videographer is to a photographer what an animator is to an illustrator. Instead of capturing and editing individual still frames, a videographer captures moving images. Videographers are usually freelancers who not only shoot the content but handle post production as well. Their portfolios, like those of animators, are likely to be both digital and analog.

PURPOSE: FREELANCE OR FULL-TIME   Technical virtuosity goes hand-in-hand with creativity in a time-and-motion portfolio. Variety is prized, as is a clever concept for editing clips of work together. Sound is a part of the palette and should be an integrated component in the portfolio. Because both animation and video projects are extremely time-consuming, work in process or personal projects are not only acceptable in the digital portfolio, but expected. So are other goodies—tutorials or personal projects—that show the work behind the scenes.

Performance

Performing artists have joined the ranks of creative professionals presenting themselves digitally. Standards for performance digital portfolios are still evolving. Aesthetic expectations are still fairly undemanding, but seamless craft and good quality film resolution can be very important. In both cases, a digital portfolio offers the opportunity for a performer to establish credibility and to provide a more professional presentation.

THE GRAIN OF SALT...

Don't be surprised if you come across portfolios of senior professionals that stretch the limits. These profiles can't represent the state of the profession for everyone at every point in their careers. When an individual moves upward professionally or carves a unique niche, he or she can salt the common wisdom to taste. If you are just starting out, are trying to improve your chances, or are shifting into a new area, you can't. That's a particularly important idea to keep in mind as you move from a general understanding of your profession's expectations to the specifics of who you are in relation to your chosen audience.

CHAPTER 2

Adaptation

You'd be surprised by how much an experienced reviewer can assume about you from looking at your portfolio. Some reviewers may react negatively to things you might not notice and pass you by, even if you'd do a great job for them. In response, you can neutralize your portfolio, avoiding examples of chance-taking work. This decision has its own pitfalls. Some art directors work closely with whoever they hire. If they can't get a sense of who you are, they may not be willing to find out after you've come on board.

It's in your best interest, then, to evaluate yourself and your work before it's done for you. Self-evaluation is tough. Although you use some of the same skills you would if you were developing a concept for a client, applying them is much harder when the product is yourself. You carry around blind spots that might make you emphasize the wrong things in your portfolio or pursue work in an area that isn't your best. What are your strengths? What will you need to overcome? Do you have the talents that your target audience wants? Where do you need to adapt to the market? Answer these questions and you have a focus that will shape your subsequent portfolio decisions.

SOUL-SEARCHING

Even if you aren't naturally introspective, don't skip this step. In fact, it's probably most important if you tend to be impatient with self-examination. You're in a profession where personality matters because it is so frequently reflected in how you approach concepts and ideas. The self-assessment checklist that follows will help you to think clearly about your abilities, needs, and goals. Not only will this help you develop an appropriate portfolio, but it will prepare you to talk effectively about yourself and your work in an interview.

Self-assessments are subjective, not scientific. You'll find this one most useful if you collate the results of each topic and use them at major decision points in your portfolio development: target market (Chapter 3, "Audience"), preparing your résumé, briefs, and other text (Chapter 9, "Creating written content"), and making the all-important concept decisions (Chapter 10, "Development basics"). It is less important to rack up points than it is to have the right points.

In general, solid experience is more valuable than training and can balance some gaps in formal education. Without it, be more flexible in your goals and prioritize your values. Look for positions that offer opportunities to learn from experienced professionals, even if those positions pay less than those that reward your technical skills.

Values should overlay your goals. The more selective your values, the less likely that you will find happiness in a large corporation, and the harder it may be for you to make a major creative change. If you have a reasonable head for detail, you might be happier as a freelancer than as an employee.

Personality is a critical component and can, in the highly subjective world of the arts, move you closer to your goals even if some of your preparation is spotty. If you've chosen one set of words to describe your work and a completely different set to describe your "true" style, you need to reexamine your answers to the other sections and prepare for many hard choices as you mold your portfolio.

Ideally, any portfolio reflects the taste and aesthetic of its owner. It supports the theory that dogs tend to look like their owners and vice versa. It should be a true representation of who that person is and what they're capable of doing.

—Michael Borofsky

Self-assessment checklist

These questions have no right or wrong answers. They also have nothing to do with how talented you are. (There's no way to judge that with a checklist.)

No one has to see these results but you, so be completely honest. Refer to this assessment at many points along your portfolio process: as a reality check against your target audience, as you decide what projects to include in the portfolio, and as you choose the type of portfolio most likely to help you reach your goals.

Strengths and weaknesses

1. Educational experience in my profession:

   ☐ Self-taught   ☐ Bachelor's degree

   ☐ Non-credit classes   ☐ Advanced degree

   ☐ Certificate or Associate degree

2. Educational experience in a related or supporting profession (check all that fit):

   ☐ Painting, drawing, or other art fundamentals   ☐ Photography

   ☐ 3D modeling or rendering

   ☐ Video and/or animation   ☐ Graphic design

   ☐ Typography   ☐ User-interface and/or interaction

   ☐ Scripting or programming   ☐ Marketing

   ☐ Writing

3. Work experience within a related or supporting profession (check all that fit):

   ☐ Painting, drawing, or other art fundamentals   ☐ Photography

   ☐ 3D modeling or rendering

   ☐ Video and/or animation   ☐ Typography

   ☐ Graphic design: print   ☐ User-interface and/or interaction

   ☐ Graphic design: identity and branding   ☐ Scripting or programming

   ☐ Writing

   ☐ Graphic design: packaging   ☐ Marketing

4. I have software training in (check all that fit):

   ☐ Photoshop and related imaging software (Fireworks, Image Ready, etc.)

   ☐ 2D illustration program (Illustrator, Freehand, etc.)

   ☐ Print design software (Quark, InDesign, etc.)

   ☐ Production software (Acrobat, color-proofing software, etc.)

   ☐ Flash or other interaction/animation program

   ☐ Web design software (Dreamweaver, etc.)

   ☐ Rendering or CAD programs (AutoCad, FormZ, etc.)

   ☐ 3D or animation programs (Maya, LightWave, etc.)

   ☐ Video software (After Effects, Final Cut Pro, etc.)

   ☐ I have no software training.

5. Exclusive of school, I have been working in my chosen profession for:

☐ < 1 year   ☐ 7–10 years
☐ 1–3 years   ☐ 10+ years
☐ 3–7 years

(Don't count time spent unemployed if you didn't freelance at least part-time.)

6. Rate your skills (not your raw talent) in your primary area:

☐ A master of my craft   ☐ Better than average
☐ Have lots to teach others   ☐ About average
☐ Better than most   ☐ Still learning

Goals

7. Why am I making a digital portfolio? Check all that apply:

☐ Creative outlet   ☐ Employed, looking for a job
☐ Required for school   ☐ Client marketing tool
☐ Need the experience   ☐ Professional project record
☐ Unemployed, looking for a job

8. If your portfolio needs are job-related, check the statements that apply to you:

☐ I'll take any job I can get in my profession.
☐ I want a job similar to one I have or had.
☐ I want a job at a higher responsibility level.
☐ I want to do specialized work in my profession. Name the area:

_____

☐ My previous jobs were unfulfilling. I want to do something different.

☐ What I haven't liked about my jobs:

_____

_____

☐ I want/need to change my creative profession.
☐ I am currently a _____ (name of profession–illustrator, architect, etc.) and want to be a _____ (name of profession).

9. If your portfolio needs are client-related, check the statements that apply to you:

☐ I am happy with the type of clients I currently have but need more work.
☐ I want to specialize in specific industries or types of work. Name the area:

_____

☐ I want to add to or change what I've specialized in. I currently specialize in (name of area) and want to specialize in (name of area).

_____

Values

10. How do you like to work?

    ☐ Alone
    ☐ Collaboration or partnership
    ☐ As a team member
    ☐ Doesn't matter

11. What's your preferred working environment?

    ☐ I can work anywhere.
    ☐ I need a private space.
    ☐ I like to have other people around.
    ☐ My colleagues must be friends.

12. Select the statement that fits you best:

    ☐ I will take jobs from any paying client.
    ☐ I won't accept some types of clients or client work.
    ☐ List exactly the type of work you won't do: _____
    _____

Personality

13. Check the words that best describe the work you've done. Choose no more than
    five from the list.

☐ Personal	☐ Trendy	☐ Thoughtful	☐ Brash
☐ Sexy	☐ Funny	☐ Playful	☐ Sarcastic
☐ Serious	☐ Sensitive	☐ Intellectual	☐ Emotional
☐ Clever	☐ Complex	☐ Detailed	☐ Impulsive
☐ Intuitive	☐ Analytical	☐ Organized	☐ Structured
☐ Elegant	☐ Crisp	☐ Boring	☐ Cooperative
☐ Confident	☐ Challenging	☐ Issues-oriented	

    You've chosen words that currently describe your work. If you feel they do not
    represent your preferred or actual style or approach, list some words from the list
    that do:

    _____

    _____

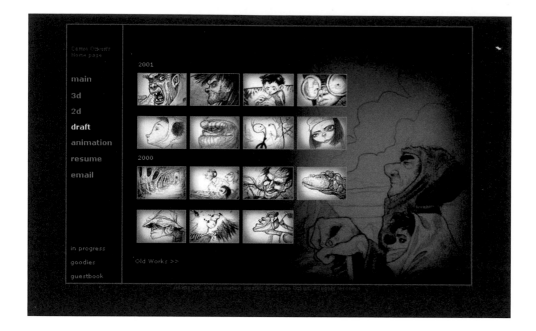

www.deluxepaint.net
Some 3D animators are very
adept on the computer but
have problems storyboarding
or making detailed sketches

with traditional media. Cemre
Ozkurt's Web portfolio has
ample examples of his ability
to think creatively off the
computer as well as on it.

Strengths and weaknesses

You have both, and you should know them well. Technical strengths and weaknesses are the most obvious and the easiest to assess. Some employers are on the prowl for specifics, like computer proficiency or knowledge of printing processes. They need evidence that you can handle their work.

> The one thing I won't ignore is a lack of understanding of typography. There are lots of pieces of advertising that we can do without photography, illustration, or even color. There is nothing that we do that is without typography. It is the single element that is omnipresent. It must be understood before a person can operate at a professional level.
>
> —Stan Richards

Knowledge is tougher to assess because it can be hard to recognize what you don't know. That's why the checklist differentiates between courses that covered the how-tos of an application and formal professional education. For example, a professional degree is most necessary in the design fields. You'll need to balance the lack with more years of high-quality work experience. Software training is most useful in areas with very high learning curves, like 3D, while sheer skill is most important for artists, photographers, and animators.

Self-confidence is important, but it should be based on reality. Without real experience or formal education or training, you may not be qualified to tackle the challenging or sophisticated projects you crave. Or you might find that you're hired for a job that becomes a nightmare because you're behind the learning curve.

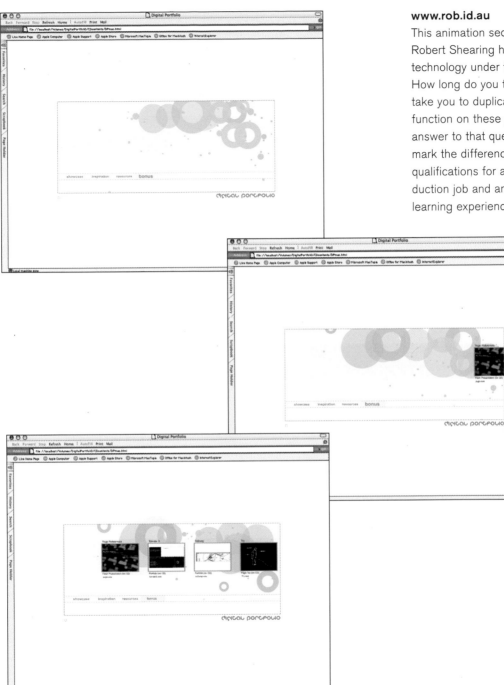

www.rob.id.au
This animation sequence by Robert Shearing has a lot of technology under the hood. How long do you think it would take you to duplicate the function on these pages? The answer to that question can mark the difference between qualifications for a Web production job and an unpleasant learning experience.

Typically with student portfolios, they're working on them for longer than might be the case in the real world. You're not sure how quick people could be on their feet or how long it would take them to actually get to a solution and produce it.

—Chris Davis

If you don't have enough training or experience to land the position you want, don't throw in the towel. Address the problem by focusing on a short-term goal—creating a portfolio that plays to your current strengths—while you upscale your skills and knowledge.

Goals

Begin a portfolio without understanding why you're making one, and it will fall prey to one of the classic portfolio concept errors (see the section, "What a portfolio is not"). A portfolio begun in ignorance or pure desperation telegraphs its weaknesses.

It's not enough to say, "I need a job!" A job is a financial requirement, not a goal. You could fix plumbing or sell real estate. It is equally insufficient to say, "I need clients!" You could do work for clients who aren't a perfect fit, but it would be a mistake to create a portfolio that will only bring in the wrong type of work for you. Never lose sight of the fact that you're in this because it's work you want to do—it is satisfying and it matters.

Set two goals now: your long-term career and your short-term job. The first should rule your portfolio's presentation format and the type of work you show. The second will determine the specific projects you include and how you customize the portfolio for individual needs. Perhaps you want to specialize in packaging and identity projects. Short-term, you need a job that gets you a step closer to that goal. That might mean creating a portfolio to interest companies that specialize in print, rather than interactive design firms.

What if you have started out in one direction, and your goal is to strike out in a new one? If you have been designing CD covers and want to design for the medical industry, you will be competing against people who are already "experts" in a demanding and complex field. When you make a risky and demanding change, you may have to constitute your portfolio from scratch. Be sure that there is a fit between how you feel about risk and the goal you choose.

Particularly if you're still young enough to stay up all night, don't squander your energy, drive, and excitement on anything other than the people you really want to work for. You want to learn the right skills from really good people.

—Nancy Hoefig

Values

Values determine what makes you comfortable and happy. You shouldn't knowingly target situations that you'll dislike unless the wolf is scratching at the door. Even when things are tough, it might be better to take a series of freelance or temp jobs than to accept a full-time position that you know is completely wrong for you. Long term, if you subvert your taste and instincts to land a client or a job, your portfolio becomes a collection of compromises, and your self-confidence can ebb. Eventually, you've done a lot of work you don't want to show and will have to work extra hard to counteract it in your presentation.

That being said, everyone makes work compromises at some point in their careers. Some are worth making. Only you can determine where you draw the line, but you should at least know where the line is, and whether it is a realistic limitation. You can't survive without a certain amount of flexibility. Not every project is groundbreaking and edgy, and you can learn a lot from projects that make you think along unfamiliar lines.

Personality

Does your work display a unique flavor? This question is subjective but goes to the heart of your portfolio. If your profession is style-based, your portfolio and all the work within it should express a personality. The words you've chosen should describe the flavor of your work. If you create images (illustrations, photographs, and so on) the words you've chosen should be strong, related descriptors. Impulsive, clever, and sarcastic might work together. Intuitive, trendy, and complex might be too far apart to provide a focussed sense of who you are.

In professions like graphic design that emphasize variety, your personality should be less obvious in a client project, although it is equally relevant in other ways. A designer works for a range of clients. A poster for a theater troupe shouldn't look like a financial firm's prospectus. The words you've chosen should describe the impression you want people to have of how you approach your work, rather than a personal or house style. Elegant, crisp, or confident are more likely to work for you than brash, sexy, or impulsive.

> In a project, you can't really ever take yourself out of the equation. You will always be present, but the percentage changes. In an art project, you're close to 100 percent present. And in a design project, that percentage is smaller, maybe 10 percent.
>
> —Yang Kim

www.jeffthedesigner.com
In a vast Internet of predictable site design, a portfolio like Jeff Kaphingst's is a refreshing taste of his distinctive design personality. You already know that he can take a fresh look at projects and might be a fun creative voice on a team.

What a portfolio is not

A portfolio is a marketing tool that can help you improve the amount and type of work you do, the kinds of assignments you land, and the rate of response to your presentations. Here's what it's not:

- **Your autobiography.** With very few exceptions, no one cares about artistic pre-history. They want to know who you are and what you are capable of now.

- **Your résumé.** Unlike a résumé, where time gaps stand out, your portfolio doesn't have to include examples from every job you've ever held.

- **Therapy.** You don't want people's sympathy; you want their confidence. Don't apologize and don't whine.

- **An inside joke.** Never forget that you are not presenting your portfolio to your friends.

- **A grab bag.** Don't throw your work in randomly in the hopes that there'll be something for everyone.

- **A check list.** No one reviewing a portfolio is keeping score to see if you have four textbook covers, three package designs, two annual reports, and a poster in a pear tree.

ADAPTING YOUR CONTENT

You've now tallied up the self-assessment and have a profile of who you are—and how the world probably sees you—as a creative professional. In creating this profile, you've defined the work you're qualified to handle, the range of work you've already done, and the type of employer or client you want. Ideally, these three areas connect elegantly. Most probably, there's an inequality somewhere that you need to address.

Quality

Your portfolio is a kind of personal statement, so you want it to say what you really mean. Every time you include a project that is clearly inferior to other work you've done, you make the worst portfolio faux pas. You've said, "I am proud of this work. I think it represents the quality of material you will get from me." By saying that, you've told the savvy reviewer that you can't tell good work from bad. Or that maybe the good work you're showing is a fluke and that most of the work you do is like the inferior pieces. Either interpretation will devalue your portfolio and all of the work in it.

Some people are aghast at this idea. "This is the only piece I have that shows I can design a website! Didn't you say I needed variety?" Project variety is never served by variety of quality.

Eliminating bad work doesn't always mean eliminating work you didn't enjoy. There's no excuse for keeping in an inferior personal or student project because of the amount of creative control a reviewer assumes you've had. But there is an occasional real-world piece that may not excite you but tells something important about your skills. If you have other work that shows your creativity and one piece that shows you can deliver a finely-crafted but boilerplate project, you might want to leave it in. In your explanation of the project, you can briefly discuss the constraints under which you had to operate.

> You should only select the material that you think best reflects you and your talents. I'd rather look at three pieces than 16, of which two are good and the rest are mediocre. I judge a person's portfolio by their worst piece, not their best piece. Because I assume that if it's in there, that could be the kind of work they could produce for me.
>
> —Bill Cahan

Quantity

There are a lot of myths about how much work you should show in any type of portfolio, let alone a digital one. There's no ideal number, but whatever it might be, people overwhelmingly err on the side of too much. Minimizing the number of pieces you show is a form of self-protection. It's a lot harder to get sucked into showing an inferior project if you limit your total number of pieces.

> I recommend under 20. If you get too many pieces, it's hard to remember anything significant.
>
> —Yang Kim

Illustrators, artists, and photographers, who are responding to a different type of market, will almost immediately disagree. To tap the stock or clip art market, they feel that they have to carry an encyclopedic amount of work on their sites. Their error is in not making a distinction between the entire Web address and a portfolio section—which should be only a small fraction of a website. The person looking through a portfolio section wants to know quickly about an artist's style and how it plays out in some example projects. This need is best served by a small, highly select collection of highlighted images. In contrast, anyone trolling through the stock section is already sold on the style and is looking for something specific. They will treat the site like a database or search engine.

Reworking, rethinking

Once you've trimmed your expectations on how much work to show and eliminated from contention any work that feels off, you may discover gaps in areas you originally thought were well covered. If you really need to have an example of a certain type of work, you can return to a less satisfying piece and rethink it—pushing it harder to show that you know how it should have turned out.

Reworking is almost obligatory for any piece that wasn't professionally produced and is particularly successful in

> For me, the ideal portfolio has about a dozen pieces in it. And that dozen pieces gives me a clear idea of how the person thinks, how that person approaches problem-solving, and how that person understands the constraints of the craft.
>
> —Stan Richards

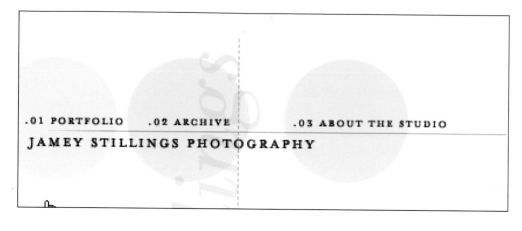

.01 PORTFOLIO   .02 ARCHIVE   .03 ABOUT THE STUDIO

JAMEY STILLINGS PHOTOGRAPHY

www.jameystillings.com
Jamey Stillings knows the difference between a portfolio and a database. He makes a clear distinction between his portfolio—a limited selection of current work—and his vast database of personal and professional images in the archive.

> I think that less happens to be more in portfolios, unless you have solid stellar work and you've done 30 pieces that you think are great. That's unlikely. I mean, I can't even find 10 in my own portfolio that I think are great.
>
> —Bill Cahan

pieces that will appear in a digital portfolio. In particular, animations and interactive projects are so comparatively easy to rework at the same level of production that you should never include a substandard one. Even with a site that was a live client project, if you clearly show how it could have been improved, you up your stock with a potential employer.

You also have the prerogative of reworking projects that were okay but suffered from built-in limitations. If your portfolio is chock full of black and white line drawings and you are bored with working in black and white, why show a digital portfolio that will never get you a color illustration? Reworking an idea with fewer (or different) limitations shows versatility and enthusiasm for your work.

CREATING YOUR OWN PROJECTS

Based on your past projects, why would someone hire you? It's possible that you love the work you do and hope a revised portfolio will help you to do more of it. But if you don't have any good examples of the work you'd like to do, and none that can simply be revised, it's time to invent your own.

Invention is not a lame response, or "make work." Creative directors often look for free-lancers and employees who will take initiative without losing sight of the project goals. If your portfolio shows evidence of these traits but you only have one four-color piece in it (the one you invented), you could very well beat out someone whose portfolio is stuffed full of pedestrian color material. That can hold true even if the other person's portfolio contains professionally printed samples, and yours is printed on an Epson. And in a digital portfolio, where all surfaces become pixels, it might be enough to get you in the door.

Not all projects are equally worthwhile as professional hole-patchers. The sidebar that follows, "Classic projects," is a starter list. Your best bet is to stick with projects that are realistic but offer an opportunity to express your creativity. Unless you are inexplicably at a loss for structure, there will be plenty of time in your life to do product spec sheets, identity systems, and Web forms. Just keep some ground rules in mind before you begin:

I'm looking for creativity, I'm looking for a designer's ability to be commercial when necessary. I'm looking for diversity. And for people who have worked for large corporate design firms, where they may not have had an opportunity to work on really exciting, edgy projects, I want to see some personal stuff that shows what they're able to do.

—Cynthia Rabun

- **Select a client first.** Having a real-world company's need to consider is much better than trying to imagine one.
- **Make your client fill a gap.** Never done a project aimed at a very different demographic? Try a company that sells to children, to retirees, or to farmers.
- **Do your research.** Take the project seriously enough to look at what your client's current material is, and that of some reasonable competitors. What fresh and new approach can you bring to their work?
- **Meet real design constraints.** If you are drawing the art for a poster, select the dimensions of a real poster to produce. If you are designing a book cover or magazine, select a standard publication size. Making an identity? Be sure to use a mailable envelope size and standard business card dimensions. Reviewers will notice immediately if you haven't done your homework.

Classic projects

Stuck for ideas? Some types of projects are the bread and butter of the creative industry. They appear in many digital portfolios and for many clients. One of them could be exactly what you need.

- **Book cover and its interior layout**. Select an already-published book and reimagine it. Create new cover art, select a different typeface, regrid the pages according to your own ideas.

www.gunnarswanson.com
Gunnar Swanson's interests in both design and text are given expression in his elegant book design for Allworth press.

- **Newsletter.** There are lots of ugly newsletters in the world. Rework one the way it should have been produced.

- **Catalog.** Catalogs are the bread and butter of the consumer economy. Some of them are luscious, but most are exercises in the mundane. Select one mundane example and redesign its cover, back cover, and an inside spread.

- **Music CD or DVD**. A classic opportunity is to add something edgy to an otherwise corporate portfolio. Even better is if you can combine it with collateral work for the artist or band.

www.wrecked.nu
Gabe Rubin's CD covers are an opportunity to showcase his ability to meet diverse client needs, even ones whose music isn't as edgy as his usual style.

- **Event poster**. Someone who is primarily an illustrator can shine with a few poster projects in hand. Designers love them because posters allow you to play creatively with many different elements.

- **Real estate or travel prospectus**. A stylish project provides a canvas for an elegant, understated approach. If your work has been youth-oriented, this might provide a change of pace.

PORTFOLIO HIGHLIGHT:
HORSEPOWER DESIGN | BALANCE

We really are bridging two very disparate client bases. We do work for snowboard and other sport companies—a very youth-oriented market. On the other side, we also do work for very corporate clients, like Microsoft and AllState. In designing the site, we were trying to find that happy medium that wouldn't turn off either one.

—Chris Davis

One of the most important issues for a designer or small design studio is variety. You cherish projects that let you express yourself as well as your client. Those types of projects exist, but the competition for them is fierce. So a talented and competitive designer also wants to be attractive to more conservative clients, who expect and deserve the same ability and commitment. If you want to attract work from a disparate clientele, what kind of Web portfolio should you build? Horsepower Design (HPD), of Seattle, Washington, asked that question and answered it successfully.

Navigation and architecture

Although a small studio, HPD has a greatly varied client base. Their depth of work extends from branding and collateral work for corporate giants such as Microsoft at one end to neon signage for a trendy Mexican restaurant at the other. Needless to say, although any good designer knows that style is dictated by the client, the style of your portfolio should be determined by your strategy. That means an architecture that any corporate client would find easy to navigate, as well as a site that's fast and focused. Fortunately, speed and focus work well for trendy clients as well.

www.horsepowerdesign.net

The balancing act begins from the very first splash screen of the Horsepower site. It's a fast-loading Flash animation—evocative enough to grab a young, hip eye yet short enough to stay below the corporate impatience threshold. After its short marketing slogan appears, the animation pulses like fire while waiting. The message: Horsepower is young and energetic but market savvy.

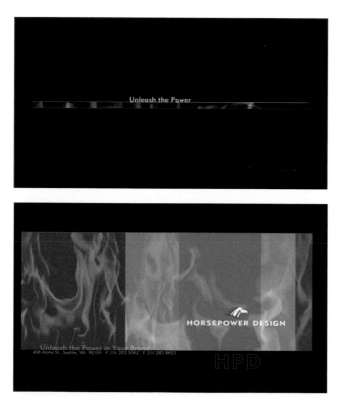

The logo initials are mnemonic links to the three RGB color-coded main site areas (H = HPD the company, P = Portfolio, D = Drop us a line). The links appear consistently but unobtrusively in the lower-left corner of every site page.

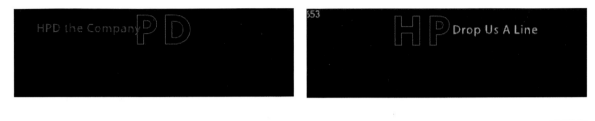

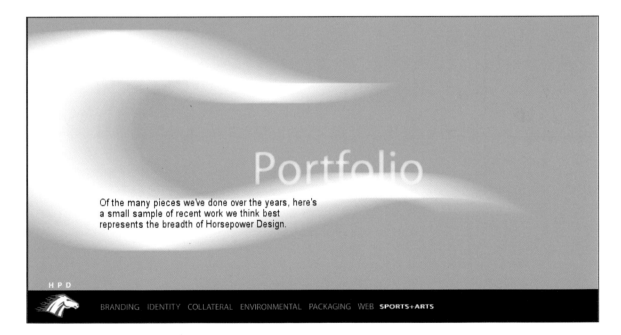

The main portfolio page carries forward the color-coding and clusters the work categories along the black bottom bar. When you roll over a link, it highlights in bold. To return to this main portfolio page from one of the branches, you click again on the P in the HPD navigation key.

Clients tend to want an overview of the quality of work that you've done, and the types of clients can be just as important as the work. A strong brand or a successful company adds perceived value to your portfolio.

—Chris Davis

Content

The HPD site page design has a distinctly corporate/professional feel. The layout is spare and tightly gridded. Many of the images are rectangular, formal product shots. The featured work initially feels somewhat weighted toward large corporate clients. This is no accident of placement.

However, if you look closely at the HPD navigation categories, you'll see that the last one, sports+arts, is not a standard design project category. This is not an error in parallel structure. It's a combination of navigation cross-referencing and client targeting. Horsepower is particularly renowned for its brand identity and product design graphics for snowboard clients. Click on this link, and you find a site-within-a-site, with work in many design categories, some of which also can be found back in the main portfolio category group.

Work for Microsoft and other corporate clients is prominent in the first portfolio categories.

Future plans

A tribute to the site design decisions, the HPD site has existed without major redesign for three years. As long as it works as a solid marketing tool, HPD will concentrate on updating the work, rather than redesigning a hard-working site. They add or replace new pieces quarterly to keep their site fresh and their examples current.

We're very comfortable working with all types of companies. And I think some of the pieces in our portfolio show a design edge that gives the portfolio flair and interest.

—Chris Davis

K2 Snowboards

CONSUMER CATALOG The inagural catalog launching the latest thrill machines from K2 had to really pack a punch and entice potential consumers. Fluorescent inks activated this catalog into oblivion, hyping their kickboards and messing with the vision of kids all over the nation.

H P D   Portfolio SPORTS + ARTS

CATALOGS ADVERTISING IDENTITY PRODUCT POSTERS MUSIC WEB

K2 Snowboards

2003 "NEMESIS" SNOWBOARD GRAPHICS Beware of the Nemesis lurking behind curtains of fire and light. Its vibrant colors and foil stamped topsheets will leave you in a trance. The Nemesis comes complete with silkscreened sidewalls and diecut-dyesublimated bases.

click on boards for detail

H P D   Portfolio SPORTS + ARTS

CATALOGS ADVERTISING IDENTITY **PRODUCT** POSTERS MUSIC WEB

The sub-site, although it conforms to the same layout as the rest of the site, feels looser and younger. The products are collaged rhythmically. The work itself has a completely different aesthetic. Even the text in the client brief is looser and younger.

CHAPTER 3

Audience

Your portfolio is an expression of who you are. But even the unique "you" changes according to your mood and situation. Kicking back with friends sparks a different state of mind than visiting family. It should. You're relating to people whose assumptions, goals, and values are probably galaxies apart. However, unless you're a chameleon, you don't become someone new with each group. You adapt your style to feel more comfortable—or to make the people you're with more comfortable with you.

Creating a portfolio that speaks effectively to prospective clients or employers might require similar adjustments. The days when companies salivated indiscriminately over hot new talent have disappeared. The current era is much more competitive, and the balance of power has shifted with a thud back to where it used to be—toward the people who hire our skills and talents. There are fewer companies hiring and fewer projects to go around. To get your share of the current opportunities, you need to be nimbler, luckier, and more aware of what your market desires.

With your self-examination fresh in your mind, this chapter will point you in the direction of tools to help you sharpen your marketplace savvy. We'll move from figuring out what you need to research, through good places to do your researching, to some practical tips on how to conduct fruitful market research. By the end of the chapter, you'll be well on your way to knowing who your target is and what they'll want to see in your portfolio.

WHY DO RESEARCH?

Part of the allure of digital portfolios is the potential they offer to craft collections of work tailored to a single market, culture, or geographical area. Unfortunately, you need to know a lot about each audience to speak effectively to it. Knowledge is key to chasing the right work, media, and approach.

> I tried to understand who my audience was, who my ideal perspective clients would be. I wanted to know what they'd be looking for and how I could package the work to interest them. I found that I needed examples of work from a number of different components—like brochure, Web, and signage—that surround the same brand expression. So, a client could look at the site and say, "Oh, OK. We could hire this firm to do everything for our brand and all of the commensurate applications."
>
> —Nancy Hoefig

Wouldn't it be nice if the people you'd like to work with would just tell you what they want? Actually, they do. They publicize new campaigns and give interviews about their strategic partners. They give talks at clubs and offer their opinions at student critiques. They put up websites with client lists and project samples that tell you the type of work they do and what types of firms they're pleased to do it for. Sometimes they even provide case studies that tell you all about their working process. This abundance of information tells an astute observer volumes about their philosophy, aesthetics, and company culture. You find this wealth of information through research.

With solid research in hand, you don't have to design your portfolio and hope you've made the right choices. An illustrator who has researched his targets' styles and clientele can showcase examples of appropriate work online. A designer can send an individually created PDF that shows her knowledge of a firm's client base or working process.

The word "research" makes some visual people twitch. Don't let it. You're just poking around for information, something you probably do for personal projects or just plain curiosity without giving it a second thought. The only difference here is that you'll be aware of what you're doing and have a long-range goal in mind.

WHAT SHOULD YOU RESEARCH?

Your research could be most effective if you move from the general to the specific. The further along you are in your career, the finer you might winnow the field. If you are already very focused and aware of your possible market, you might simply research individual prospects.

Depending on why you are creating a digital portfolio, you may pause at, stop on, or skip directly to any of four progressively more detailed research stages.

1. Who's your target audience?

Savvy creative professionals always ask this question of their clients. Design and advertising are driven by market forces. Each individual market needs to be approached in a unique way. We all know—or we should—that it's hard to develop a good logo, design effective communication, or create a killer game if you haven't a clue about who you need to sell to, speak to, or impress.

We may complain about our clients' myopia, but we can be guilty of the same career crime. Although you can do every type of work for everyone, you are probably better at some types of projects than others. The end result is more satisfying, better produced, and you're proud to show it. Why not make yourself more attractive to people who can offer you that kind of project?

When you aren't consistently getting the work that you would like, you either have to look closely at yourself (as we did in Chapter 2, "Adaptation") or your working environment. If you're not sure how to define your audience or what type of audience matches you best, the Market Assessment sidebar provides a list to spark your thinking.

Which of these items is most important to you? Priorities matter because your ideal situation may not exist. Refer to your self-assessment in Chapter 2 to help you prioritize and narrow your focus.

You might not be sure of how some factors play out—company size, for example. A large corporation may put you to work on one mammoth project, giving you an overview of process and production. Or if you're looking for clientele, you may have prior experience with certain demographics. Should you look for a client that sells to that market? If you're not sure how some of these topics affect your job or client search, you've found a good subject to research.

For example, let's say that you want a better idea of how company size is likely to impact your project opportunities. You could move forward by selecting a small group of companies that do your type of work—half large (advertising companies or design firms listing more than one branch) and half small (firms with a single principal's name or with a creative or unusual identity are often small, personal concerns). Go to their websites and poke around to see how you respond to the type of projects on view, the type of clients (big corporate names or small local companies), and the design of the website itself. A large firm will only show work from a small client if the work represents their most creative effort—a good gauge of their creative range. A small firm may display fairly pedestrian projects if they've been done for a prestigious name—a good measure of their long-term growth aspirations.

Most people don't seem to be able to identify anything specific about their clients. For years, I've asked, "Who's your customer?" and got "everybody" as the answer. My favorite "everybody" came from the owner of a chain of stores that sold tires and wheels for lowriders. So I said, "You're telling me that obstetricians' wives from Encino are going to drive down to Englewood to get light pipes put on their Mercedes?" It turned out that "everybody" was 19- to 25-year-old males—85% African-American, 15% Latin-American...somewhat more specific than "everybody."

—Gunnar Swanson

Market assessment

Looking for a job:

- Geography: Where am I looking?

- Independent studio/agency or in-house department?

- Company size?

- If independent, what specialty? (design/concept, integrated branding, advertising/selling, and so on)

- Client or company industry category or categories?

- Type of projects? (packaging, editorial, marketing, entertainment, for example)

- Specializing in a specific media? (such as print, interactive, mass media, or entertainment)

- Specializing in specific activities or sub-cultures?

Looking for clientele:

- Other creatives, individuals, or corporate?

- If corporate client, specific industries?

- Type of work they purchase? (identity, packaging, magazine advertising, and so on)

- Specializing in a specific media? (for example, print, interactive, mass media, entertainment, and so on)

- Type of audience each client targets?

2. What categories should you search?

After you have created a basic definition of your portfolio's target audience, you're looking for general data about this target. Some typical questions to answer might be:

- Is my target realistic? Are there companies that do exactly what I'm looking for, or should I be more general?
- How many companies fit my target? Can I narrow it down?
- How many companies are local? Does the geography matter to me?

In doing a general category search, you should come up with several pages of possible company targets. If you're in the triple digits, you need to be more selective. If you have only five to ten options, you've narrowed your options too far and too fast.

3. What specific companies should you approach?

Now you're honing in on companies that exemplify the type of work you'd like to do.

You may have found these companies initially by exploring links from the general search or developed a separate list from directories maintained by professional organizations. (See Appendix A, "Resources.") These companies will become the target audience against which you will "test" your portfolio concepts. You'll ask more specific questions about this group:

- What do the companies I've short-listed have in common?
- What do they have to say about their process or client relationships?
- What types of clients do they specialize in?
- What is the range of work they do?

The more these companies have in common, the easier it will be to create a digital portfolio that will be appropriate to the group, yet feel individually crafted when you approach each one. Understanding the visual language and work culture of the companies you admire will make it easier to winnow your existing work and develop ideas for your portfolio presentation.

If you are in possession of this information, you can use it to answer a broad range of vexing questions about your portfolio format, content, and design. Here are some examples of questions that you can find answers to through networking, periodicals, school contacts, websites, or other research sources:

- Should I put that group of photographs in my graphic design site?
- Will they appreciate my sense of humor?
- Which illustrations are likely to get me more book work?
- Will they be put off by the ad campaign work?
- How much new media work should I bring compared to print?

Like anything else—just like buying shoes—it's important to buy the one that fits. Some companies really push innovative work. Other companies are set up for larger, risk-averse clients and they know how to service them. It's a different business. One incredibly talented guy we hired got frustrated because it was difficult to sell his really edgy, unique work. He wound up the straw man—the solution that demonstrated to the client that, yes, we could push the envelope but that never got used.

But in the long run, I don't think he had any regrets. By working in a large place, he had the discipline of a business and a branding program. When he left, he owned a very impressive portfolio of large clients.
—Nancy Hoefig

4. What do these organizations want from you?

Defining your audience and determining their basic category information should always take place before you begin your portfolio. They may be all you need. But in some situations, you want to impress an audience of few—or one. If you've done a good job in organizing yourself (see Chapter 5, "Organizing your work"), you may be able to quickly pull together a version of your portfolio for one special company.

Search questions to answer about a specific company:

+ Are they busy? Are they hiring?
+ What is their aesthetic? Do I like it? Would I be proud to work with them?
+ What's their philosophy or way of working with clients? Could I work within it?
+ How do they like to be approached? Email? Letter? Phone?
+ Who are their decision makers? What does their personal work look like?
+ What are they like to work for?

A designer or potential designer should know why they're presenting their work to that particular design firm, what it is that interested them, and what they're looking to do. I hired a guy, many years ago, who worked at a great design agency in Minneapolis. His was quite frankly the best portfolio I think I'd ever seen in my entire life. We hired him and in getting to know him and understand his philosophy, we started to realize that we weren't in sync. We were more about strategy and solving business problems. He was more about formal design aesthetics. It didn't work at all.

—Bill Cahan

You may wonder why you need to ask these questions. You're applying for a job, not marrying the company. Yes and no. If you're hired, you'll probably spend more time at the office than you do with your significant other. You need to know that so many hours will be well-spent and that the projects you take on will enhance your next portfolio. Also you should consider the other side. If you are hired, but it's not a good fit, you might not stay hired for long. You could have used that time to find a more compatible situation.

You will need a slightly different approach for a full-throttle search on a specific company. Word of mouth information is the most precious and useful way to learn about a specific company that you want to work with or for. Personal and local contacts will be most important, particularly to find out if the company represents a solid work opportunity.

SEARCH TOOLS

No matter how general or specific your search looks, you'll be using tools you probably take for granted: personal contacts, periodicals, and the Internet.

Personal contacts

A personal network can be your best resource. Do you know anyone who has the kind of job you want? If they are secure there, they might tell you what people at their firm say about the portfolios that get passed around. Creative professionals in related areas can be excellent contacts because they talk to the same people you would—but about different work. They might give you the name of someone in the organization who would be willing to look at your current material and give you direct feedback on it. (See Chapter 13, "Presenting your portfolio.") Other surprisingly good contacts are representatives of supplier companies such as printers or service bureaus. They can often tell you who in your city is busy and might be ready to hire new talent.

If there is a professional association in your field, join it. Most large national associations, like the AIGA (American Institute of Graphic Arts) and the IDSA (Industrial Designers Society of America) have regional chapters with contact information listed on the associations' main websites. (You'll find a list of professional associations and their websites in Appendix A.) Very active chapters will have their own websites, brimming with useful information about the local scene. Go to the meetings, and take advantage of any career events they sponsor. If you are new to your profession, volunteer your time, particularly for events and projects that will give you the opportunity to work with people at different levels of experience. People are more likely to go out of their way to answer questions for someone they've met (or for the friend of a friend).

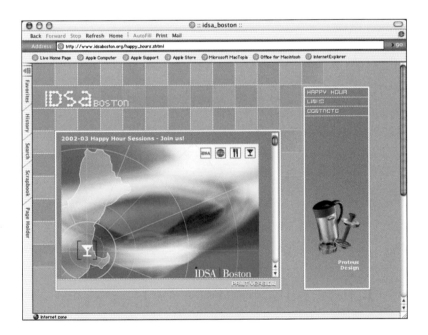

www.idsaboston.org
Each active local chapter should offer special meet-and-greet events, like the ongoing "Happy Hour" meetings at IDSA:Boston. Really large chapters may offer local lectures, special events, and local job listings.

Although it's not the same as a face-to-face encounter, you can also learn a tremendous amount by visiting online forums (see Appendix A). People are always interested in discussing professional practice and willing to offer advice and a reality check. A good source for a list of forums and discussion groups specific to your chosen career is Yahoo (groups.yahoo.com). There are often several groups dedicated to your interest area, so look for the ones that have the largest number of members and have many recent postings.

dir.groups.yahoo.com
A search on "graphic design" in the Yahoo Groups section turned up over 400 groups, but Yahoo sorts them in order of membership size. The most useful groups will almost always be found within the top 20 listings.

YAHOO! Groups

Welcome, Guest

Yahoo! Groups

Top > Entertainment & Arts > Fine Arts > Design Arts > **Graphic Design**

[   ] [Search]

1 - 10 of 430 | Previous | Next [First | Last]

1   **Bashar Designs**
    \<center> \<MARQUEE bgcolor="white" loop=
    "-1" scrollamount="2" width="100%"> ... **more**
    Members: 1154 | Archives: Members only

2   **AIGAExperienceDesign**
    The mission of AIGA Experience Design is to
    investigate, innovate and advocate the best
    understanding and use of design in a world in
    which experiences are increasingly digital and ...
    more
    Members: 1130 | Archives: Public

Most professional organizations have statistics and surveys about your profession, from pricing structures to presentation standards, often broken down by geography or industry. While some of this material might be published for general use, other parts of it might be for members only. Contact information for a selection of relevant organizations can be found in the Appendix A.

Schools, universities, and alumni associations

Did you graduate from an art school or from a university with a large department or school in your specialty? If so, you could have an invaluable resource at hand. A specialized school might offer career counseling and even placement services for alums. As a service to their students, schools often offer great career links. Even if they don't, they're usually well-connected with firms in their local area and committed to offering useful information that can be exactly what you need for your target audience search.

Some art and design schools have an intricate network of alumni associations in major cities throughout the world. Local alumni clubs often have lists of companies with established professionals who are willing to offer informational interviews—or even a shot at real jobs—to other alums. They can help you match your skills and interests with companies whose style and interests are compatible with your own. Even nongraduates can sometimes find these organizations helpful. Their list of prestigious firms and contact names can help you in a category search or to find possible targets in a geographical area that interests you.

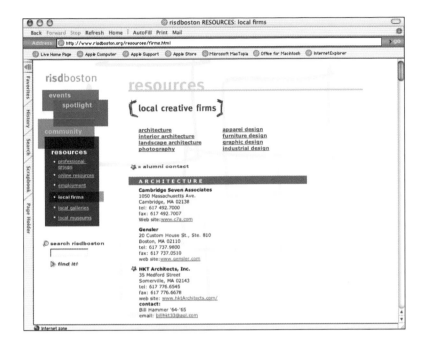

www.risdboston.org
RISDBoston is a very active local chapter that lists local firms with a special interest in RISD graduates. Ones with alumni contacts are starred and listed with their year of graduation.

Internet

Unquestionably, the Internet has become the first and best tool for capturing information. There's almost nothing you can't find out about potential clients or employees—in general or in specific—by using Internet resources.

One of the easiest ways to find out about a specific company is by Googling (**www.google.com**). Phrases such as "working for (target company here)" or "(target company here)," and "resume" will get you job listings and contacts, as well as articles about the company. In addition, if you've targeted a large and well-known company, you can visit a career website (like **www.vault.com**) and search their name on its message boards.

Remember to make bookmarks so you can return to them later and organize your bookmarks into categories, like "job directories" and "art schools." Half of the battle in making your way through research is knowing where to look for answers. If you have to reconstruct your sources every time you have a problem to solve, the process will take much longer.

Designing a general search

The problem with the Web is that it offers too much information. Between Google, Yahoo! and all the searchable design- and art-specific websites, you could waste hours looking for data. You need a strategic approach.

Imagine that you're a designer looking for firms that do branding. One good place to start is Yahoo!, because its format makes it easy to find things by category. Go to Yahoo! (**www.yahoo.com**) and type in "graphic design studio." Oops. It sends you to Studio City in California. Well, your real interest is in design firms that do branding. What if you replace "studio" with "branding?" Well, you're out of Studio City, but you still have 85,000 results to wade through.

search.yahoo.com
Not only is Studio
City the wrong area,
it's way too big a
category—with
625,000 results.

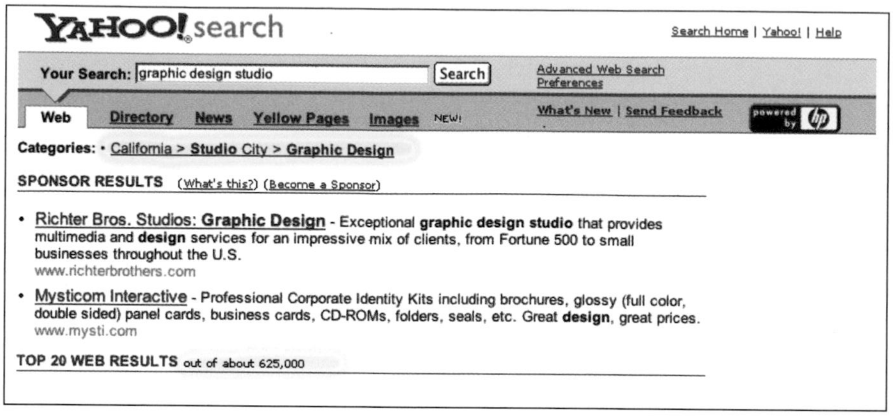

YAHOO! search   Search Home | Yahoo! | Help

Your Search: graphic design studio   [Search]   Advanced Web Search
                                                    Preferences

Web   Directory   News   Yellow Pages   Images   NEW!   What's New | Send Feedback   powered by (hp)

Categories: • California > Studio City > Graphic Design

SPONSOR RESULTS   (What's this?) (Become a Sponsor)

• Richter Bros. Studios: Graphic Design - Exceptional **graphic design studio** that provides
  multimedia and **design** services for an impressive mix of clients, from Fortune 500 to small
  businesses throughout the U.S.
  www.richterbrothers.com

• Mysticom Interactive - Professional Corporate Identity Kits including brochures, glossy (full color,
  double sided) panel cards, business cards, CD-ROMs, folders, seals, etc. Great **design**, great prices.
  www.mysti.com

TOP 20 WEB RESULTS out of about 625,000

You could continue to add words to the search list, but the curious thing about adding raw
criteria in a search is that it can lead you away from your actual interest. You need to search smarter
by using the Advanced Web Search, as shown in the figure below. Here you can search the exact
phrase "graphic design studio," along with the individual word "branding." For good measure, you can
add your own city in the "any of these words" box to scope out local options.

search.yahoo.com
Yahoo!, Google, and most
other good directory and
search sites have an advanced
search function. Turn to it if
your first easy search turns
out to be too general.

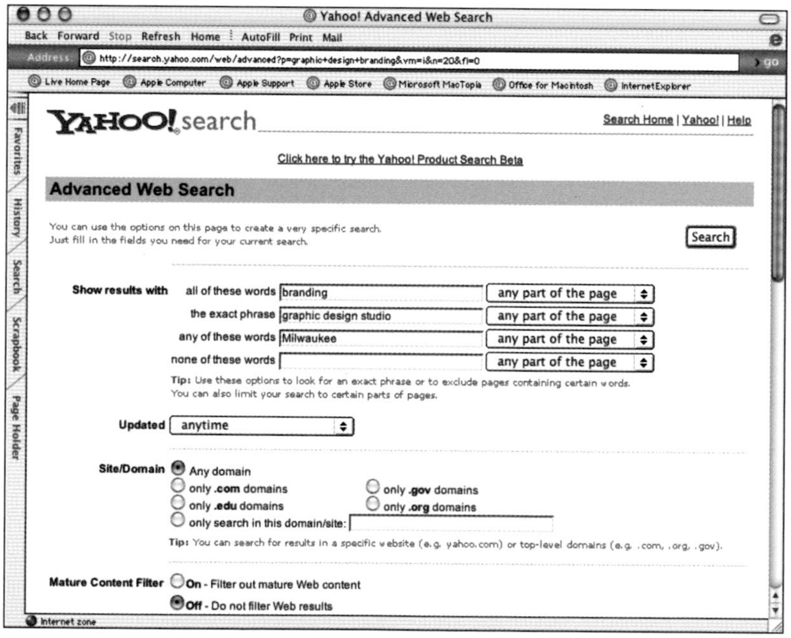

Yahoo! Advanced Web Search
Back Forward Stop Refresh Home   AutoFill Print Mail
Address: http://search.yahoo.com/web/advanced?p=graphic+design+branding&vm=i&n=20&fl=0   go
Live Home Page   Apple Computer   Apple Support   Apple Store   Microsoft MacTopia   Office for Macintosh   Internet Explorer

YAHOO! search   Search Home | Yahoo! | Help

Click here to try the Yahoo! Product Search Beta

Advanced Web Search

You can use the options on this page to create a very specific search.
Just fill in the fields you need for your current search.   [Search]

Show results with   all of these words   branding   [any part of the page ▼]
                     the exact phrase   graphic design studio [any part of the page ▼]
                     any of these words Milwaukee   [any part of the page ▼]
                     none of these words   [any part of the page ▼]

                     Tip: Use these options to look for an exact phrase or to exclude pages containing certain words.
                     You can also limit your search to certain parts of pages.

Updated   [anytime ▼]

Site/Domain ● Any domain
             ○ only .com domains   ○ only .gov domains
             ○ only .edu domains   ○ only .org domains
             ○ only search in this domain/site:

             Tip: You can search for results in a specific website (e.g. yahoo.com) or top-level domains (e.g. .com, .org, .gov).

Mature Content Filter ○ On - Filter out mature Web content
                       ● Off - Do not filter Web results

Internet zone

You might wonder, why not put the city on the same line as branding? Sometimes it doesn't
matter, and you'll get identical results both ways. Other times, particularly if the words in the first
box combine (like "west" and "branding" might), you could end up with something totally different
than what you intended.

When you do a search using a general tool like Yahoo!, your results will fall into two categories. One will be specific names of companies that meet your criteria. The other will comprise other directories, some of them branches of Yahoo!, others completely independent. (See Appendix A for a list of some good directories to start with.) Sometimes these independent directories contain a better list of results than Yahoo! does, so check them out when they appear in a search list.

For example, although it's purely alphabetical, I particularly like **www.design-engine.com**'s directory of ID firms because it gives you a thumbnail description of each company in the list. On the downside, you could waste hours skimming the almost 300 listings because it has no search function. That failing is shared by many industry-specific directories.

Additionally, by looking at the brief descriptions, you might be able to eliminate those that don't sound right for you. Find a keyword that appears in the useless results. Return to the advanced search page and add the word or words to the "none of these words" box. In our hypothetical search, we've done this and slimmed down to only 51 results. That's a reasonable number to explore.

www.google.com

Use Google to search sites without their own search functions. In the Google search box, type your criteria (NY), then a space, and then **site**: followed by the site URL (in this case, design-engine.com). You'll get a list of links only from that one site that contain your search criteria. It's so much easier to assess 19 responses than to struggle through a list of hundreds of items.

search.yahoo.com

If the directories turn out to be a dead end and you want to limit your search to companies, you can shorten your list by clicking the "only.com domains" radio button.

> Site/Domain ○ Any domain
> ⦿ only **.com** domains   ○ only **.gov** domains
> ○ only **.edu** domains   ○ only **.org** domains
> ○ only search in this domain/site: |.com
>
> **Tip:** You can search for results in a specific website (e.g. yahoo.com) or top-level domains (e.g. .com, .org, .gov).

DESIGNING A TARGETED SEARCH

Imagine you are still the designer interested in branding. Always on the lookout for good work, you're wondering who designs Williams-Sonoma's material. How can you find out? Again, an advanced search can help to answer that question. To find out what firms have the company as a client, you combine several descriptive words, including "client" and "branding." (See the figure below.)

Of the top five responses, only one—the second result—gives you an agency, but it looks promising.

search.yahoo.com

"Williams-Sonoma" must be input as an exact phrase to avoid getting sidetracked by people named Williams or Sonoma County.

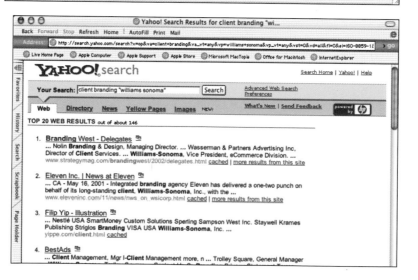

search.yahoo.com

Next stop is the Eleven, Inc. site, where you can examine their portfolio and client list and see if you are on the right track.

Hit the books

Creative professionals frequently pour through *Graphis*, *Communication Arts*, and other magazines for inspiration. These publications are also useful for research. It is still much easier to flip through a book than search on the Web, so you should glean as much information this way as possible. Look for work you admire and see if the companies or studios who've done the work fit your general audience description.

You also can use these books to create a Web search, a particularly fine strategy if the companies you love don't happen to be anywhere near where you live. Go to their websites and look at the source HTML code, as shown below. There should be a descriptive list of words inside a tag called "meta." Use these words for your local area searches, and you should find companies that describe themselves the same way and hopefully do the same type of work.

```
<meta name="keywords" content="branding, strategy, advertising, design,
interactive, web, brand strategy, advertising agency, ad agency, graphic
design, graphic design firm, design firm, design studio, interactive design,
interactive agency, design services, brand communications, brand consultants,
multi channel retailing, strategic design, corporate identity, logo design,
collateral, annual reports, e-commerce, packaging, package design, online
strategy, web strategy, web design, web development, web site design, website
design, marketing strategy, i-shop, web shop, online marketing, interactive
marketing, online branding, banner ads, point of sale display, point of sale
design, pos, pop, flash design, flash, direct mail">
```

Meta tags are used by Web search engines to find sites that meet your criteria. Someone at the company has deliberately chosen these words to make their site come up frequently in a Web search.

WHEN ARE YOU DONE?

One of the dubious delights of research is that it is never completely finished. There are always little tidbits of information that can teach you more about your target audience or change your focus. Once your portfolio is underway, it's a good idea to revisit individual websites and check for articles that might have been recently posted.

In the meantime, you should have developed a feel for the market you want to enter or entice. Looking at their work has helped you judge what of your own work might be most effective. Reading about their philosophy and comparing it to their client lists will tell you whether you should be conservative or try for a tour de force. If you've been researching potential clients, you'll know who they've used previously, why they continued to use them (or dumped them), and whether they might find your approach compatible.

In short, you'll know your subjects well enough to have built a little target audience construct in your head. Based on your self-assessment from Chapter 2, do your current skills and work fit that picture? If not, you'll need to determine the changes you need to bring your portfolio into the right ballpark. If they do, you can steam confidently ahead.

PORTFOLIO HIGHLIGHT:
BBK Studio | Know your market

www.bbkstudio.com

How well do you know your market? If you know it well enough, you can create a site that meets all of a website's general purposes while still attracting the type of client you most desire. BBK Studio, a design consultancy in Michigan with three award-winning designers, illustrates how to keep your options open while still fielding a client-centric site.

> The primary audience for this website is a potential client. The work on our website is its eye-candy. But you can also see *how* we work and how we understand the client's problem.
>
> —Yang Kim

Navigation and architecture

Speed and efficiency are important to corporate clients. The BBK Studio site has no opening Flash animation or other titling function. The viewer comes directly to the meat: a navigation system that maps the whole site, a fast-loading image, and some constantly updated news-bites in simple HTML text.

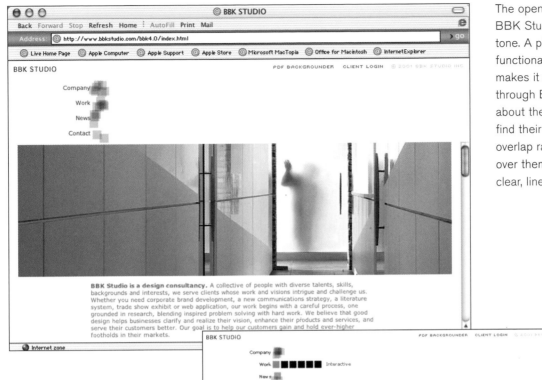

The opening screen of the BBK Studio website sets the tone. A playful, but extremely functional navigation system makes it easy to either browse through BBK's work, read about their process, or skim to find their clients. The boxes overlap randomly until you roll over them, when they become clear, linear signposts.

Click a box, and it brings you to the link. The navigation persists on every screen. The Work section has two parts. The grouping on the left represents the categories. The group on the right-hand side represents individual examples within the categories. Roll over any box, and it's identified at the right-hand end of the row.

Each box changes color as the page or section it represents is visited, making it easy for the user to tell at a glance how much of the portfolio she's seen.

The portfolio page gives a representative view of a project, with the simplest possible client brief. The companion case study goes into more detail, in both word and image. It also allows a much better representation of the work than the bandwidth limitations of a website allow.

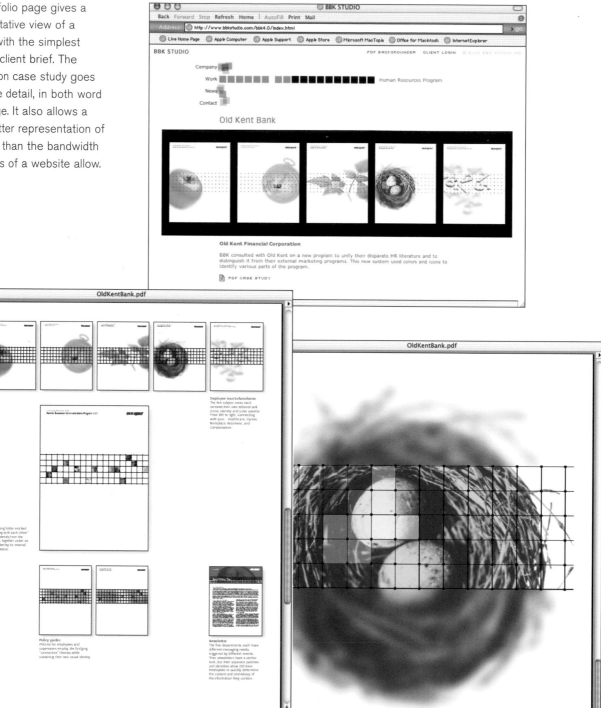

The site offers several well-stocked project categories that reflect the way clients purchase. Says principal Yang Kim, "We do about fifty percent new media and fifty percent traditional design. We try to represent both by picking a good cross-section of our client work. We picked categories that people who buy design can relate to, like annual reports or print collateral." The breadth of categories tells potential clients that BBK can handle integration of a variety of projects and in a wide range of media.

Content

BBK does not simply display a historical record of projects. It uses the website as a tool to help deliver more specific, client-oriented messages. Every portfolio page offers a case study that documents how BBK approached the project.

Through the combination of media, BBK gets the best of both worlds: a website for the general viewer and an opportunity to tell a new client how the principals think and work. "The case studies are written from the client's perspective," explains Yang Kim. "They show what that particular client's problem was and how it was solved. The potential client can relate to that a lot faster than they do to an esoteric photo of an annual report."

Future plans

Portfolio sites are always in flux, and you learn from what works. The PDF case studies have been a great success. BBK plans to use some elements from them in the new version of the site. As Yang Kim says, "We often now have both a digital and a print component in the same series. So, as with the case studies, we'll be making version 5.0 more dynamic by cross-referencing the components. The cross-referencing will help to emphasize that our projects are a collaborative effort."

CHAPTER 4

Format

One of a digitally based portfolio's conveniences is its flexibility. The same content can be packaged in a delightful variety of ways, depending on your needs and your available time. You can begin simply with a small selection of work collected in a PDF, opt for a short slideshow presentation for a client pitch, or move to an interactive website or CD. A well-organized digital file lets you shift elements in and out for multiple presentations almost as easily as you might slide something into and out of a binder. Even nicer, the work you collect in one format can become the basis for a more comprehensive and sophisticated portfolio as your technical knowledge broadens and your body of work increases.

There is no "right" format for a portfolio. Nonetheless, there are preferred formats and preferred combinations of formats. And there are definitely wrong choices—decisions that might look attractive initially but for various reasons are poor decisions for your market. All choices boil down to one of two types: portable or online.

PORTABLE MEDIA

If you want to make your digital portfolio a part of your in-person presentation, or need to send large-sized files to prospective clients or employers, you can select from a variety of materials.

Zip disks

In one word: don't. Zip disks have been a popular portable format, but their limitations are more obvious as CD burners become standard computer peripherals. They are undependable and fairly fragile. They do not cross platforms easily. A PC-formatted disk viewed on a Mac will often have a corrupt desktop—a very frustrating experience for the unsuspecting. Zips hold very little material for their price. And most importantly, your portfolio can be zapped off them in a busy shop that needs a disk quickly. Do yourself a favor and avoid them.

> When designers or illustrators send me a disk, I often find that either I don't have the correct software installed or the disk crashes the computer. Either way, in the trash it goes. In case you're wondering, I'm not a Luddite, but I know I'm not the only designer who feels this way.
>
> —Alex Isley

CDs

The CD is by far the most common choice for a disk-based portfolio. CDs are familiar, easy to integrate into a traditional portfolio, and fairly sturdy. In addition, they can be attractively packaged.

If you decide to put your portfolio on a CD, you can choose between a CD-R (write once, no deletions or changes) and a CD-RW (write many times, like any hard drive or Zip). I recommend that you keep your template on a CD-RW to make it easy to update as you complete new projects. When you're ready to send out a copy or to bring a disk with you for a presentation, copy the material onto a CD-R.

People feel strongly—pro and con—about receiving a CD portfolio. The people who dislike them usually do so not because of the format itself, but because so many people do a bad job of creating them. Typical complaints range from bad organization to unreadable file formats. Unlike a website, which can be revised to address these types of problems, a badly conceived or executed CD will simply be tossed—or tossed around a shop as an example of bad form. Chapter 5, "Organizing your work," Chapter 10, "Development basics," and Chapter 13, "Presenting your portfolio," address these issues head-on, and will help you create a CD portfolio that won't frustrate an art director.

You may also run into the laziness factor. It isn't fair, but for some people —more in the design world than in ID or animation—having to put a CD into their drive, look through it, and then find your contact information seems like too much trouble. Don't let that prevent you from creating a CD portfolio, but if you are in design, keep another digital sampler in the wings. PDFs and email may be your best first contact.

> Most artists send image files as attachments. My preference would be a CD. I could easily archive the material somewhere other than my own hard drive. In addition, a CD would normally contain a more extensive overview of the artist's work.
>
> —Mary Ann Kearns

In contrast, people with positive experiences with CDs swear by them. Unlike a website, which must be designed around bandwidth considerations, a CD can be viewed anywhere, anytime, even without wireless access. You can create the material on it at a much higher resolution, so typographic or composition details that you're proud of become accessible. It's already a compact package that a creative director can archive and pull out again when the right project comes along.

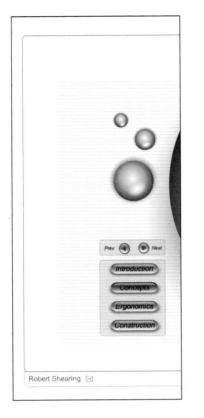 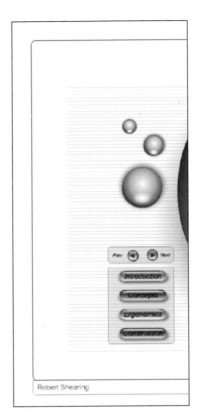

www.rob.id.au
These two images are details from the same portfolio page in Robert Shearing's portfolio. The one on the left is a high-resolution image from the CD version. The one on the right is a screenshot of the same page on his Web portfolio. It has been zoomed to the same pixel dimension as the first one for comparison. The CD file is much too large for a website but clearly displays far more visual information.

Mini CDs

Mini CDs are not often used by visual creatives, although performers have found them so useful that they have taken the place of the actor's traditional demo reel and glossy head-shot. This is not surprising because they are inexpensive and sleek.

Mini CDs are just the right size for a high-resolution presentation or a tasty selection of work that fits in a coat pocket. This smaller CD format has another, less obvious plus—it prevents creative diarrhea. A standard CD has such a large capacity, there's the temptation to put "just one more project" on it. People who succumb to this temptation are the ones whose CDs end up in the trash.

So why not switch to the mini-CD format? They do not play nicely with any slot-loaded CD player. Slot-loaded CD trays are the skinny ones that you slide a CD into and the mechanism drags it the rest of the way in. You'll find them on iMacs and some Compaq workstations, among others. A mini CD will destroy a slot-loaded CD player in lightning-fast time.

Robert Shearing's hand-crafted
packaging of his mini CD is an
irresistible leave-behind.

DVD

DVDs are the best choice for demos of moving image work. On CDs, you'll have to make compromises in image size and quality.

Most demo reels are still distributed on standard VHS tape, but more and more animations and videos are created or edited digitally. Having to convert down to analog is inconvenient and extremely time-consuming. Now that DVD players are becoming standard computer options, the tide is quickly shifting to DVD disks.

Laptop

Besides being an extremely compact and elegant way of transporting large volumes of work, the laptop gives you ultimate control of your presentation. You're less likely to be plagued by technical gremlins because you've controlled and tested your environment. You never have to worry about platform issues or care if the people you are presenting to can tell the difference between a DVD and a coaster. There are no surprises in type size, player speed, and image color. You can show your work in an intimate setting or hook the computer to a projection system and present it to a filled room. For all these reasons, laptops are a great way to present your portfolio to a client.

On the downside, walking in with a laptop sets high expectations that the presentation itself can negate. Unless you have access to a projector and screen, you'll have to choose between watching the screen and connecting with your interviewer or client. The only way around that is to have rehearsed your presentation so frequently that it's practically memorized. You also have to take the flat panel display's limitations into consideration. Anyone at an angle from the screen won't see it at all.

For an individual, buying a decent laptop simply to present your portfolio is an extravagance, to say the least. Using one you already have means toting to interviews what may be your one-and-only computer, the repository of your entire creative existence. If something goes wrong, failing to land a job may be the least of your concerns. And it doesn't save you from creating some other form of portfolio, since you won't be dropping your Powerbook as a leave-behind.

ONLINE

An online portfolio is one that people can view from their very own desktops, on their own time. Online portfolios are like free samples in a supermarket. They enable the potentially interested client or employer to taste-test your work anonymously. If they like what they see, you'll hear from them. If it's not their style, both you and they are spared a painful face-to-face experience.

Although most online portfolios get lumped together as a category, there are actually a variety of distinct types that provide a range of exposure and make different statements about you.

Email

When done correctly, the most effective free sample can be a little email attachment. Its plusses are those of any direct mailing: You can target prospects individually with a fairly small outlay of energy. Because you don't have to create an interface or struggle with a technology learning curve, almost anyone can send an email portfolio.

There are few negatives to email attachments, but they are worth considering nonetheless. First, attachments are a poor second to a website for anyone with substantial online design work. Second, not everyone has enough free space on their server to accept them. This last issue shouldn't be a problem if you are sending to a large company, but it can easily crop up when you're dealing with a boutique firm or emailing to a gallery or client. Third, if sent unannounced they can be viewed as spam—very bad press for the aspiring creative.

> If someone's emailing me their work, it demonstrates that they are really interested in working for the firm, and they've taken the time to research who I am and how to reach me.
>
> —Cynthia Rabun

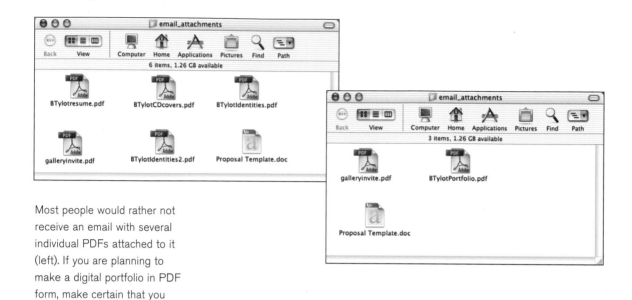

Most people would rather not receive an email with several individual PDFs attached to it (left). If you are planning to make a digital portfolio in PDF form, make certain that you gather all of your material into one PDF file (right).

Personal website

Although creatives use a variety of media, websites are by far the most popular digital portfolio medium. A personal site creates an avenue for creative expression, is constantly available, and through linking can bring you to the attention of prospective clients or employers that you would be hard-pressed to reach otherwise.

> Surprisingly, a fair number of artists who contact me do not have their own website to refer me to and are looking for Web representation.
>
> —Mary Ann Kearns

In practice, a personal website is somewhere between a mailing and an in-person presentation. It allows a much larger work sampling than most mailings and lets you inject personality into an otherwise anonymous experience. It does not allow you to adjust your tone, emphasis, and pacing the way you can easily do face-to-face.

When I discuss personal websites, I include studio portfolios. The line between an individual portfolio and a studio one begins to blur as soon as an individual talent begins to hire freelancers or artists on commission or plunks the phrase "and associates" at the end of his name.

Group presentations

There are two kinds of online "group" portfolios. The first is like a traditional gallery, where one person chooses and organizes the disparate work of individuals. The second is more like a visual source book—an unmediated "mall" of disparate portfolios.

GALLERY

Many artists want a Web presence but are intimidated by the technology or lack the resources to hire someone to create their site. For them, a gallery site can be a substitute for a personal site—a way of establishing a foothold in the virtual world.

JPGs versus PDFs

When it comes to attachments, there are only two good formats: JPGs and PDFs. PDFs should be the file format of choice for graphic designers and illustrators, particularly those who specialize in editorial, identity, or package design. JPGs can be an excellent way for fine artists or animators to give a prospect a taste of their style.

JPG: Pros

JPGs can display correctly in an email—no need to find and launch a file.

Digital cameras make JPGs—great for photographers, artists, and other creators of 3D art and design.

JPG: Cons

JPGs are too useful. They can be digitally stolen and used without your consent.

JPGs do not scale—details are pixelated when zoomed.

Loose JPGs cannot be arranged in sequence or clustered.

PDFs: Pros

The PDF format is almost as universal as JPG. Almost everyone has Acrobat Reader in his or her browser.

PDFs can be generated from page layout programs. You can output directly from the digital art you created in a design project.

PDF windows can be scaled to fit any size monitor without loss of quality.

PDFs allow you to present your work in a specific sequence that mimics a traditional print portfolio.

PDFs can be locked to prevent your work from being easily extracted and appropriated.

PDFs: Cons

You might need Acrobat Distiller to create a PDF. OS X creates PDFs natively, but you have no control over their quality.

To take advantage of PDFs' best features, you need to know a page layout program.

Multi-page PDFs can sometimes end up too large for easy email download.

There are both fine art and commercial gallery sites. In both cases, the site is the product of an individual's personal vision—the curator in a fine art gallery, the rep/curator in the commercial site. An artist has to come to the curator's attention, and the curator has to want to represent that artist. Assuming the chemistry is right, the artist gains immediate increases in visibility, as well as a personal advocate.

Resource book

At the other end of the spectrum from a gallery is the sourcebook site, an unedited, paid listing. Separate ones exist for photographers, illustrators, designers, and artists, although a few (like the Communication Arts portfolio site) cover a range of professionals.

The plusses of this marketplace-based approach are that it is usually inexpensive and practically instantaneous. In minutes, you can have a Web address with your work uploaded into a template. You need to know nothing about design or technology. The template takes care of visual decisions like layout and fonts, as well as shielding you from HTML. It also can be the best way to get your work online when you are unexpectedly let go from a full-time spot.

The downside of such a big site is that your work could get lost on it, unless the site features your portfolio or has a premium portfolio level that makes you more visible.

Any resource book site requires a terrific searchable database to drive work in your direction. Even with a great search engine, you might be judged by chance association. You have no control over the context of your work, and there is no curator to exercise quality control. If a search turns up ten people and the first five are mediocre, your work may not be seen when you're number six.

wwar.com

Typically, artists and designers have a variety of levels to choose from on a resource site. The free portfolio at the basic level is usually extremely limited in the number of images and their size. You'll have to pay a yearly fee to have a more complete portfolio presence.

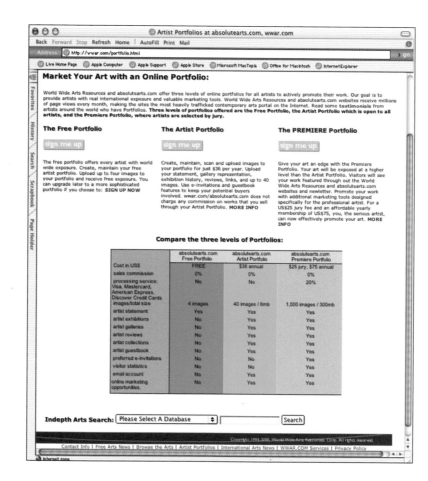

Portfolio highlight:
Sharpe Online | Gallery format

www.sharpeonline.com

Most portfolio gallery sites are personal projects. Each artist devotes significant time to create his or her share of the site, often by making it from scratch. Some gallery sites are curated by a person who bears the burden of maintaining it and who sometimes acts as an agent for the artists. In both cases, the sites are often delightfully anarchistic, non-commercial destinations.

In contrast, professional portfolio sites tend to be distinctly corporate—strictly formatted, plain-vanilla objects. The ones that break this mold are often remarkably amateurish-looking in comparison. Sharpe Online, the site for Sharpe & Associates, is neither. It is several cuts above most gallery or photography or individual. It takes the best elements of the artistic and commercial extremes and adds a large dollop of beautiful design. More so than most fine art destinations, it captures the mood and experience of visiting a collaborative gallery.

John Sharpe reps a decidedly upscale group of image-makers. Prior to launching this website, he reached his target market through striking promo pieces. The website is in keeping with these prior campaigns in being attractive, professional, and one-of-a-kind.

> Sharpe Online launched with seven people. Each talent basically got their own site for about a third of what one artist paid for his individual site. You can't get the same sort of involvement from a design studio or agency that we received without the numbers of people or the significance that we have in the marketplace.
>
> —John Sharpe

Navigation

The Sharpe site is driven with Macromedia Flash. There are pros and cons to this approach. When marketing to corporate clients, it can simply add an extra layer between the client and the work. In this case, Sharpe had an appreciative audience. His clientele are creative directors at studios and advertising agencies, so they are extremely sensitive to a well-designed presentation.

Although fast, functional, and a visually delicious feast, the site's marketing purpose is clear. In the upper crust of the photography market, personal style and concept are major selling points. On this site, each photographer's uniqueness is emphasized to provide eight very focused messages.

> Our site definitely positions us in a unique place vis á vis our competition. All the portfolios function in highly individual ways, and they are all designed conceptually from the talents' work. We try to meet the highest benchmark in everything so that when things get tighter, we'll be the high end that people still come to.
>
> —John Sharpe

On the Sharpe site, the simple gateway page gives way to a cleanly designed new window dominated by a randomly generated image by one of the featured photographers (below). In this case, the image is one by Hugh Kretschmer, but it could just as easily be the work of any of the others in the collaborative group.

If you click on the animated icon near the bottom of the page, you'll go directly to the work of the randomly featured artist whose name appears next to the icon.

Click ARTISTS in the main navigation bar running across the page, and the artist names appear as links to their respective areas.

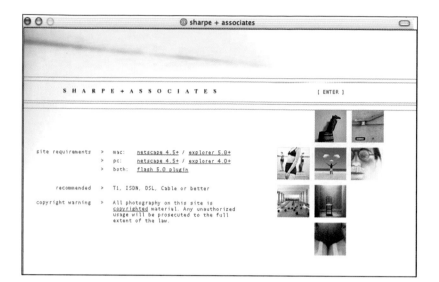

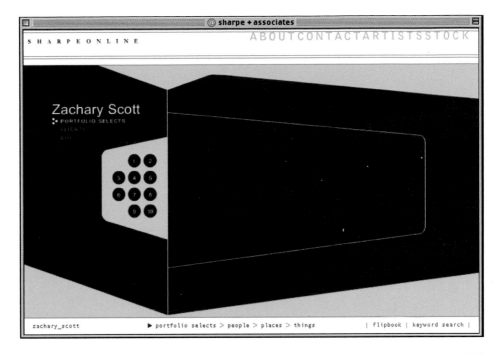

These are the interfaces for
Zachary Scott and Ann Cutting,
two other photographers on the
Sharpe site. Although they
appear radically different, they
are very alike under the skin.

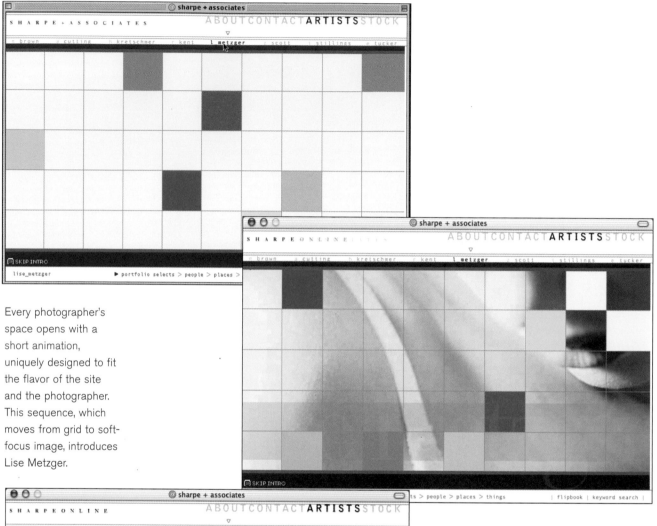

Every photographer's space opens with a short animation, uniquely designed to fit the flavor of the site and the photographer. This sequence, which moves from grid to soft-focus image, introduces Lise Metzger.

Flash makes it easy to create a site with consistent interaction and architecture but radically differing interfaces. Each talent has his or her distinctly individual "room," sporting a unique interface with a personal feel consistent with the style of work, whether it's quirky and humorous, quiet and organic, or something in between.

Despite the radically different flavor of each area, a visitor never gets lost because the Sharpe interface persists at the top of the page. There is an elegant but neutral "wrapper" for the common areas, like a virtual entrance and hallways.

Content

Unlike other sites, which can include case studies and other tangential material, Sharpe Online remains true to its gallery concept. It is all about the work. The site content is sensibly straightforward, despite its visually rich and textured appearance. Each room comprises two parts: "portfolio selects" that offer ten representative highlights of recent work and a collection of stock photos accessed through one of three mail categories. The highlights are often very different in subject and approach, with a view toward exposing as many of each photographer's specialties as possible. Each mini-site also includes an artist bio and a list of selected clients.

Future plans

Even though the site has been enormously successful for the group, Sharpe plans to take advantage of Macromedia Flash's new database management tools to expand it. The current site has too many growth limitations. First in line are improvements to the keyword search and a better backend function. When part of your income comes from topic variety, it's important for potential clients to be able to see a wide range of subject matter. Second, like any gallery owner, he'd like to expand his featured artists, and the current design and its technology limits his options.

> No one side has total control over what shows up where when. I have a strong opinion about what should go in, as do the artists. We usually agree. But my idea for the portfolio selections is that we keep them updated so that one of the first things people see is new work. That's why we call it Portfolio Select—because it's an opportunity to show the latest and greatest.
>
> —John Sharpe

PORTFOLIO STRATEGIES

Not every need can be served with one format. In fact, many creatives need some combination: an online presence, a disk they can mail, and a traditional book to show print work in interviews and personal presentations. There are four ways to approach the multiple portfolio problem: duplicating, dividing, doubling, and developing.

Duplicating

When you duplicate, you have a single body of work in many formats. You develop your portfolio themes, choose the best pieces to illustrate them, and create one portfolio version—the easiest to create or the one you need immediately—first. After this portfolio has been tested, presented, and, if necessary, refined, you duplicate it in other media. The plus of this approach is that it's very fast. Updates happen in tandem, and you never have to remember who saw which version of your work. The minus is that you may be showing some work in a medium which compromises its effectiveness or weakening a piece that plays very well in one format but seems redundant or weak in another.

Dividing

The divided portfolio is a compromise and demands more thought and preparation than simple duplication. Material that doesn't look right on screen and can't be zoomed into or manipulated remains in your traditional portfolio, which you use only in personal presentations. Anything that is effective on screen stays there. The few pieces that sparkle both digitally and traditionally remain in both versions but may be highlighted differently onscreen and off.

Doubling

Doubling—maintaining two completely different portfolios—is not just useful, it's required if you do more than one thing well. Fine artists who actively solicit commercial illustration, designers who also photograph, or illustrators who design are usually best served by keeping these specialized skills separate. It is possible to create distinct areas on a single website, but think twice before you try. This tactic only works if you are truly expert enough in both areas to give them equal attention and treatment.

Designers have dropped off their portfolios with me and the last two pages are a bunch of photographs. The question is, do you think that somebody's going to hire you on the basis of your hobby? I don't want to be negative, but if you're serious about your other skills, then do an extra portfolio and show what kind of photography you specialize in. Don't just put it into your portfolio of design work.

—Layla Keramat

Developing

When you develop, a small selection of older material may combine with new work—revisions of older projects or brand new ideas—explicitly created for the new portfolio. Developing allows you to reinvent yourself. You can revisit ideas and show how you translate concepts with new constraints.

This strategy can be good for a first digital portfolio. It also works for designers moving from a PDF of print work to a sophisticated online presentation. If you want to move into a specialty within your profession—like a photographer moving from product to editorial shots—developing may be the only way to do it.

The negative points of developing come down to two little words with big impact: money and time. Developing from scratch is by far the hardest strategy—short term. But it's often best to take the long view with your portfolio. Everyone has periods of feast and famine, even during good economic times. The quiet periods are ideal for developing new material, which will hopefully help to minimize downtimes in the future.

PORTFOLIO HIGHLIGHT:
JAMEY STILLINGS |
WHEN ONE PORTFOLIO ISN'T ENOUGH

www.jameystillings.com

People who maintain multiple portfolios usually do so for one of two reasons. Some are trying to separate two types of creative work, such as an artist/teacher who keeps a college fine art site but maintains a commercial site for illustration work. Others do so for marketing outreach. They buy inexpensive space on one or many resource book sites in addition to maintaining a personal website.

> I really wanted an independent site that gave me the autonomy to do what I wanted with it.
>
> —Jamey Stillings

In the case of photographer Jamey Stillings, the marketing rationale takes an intriguing twist. He is a photographer represented on Sharpe Online. All of the other photographers use that site as their primary—or only—Web presence, and yet Stillings has spent considerable time and money also developing a website with its own portfolio and personality.

For Stillings, both sites are important, but they serve different purposes. In any collective site, you risk being seen as part of a package deal. If it's a beautiful package, all parts benefit—but not always equally or at the same time. By having his own site with a broader selection of easily updated material, he improves his studio's chances of standing out as an individual entity.

Stillings wanted three important things from his own site. First, he wanted to be able to update and change it immediately. Second, he wanted to broaden the range of material he could display by bringing his library archive of images to life. The Sharpe site doesn't let members make fast changes to their portfolios; it has a ceiling on how much material they can display, and it dictates the format.

Third, and most important, Stillings wanted to present more of himself, especially his non-commercial work—to the world. Both site navigation and site content were influenced by these requirements.

> Reps and photographers have different marketing models, although their relationship is symbiotic. There's a balancing act for me between the collaborative marketing: "Sharpe & Associates reps these people," and the individual marketing: "I'm Jamey Stillings, a photographer who happens to be repped by Sharpe & Associates, and this is what I do."
>
> —Jamey Stillings

Navigation

Stillings set his personal site's functional criteria and goals and worked very closely with the graphic designer responsible for his look and feel. Even prior to Sharpe Online, Stillings had developed very strong feelings about what he liked—and didn't like—about Web interaction and navigation.

It's useful to compare Stillings' own portfolio section (top left) with his portfolio select space on Sharpe. The two sites look comfortable next to one another. Their palettes are similar: neutral shades combined with white background and black type. The logo typefaces and their treatments are different, but the differences are insignificant to the untrained eye. Even some of the stylistic effects are similar, such as hairline rules and small iconic links.

The major difference is the balance between interface and image. In the Stillings site, the interface recedes far into the background, bringing the image starkly forward. Because you can click the magnifier icon to launch a window with an enlarged image, you are constantly reminded that the image and interface are separate. In the Sharpe-Stillings site, the image merges with the background, making the two more equal partners.

.01 PORTFOLIO   .02 ARCHIVE   .03 ABOUT THE STUDIO

JAMEY STILLINGS PHOTOGRAPHY

featured projects

.02.A

.02.A

.02.A

All Images © 2002 Jamey Stillings - Contact Info

Communication Arts
Feature Story

The large circles in the upper left are connections to the three main sections of the site—the portfolio, the database archive, and the studio information area. On rollover, they quietly change to colors sampled from the homepage image.

Rolling over the smaller boxed circles gives you a thumbnail of a featured project from the archives. A click brings you to the archive page.

Lincoln Financial Group - Affluence

.02.A

.02.A

.02.A

Communication Arts
Feature Story

.01 PORTFOLIO   .02 ARCHIVE   .03 ABOUT THE STUDIO

JAMEY STILLINGS PHOTOGRAPHY

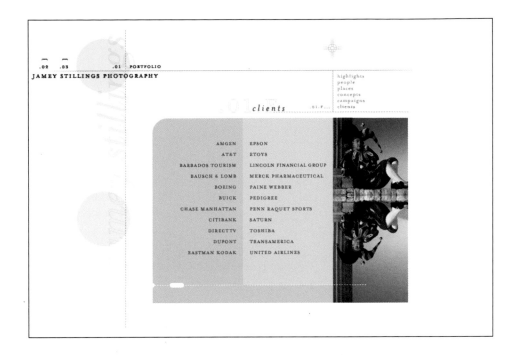

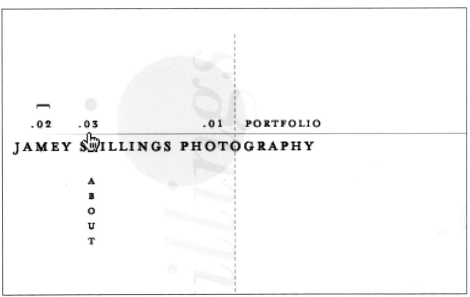

In each area, the large navigation circle is rendered in its coded color, as are all other type and graphic elements on the page. The other two circles disappear, leaving only their section numbers. When you roll over the section number, a small version of the circle and a vertical label appear.

I didn't use Flash in my site because I figure, if somebody's in there, they want to look at images, get through the site, and get out. They want to have a good experience, but they're not there to entertain themselves.

—Jamey Stillings

The home page opens and loads very quickly with an image from one of Stillings' featured projects. The compelling photo makes an immediate statement that this site is all about images. The navigation is less obvious at first glance, but you quickly discover as you roll over the page that both text and circles are active links. The organization is simple and logical.

Unlike the Sharpe site, which is a seductive, playful, tour de force of design, Stillings has deliberately opted for functional simplicity, relying on the force of his images for visual intrigue. Strategically, the site relies on HTML and JavaScript, not Flash, for its interactivity.

Content

As in the Sharpe site, Stillings has a 10-image portfolio highlight, chosen to quickly reveal the range of his work. For people who want to browse further, he has also collected images in four standard project categories: people, places, concepts, and campaigns.

The site is driven by a very powerful and intelligently-coded database. It is very easy for Stillings to update the material on his site without having to do any coding. Both of these facts are extremely important to a site that archives close to a hundred different projects, each with as many as 45 images. You can access the projects through the project list or go to the image search page of the archive and search within one of three main topics and their subtopics.

One of the ways that Stillings personalizes his site is through the About the Studio section—an area unique to his own site. His studio has a great sense of camaraderie, and Stillings has a playful sense of humor that surfaces in his working style but would be hard to show in a straightforward digital portfolio.

Since the site was going to cost the same amount either way, why not put up what I want? I can show a little fun project I did just for myself, or a big campaign. I don't have to tie images on the website to whether or not they're going to make money. My criterion can be just—is it something I want to share?

—Jamey Stillings

Future plans

On the Sharpe site, Stillings often consults with John Sharpe on what to put in the Portfolio Selects section. On his own site, he follows his instincts, updating frequently. His own site is obviously an extension of his aesthetic and personality—quirks, humor, and unique world view. Stillings is satisfied with both sites and the different ways that they perform for him. As all good portfolio sites should do, they grab prospective clients' imaginations and get their creative juices flowing.

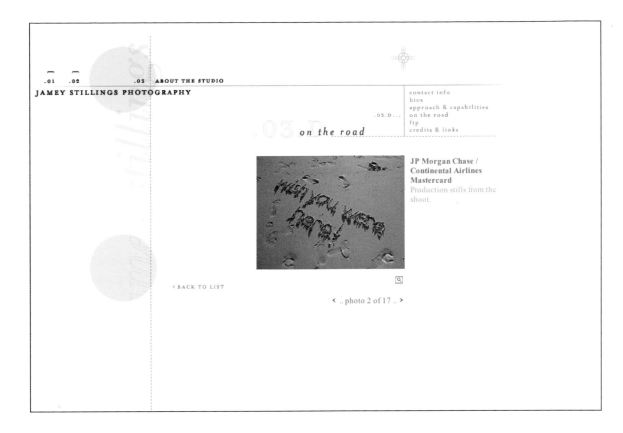

The "on the road" portion of this personal section includes digital snapshots and little QuickTime movies. Although most of the images are well-composed, they have a looser feel than most commercial shots.

PART II

Collecting

and Preparing

CHAPTER 5

Organizing

your work

Good portfolios are not created the night before you present them. You need to look at your entire body of work to evaluate its condition and current relevance. And that's hard to do when it's scattered on multiple disks, file folders, and flat files.

Let's face it: Organizing isn't sexy. Creatives aren't supposed to be organized…it's part of our mystique. But wouldn't you rather be a little less cute and a little more rested? When developing a portfolio, being organizationally challenged will set you up for extra work every time you need to redo or revise. If revising is a chore, you'll wait until the eleventh hour to do it. Unpaid work on a personal deadline is just about the worst creative nightmare. Inevitably, you'll cut corners, make mistakes, and miss important details.

It's far better to approach your working process with the idea of making your work "portfolio ready." Take the time to organize as you work—it's only hard at the beginning. Once you get used to the process, organizing your work becomes second nature.

COLLECTING MATERIAL

Unlike people in other lines of work, everything you do results in a unique creative product. Don't trust your employer or client to archive your work. Everything you do should remain in your possession in some form: original, sample, slide, print, or disk. For some professions, ideas and work leading up to the finished piece also should be retained. This might seem obvious, but it bears emphasis. To keep your work secured and up-to-date:

Keep process materials

Ask yourself at the beginning of every new project if this piece might be a keeper. If so, hold onto your process work. From quick pencil sketches to detailed storyboards, the first stages of creativity are seldom found on disk. Your concepts can be a powerful tool to help you illustrate your creative process in your portfolio.

Keep editable backups of computer files

If your artwork is digital, keep the original, editable files, not just player versions or PDFs. You may want to change frame rate or scale the dimensions later. If your final product is a printed piece, don't assume that's all you need, especially if the work is product packaging or oversized flat art. As you'll see in later chapters, original art is sometimes more useful in a digital portfolio than a shot of the real piece.

Students: retrieve your graded work

Between summer break, co-op stints, and requests by faculty to borrow student work for their own needs, student pieces often fall into limbo. (Limbo is also known as the trash pile.) Art instructors often don't have a permanent affiliation with the schools where they teach, and work left with them can easily be misplaced. In addition, most art and design departments have policies for discarding unclaimed student work. Does it sound as if you shouldn't trust your school and faculty to get your work back? Exactly. Be responsible for your own career and get your work before the school year ends.

Request samples when working for hire

If you're doing work for hire, don't be shy about asking your employer about sample copies before you start your work. Even if you are not retaining copyright (see Chapter 12, "Copyright & portfolio"), in most situations you're entitled to add a sample to your portfolio. If you can't, you'll know the limitations before you imagine the project as your portfolio's centerpiece.

Get plenty of samples

You can never be too rich or have too many samples. Speak to the printer directly if you can. If the client is handling the printing, request your samples from them in advance. Print runs are not an exact science and most jobs result in more finished impressions than the quote specified.

Photograph artwork

Most artwork is one-of-a-kind. Even computer art is often output large in a variety of individual forms or on special materials. As soon as the piece is dry, shoot it yourself, even if you plan to hire a professional later. If the worst happens and your artwork is stolen, damaged, fades, or ends up sold to someone who disappears, you still have a portfolio record. See Chapter 6, "Digitizing traditional work," for the best ways to get your work into the computer.

STORING ORIGINAL ART

Mounted boards curve, glues lift and yellow, and prints badly framed bubble with moisture. You learn these lessons in school or from miserable experience. Yet people who are very craft-conscious in traditional media can be remarkably careless with digital output or printed samples. Yet how many designers can afford to reprint a poster? If you are keeping material for portfolio use, no matter what it's made of, store it with care.

Storing traditional materials

Always store your two-dimensional work flat, between acid free paper, out of direct light, and in a cool place. If you must roll the work, store it in a closable tube with as large a diameter as you can find. If you have a portfolio case full of work, store it on a shelf without any bulky items or additional folders inserted, and never place anything on top of it.

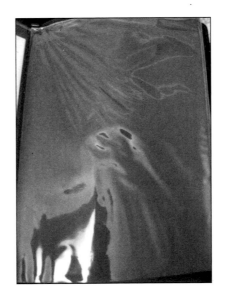

Garbage bag? Ink blot test? Nope. This portfolio was stored in a basement over a muggy summer. Similar bad performance art is created in the storage hold of airplanes and car trunks in the summer.

If you are storing process work, set aside a sketchbook or file folder for these non-computer project materials. Keep these folder materials off your working surface. Coffee rings and grease smears do not improve marker sketches.

Storing digital output

Some work is only output on a digital printer, not professionally offset or chemically developed. The quality may look great initially, but some inks, toners, dyes, and even the papers you print them on are unstable. If you are unsure of your digital printer's (or its inks) archival quality, see the sidebar, "Is your digital output stable?," that follows.

Other problems can arise with stored digital output, even when the ink and paper archive well. Some inks chemically react with portfolio books' plastic sleeves. Copier and laser prints can stick to the inside of vinyl, ruining both the sample and the portfolio page. And almost all output—even the very best—will eventually fade, especially if left in full daylight. If your only original version of the piece is a digital print, store it just like traditional art.

Is your digital output stable?

To check for fading, run a CMYK bar test (a full page of output with each of the four printing primary colors running vertically) on the paper you're using for output. Cut the output in thirds so each portion has all four ink colors. Pin one up on a sunlit wall. Put one in a flat box with a lid, and put the box someplace dark. Leave the third one out of direct light, but uncovered. A month later, run the CMYK test again.

Now pull out all three pieces and look at them, using the newly printed copy as a guide. In many cases, there will be color degradation in the print that was hung in unprotected bright light. (That happens to traditional photographic prints, too.) Has there also been a shift in the other two pieces? If you see color problems in the third piece, you should use a different printer for your portfolio work. If you see any change in the copy you left in the dark, the inks are chemically degrading. Not only is the printer wrong for your portfolio, you shouldn't use it for anything other than quick proofing.

Organizing samples and artwork

Keeping your work in prime portfolio condition is an imperative first step, but it isn't enough. You need a storage or documentation system as well so you can find a piece later, either for a traditional book or to shoot or scan for a digital portfolio. Being organized is particularly important if you create unique works of art. If you ever have to put in an insurance claim because of theft or damage, you'll need to show physical proof of its existence before you can recoup any losses.

The simplest and easiest way to handle small-format printed pieces is to use a good, old-fashioned file drawer with Pendaflex files and folders. Most people file work either alphabetically by client or consecutively by date. Some people create folders based on the type of work (like annual report or identity) or client industry (like biotech or fashion). You can use the quirkiest system you like, as long as you apply it consistently.

Store original, non-printed art, or printed pieces too big for a file folder in flat files, shelves, or artist racks. But wherever you put it, keep a record of it (see archiving strategies in the next section) as well. With a cheap digital camera, you can shoot the piece for identification, add text (including where you've stored it if you're absent-minded!), and print the page.

Document now: the further you are from creating the artwork, the more you won't remember. It's most efficient to do this all at once—scanning batched photos, or hiring someone to shoot your work—but it's better to do this work in smaller clumps than to be caught empty-handed.

ORGANIZING DIGITAL FILES

Keeping traditional materials in good order is painless compared with computer files. They are hard to recognize, harder to find than a buried piece of paper on a messy desk, and all too easy to delete. Even if today you start naming and filing every project with the zeal of a librarian, there's all your previous projects to consider. Going back months later to reorganize your files is exquisite torture. Fortunately, there are useful strategies that can at least deaden the pain. Most of them work best if you combine them with an archive made with database or catalog software.

To organize your files, you'll have to master five disciplines:
+ Group
+ Name
+ Show
+ Weed
+ Backup

Group

The first step is to keep your working files in order. Everyone is occasionally guilty of putting a new file out on the desktop when in a hurry. But if your desktop becomes the home for all your files and folders, you'll waste valuable time hunting for work when you need it, and even more time trying to clean up between projects. Here are some grouping guidelines:

+ **Use folders.** Create a separate folder for each client or project series. Each time you start a new project, create a new folder inside the client folder. Put new files in the appropriate folders when you save them the first time.
+ **Link folders.** Make aliases of your major folders so you can jump directly into them. Put one set of aliases on the desktop, but don't stop there. Make multiple aliases of each folder, and put them inside each of the other folders of live jobs. You'll be able to reach any folder almost immediately, and you won't be tempted to put files in the current directory or on the desktop to "save time."

Name

After you've found the folder, you still have to find the right files inside it. One of the best ways to save time is to develop a method of file naming. Here are some guidelines:

- **Name uniquely.** Avoid generic folder and file names. Be concise but descriptive. Filling a disk with multiple versions named "image1," "newproject," or "brochure" can be almost as useless as deleting them.
- **Name descriptively.** Avoid numbers in file names unless they refer to a series (like pages or book folios). Otherwise, use them only as "save as" devices for chronological stages of a working session. If you are designing a home page image for a new website, HomeHeader-DVA—what the image is, and the client it's for—might be a good naming convention. At the end of the session, you can delete all the transitional versions.

If you create an alternate version of a file, describe what's different in the name. These file names document variations in typeface and color.

● ● ●	LOHPDesigns	○
OralHistV2.psd	OralHist-Meta.psd	OralHist-Red.psd

- **Name briefly.** Really long names truncate (get cut off) in directory displays and make confusing icon labels. If you must use a long file name, start it with the most unique information, moving toward the least unique. For example, if you are archiving artwork for specific pages of a book, try "Fig57ARev-P210-Ch5-DDP.psd" rather than "DDP-Ch5-P214-Fig67Arevision.psd." You'll be able to scan for the most unique portion of the name more easily.
- **Name inclusively.** You might need to show your digital portfolio on different platforms. Whenever possible, use naming conventions that are legal on all likely operating systems. For example, avoid colons, semi-colons, and slashes.

Long file names are easier to read in list view but are still not always clear. Some OSs truncate in the middle like this one, others at the end. Since the bottom three names start with the most important information, it's easy to identify them in any OS.

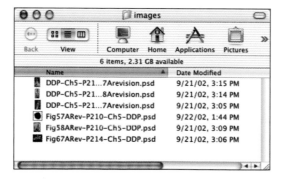

Name	Date Modified
DDP-Ch5-P21...7Arevision.psd	9/21/02, 3:15 PM
DDP-Ch5-P21...8Arevision.psd	9/21/02, 3:14 PM
DDP-Ch5-P21...7Arevision.psd	9/21/02, 3:05 PM
Fig57ARev-P210-Ch5-DDP.psd	9/22/02, 1:44 PM
Fig58ARev-P210-Ch5-DDP.psd	9/21/02, 3:09 PM
Fig67ARev-P214-Ch5-DDP.psd	9/21/02, 3:06 PM

If you haven't been very good about file naming, you aren't condemned to disorganization. See the following sidebar, "Bulk renaming," for strategies for name cleanup.

Show

Since you're probably a visual person, the best way to find files is to use a visual method—icons.

- **Use catalog thumbnails.** You can't depend on the little image icons on your files. It's too easy to confuse images that look the same but have radically different resolutions or sizes. Cataloging software (more on this under the "Backup" section) creates bigger thumbnails, and can read the file dimensions from many formats. If your work is cataloged, it's really easy to pull up a file in the middle of a presentation, even if you hadn't originally planned on including it.

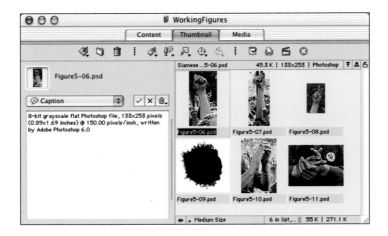

In iView MediaPro and other cataloging software, images are large enough to recognize. To look at them even larger, you can use iView's Scale to Fit function in the Media tab. As a bonus, on the left is information about the file's pixel size, output size, and resolution.

- **Customize folder icons.** Most OS versions allow you to replace a generic folder icon with a custom one, although older ones (such as the classic Mac OS and Windows versions prior to XP) limit you to specific file icon types and work best with square images. Windows XP and OS X give you wide latitude on what file format you use for the icon and will display rectangular images without distortion. See "Making a folder icon" for the basic how-tos on each platform.

Weed

Sometimes the best way to stay organized is to throw things out.

- **Simplify.** When you're certain your project is finished and billed, review your project folder and disk. Put any process ideas in a "process" folder and then throw out errors while the project is fresh in your mind.

- **Update.** Sometimes last-minute changes are made while a job is on press. It's tempting to say, "Whatever," and be glad you didn't have to do the changes yourself. Don't give in to temptation. Unless the correction won't effect some future version of the piece or is work that was not your responsibility, make the edit in the original file. You won't remember the change if you need to output the file again.

Bulk renaming

There are strategies on both Macs and Windows computers to rename groups of files.

Windows XP offers a very limited way to rename multiple files. It maintains the file extensions but replaces the actual file names with whatever you type, adding a sequential number in the order in which the files appear in the display. That means you need to sort the files however you'll want them to be numbered (alphabetically or by date).

To do more sophisticated renaming in Windows or any bulk renaming at all on a Mac, you'll need software program for batch conversions. Several programs can do this for you, iView Media or MediaPro among them. You can browse a file download site such as **www.shareware.com** for others.

Find the files you need to rename. (Moving them all into a folder first will make this task easier.) Select them all and then press the F2 key. Type the string of characters you want all of the files to contain. The files will retain their file extensions, but all of their names will change to the same as what you've typed, including a number.

One of my favorite uses for batch renaming is to renumber book figures. I put the figures that need renumbering in a folder and then drag the folder to the Catalog dialog box and highlight them all. Using iView, I select Incremental and type any change in the rest of the file name. I type the number the figures should count up from in the box and click Rename, making sure that I'm retaining any file extensions.

Making a folder icon

Anything that you can copy into the OS X clipboard can be used as a folder icon, including text. The process is simplicity itself. Open the file in an application and then select all or part of it. Highlight the folder you want to change, and press Command+I to Get Info. Click the folder icon in the Get Info box to highlight it, then paste (Command+V).

Replace generic icons with unique ones, and you can quickly zero in on what you need. In the top row of icons, the first is Postscript text from Illustrator and the second came from a Word document. In the next row, the left icon is a .JPG and the right is a Photoshop file.

You can use a similar strategy in Windows. File icons themselves must be .ICO files, and you'll need third-party software to create them from .BMP artwork. The artwork will have to be square and created to the right size. But Windows XP lets you add a picture to the generic folder icon instead of completely replacing the icon with another picture.

To make a folder more visual in Windows XP, right-click the generic folder icon you want to personalize, then click Properties. Click the Customize tab and then click Choose Picture from the Folder pictures box. Browse to the image and select it.

Backup

All of these techniques make it easier to find and retrieve your files for portfolio building. But the job is even easier if you file copies of portfolio pieces in one place. (No one needs to tell you that you should have backups of your work anyway.) As you finish each project, copy the final version to the dedicated disk. If you have to create your portfolio in a hurry, everything you need will be in one place, ready to be output, moved into a presentation format, or converted for the Web.

Make a catalog of your work

If you are a prolific image maker who plans to upload all your work to a website (as some photographers do), I'd recommend archiving your images using a database program. I much prefer FileMaker Pro (**www.filemaker.com**) to the alternatives because it doesn't require you to sacrifice all your spare time on the altar of database programming.

If you don't want to use a database, try catalog software. iView Media is available in Windows as well as on both Classic and OS X Mac platforms (**www.iview-multimedia.com**). As a graphic designer with a preference for Macs, I use iView MediaPro (unfortunately, not yet available on the Windows side), which recognizes and manages not just image files, but also Quark, InDesign, and other program-specific software files. It's the software I used for the examples in this chapter.

A bonus to using catalog software is its slideshow feature. If you're in a desperate hurry, are in the midst of designing a portfolio that isn't finished yet, or are not in a field where portfolio technology and sophistication are crucial, your archive can become a portfolio in minutes. All you need is a disk containing the portfolio images you want to show and the cataloging software.

You can drag whole folders into the catalog or bring in individual files. As long as the original images remain available where the cataloging software can find them, they can be displayed at full size on screen. If you change your mind and don't want to show something, you can just delete it from the catalog. (It won't delete from the disk.)

After you've arranged your material, it's easy to set the slide show options for how long each image remains on screen or whether there are transitions between images. You can even choose a typeface and font size for any caption material.

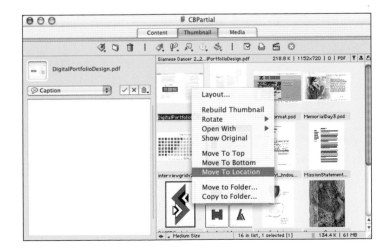

By dragging the thumbnails around in the display area, you can determine what images will display and in which order.

PORTFOLIO HIGHLIGHT:
GABE RUBIN | LEFT BRAIN, RIGHT BRAIN

wrecked.nu—Gabe Rubin

Are creatives hopelessly left-brain challenged? Are organization skills and first-class creativity mutually exclusive? No way. In fact, one of the hallmarks of a really talented designer is his or her ability to wrap a striking new look around the bones of a lean and logical concept. Gabe Rubin's personal portfolio site proves that the two sides of the brain can exist in perfect harmony. Its unusual layout decisions and color palette dazzle, while its intuitive navigation and clearly presented content make it easy to appreciate.

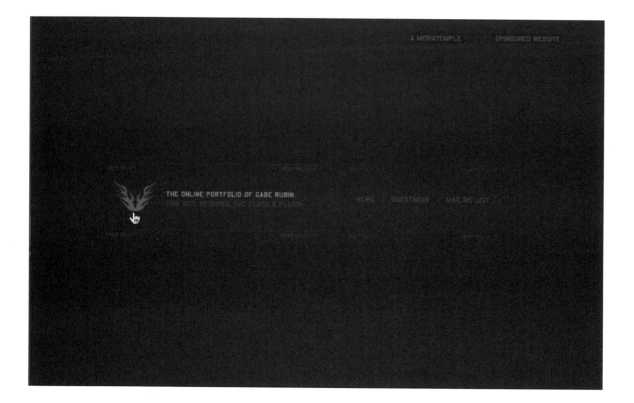

When so many portfolio website backgrounds are white, black, or a well-behaved neutral shade, it's a visual shock to open a page that uses such a rich, bold color. Yet the opening palette is actually very restrained with a tight range of analogous colors—colors right near each other on the color wheel. This device makes the bright orange graphic rollover easy to recognize as the access to the portfolio itself.

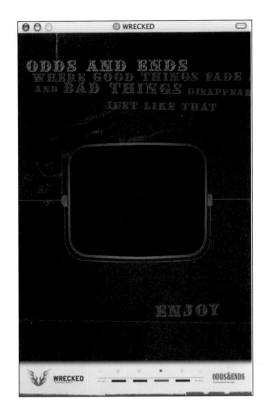

Textures can convey a mood and sense of place not often seen in a personal portfolio.

Gabe Rubin's rich textures, reminiscent of the American West in the 1800s, are an effective design surprise. This intelligent adaptation serves more than an attractive visual purpose. It cleverly tells the viewer a little about his interests and personality and telegraphs his historical knowledge.

Navigation and architecture

The vast majority of portfolio websites are designed horizontally, with the traditional screen aspect ratio of 4:3. Some play clever geometric games within this space, but very few people dare to play out the possibilities of a vertical layout. Rubin's portfolio is striking for many reasons, but certainly its most obvious difference is its vertical orientation. For him, it was the type of design constraint that sparked creativity.

One excellent advantage the layout presented was the ability to keep the site very linear. All of the elements within the site serve a purpose, and as your eye works down the page vertically, there is not much room to stray from what's being presented.

—Gabe Rubin

As you might expect, the Work section of the portfolio site is the deepest because it contains subsections with project categories. Like the much larger BBK Studio site in Chapter 3, "Audience," it uses the classic navigation concept of a group of categories linking to their group of individual projects.

A mouse click launches a short but visually compelling animation that wipes down to the bottom of the screen and introduces the title page. It accustoms you to the space in stages—first to the portfolio's vertical orientation and then to its navigation elements. The windowshade animation reappears each time you move to a different section, moving up to indicate that you are leaving one area, pausing to keep you engaged while the next section of the Flash player loads, and moving down again to introduce the new section.

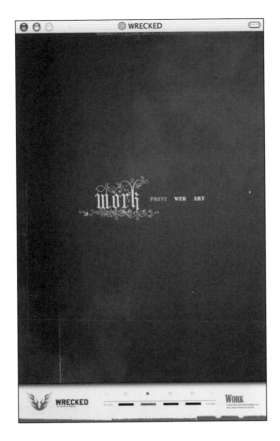

The Work section is visually distinct. Its teal opening page is a color complement to the earlier reds and browns. Links to three categories are distinguished by their color-coded navigation layer.

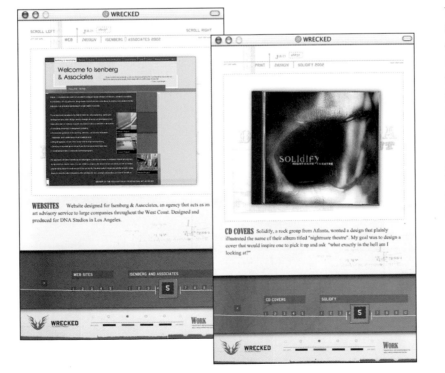

The navigation concept is unusual but easy to comprehend. A live link is magnified under the floating box and labeled in the rectangle above. Click a category, and the projects within it become live as well. At any time, you can return to the main Work page by selecting the box on the far right of the navigation strip.

The portfolio content is literally still a work in progress, which is exactly as it was planned. The navigation indicates placeholders—categories that have yet to be experienced, numbers for projects to come—with Xs over their links.

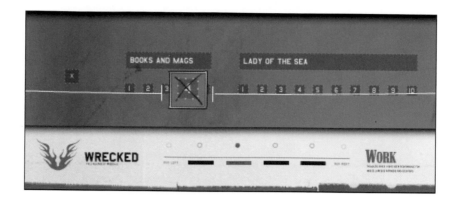

Content

Most people create their portfolio sites the way they would another Web-based project. It has a purpose, and it needs to be complete when it goes live. That's partly self-defense because to keep a portfolio project open-ended can often mean that it never gets finished. You need to be very much in control of your process and be organized to handle portfolio maintenance.

> I thought about why the site was being created in the first place. I wanted people to know about me, I wanted them to see my work, I wanted a place to put things that didn't have any real significance, and I wanted people to be able to get in touch with me. Simple: About, Work, Odds & Ends, and Contact.
>
> —Gabe Rubin

Gabe Rubin considered that pitfall at the beginning. He avoided the problem by making his big categories general. By keeping his major work categories on a second level and several detailed categories completely unlabeled and even unplanned, he can quickly add a new capability or new projects to existing categories.

Future plans

Having recently finished this version of his portfolio, Gabe has no immediate redesign plans. As he says, "I knew I needed to structure the work section so that I can add to it as I further my career. I wanted to keep the site relatively small in scope with the notion that as time went on, only the body of work would grow." Any future redesign will be driven by a desire to change, not the need to squeeze more work in.

No matter what Gabe Rubin adds to his expandable portfolio, he'll have no problems locating materials or adding them quickly to his Flash project file. He takes staying organized very seriously and never allows himself to take the easy and sloppy route. In fact, he brings the same clean simplicity of organization to his archive as he does to his design. From process through finished work to legal rights, Rubin has covered all the bases.

> My work is filed in one "Work" folder. When I get a new project, I create a new "client" folder in the work folder. This folder usually contains five more folders: "Legal," "Assets," "Designs," "Site," and (possibly most importantly) a "Backup" folder, where variations of the designs and site get filed.
>
> —Gabe Rubin

CHAPTER 6

Digitizing traditional work

If all or most of your work was created (or printed) in traditional media, getting it into digital form will be a major project. Like any other task that is light on creativity and heavy on production, it can take an effort of will to begin. It's also tempting to underestimate how important it is to digitize well. Failing at this crucial stage can make the rest of your effort a waste of time.

In the end, your portfolio is all about your work. Digitizing that work successfully is the first step to a quality portfolio. Fortunately, you probably already have the technology you need to do it right. Your skills and some patience will take you the rest of the way.

This chapter will outline the best methods for capturing different types of material for a digital portfolio, and how to move your work most effectively into a digital file.

DIGITAL CRAFT DEFINED

Craft is just as important in making digital files as it is when doing everything by hand—in some ways, more so. People are far less forgiving of bad digital craft when they see it because it is so much easier to fix a digital image than it is to repair a dinged or folded corner on a sample. You owe it to yourself to keep the focus on your samples, not your production.

Images in digital portfolios are judged by how faithfully and effectively they communicate your work. Not having the original at hand, people will judge you by two criteria: image quality—sharpness, cleanness, size, and speed and image appropriateness—whether what you've chosen to show actually helps them judge your work.

Unlike your traditional portfolio, whether your work is appropriate for your digital book doesn't depend just on its style or subject; some of your portfolio material might transfer poorly to the digital medium. Be prepared to evaluate your work twice: before you scan it and when you see the scanned images themselves. No matter how much you want to have a digital portfolio, trying to doctor a terminally ill file will just make you frustrated.

> A very important thing to remember is that almost anybody interviewing someone is thinking, "Is this person going to make me look like a chump? Cost me money, reputation?" So you're looking for reassurance in a portfolio. You're looking for a portfolio that says, "I do everything perfectly."
>
> —Gunnar Swanson

www.jeffthedesigner.com
Jeff Kaphingst's portfolio images present his work at a readable size with excellent sharpness and color fidelity.

Photograph, scan, or digitize?

Should you use a flatbed scanner or a film scanner? Or should you photograph your work? The answer to these questions will differ based on the exact type of work you have.

Garden variety flatbed scanners are happy with flat, low contrast images. That makes them extremely useful for printed art and illustrations but less effective for images with a broad value range. If you scan to hold shadows, you'll lose the highlights, and vice versa.

If you have strong highlights and shadows and comparatively few midtones, you may lose detail at both ends, as happened in this image. The bright foam is too bleached out (center of the image) and there is no detail in the rock shadow in the lower-right corner.

Although you can scan printed photos on a flatbed scanner, if you are a professional photographer, you should go direct from film when you can. You should also look for a slide scanner, not a flatbed with an attachment.

Flatbeds marketed as photo scanners have better dynamic ranges than standard flatbeds, but even with transparency attachments, they are no competition for a good film scanner unless they cost thousands of dollars. Use them only if you print on special paper or make post-developing changes to the print.

If you are trying to capture a package design or sculpture, you will maintain the best quality by taking the fewest steps between the original and your digital presentation. So if you own or can put your hands on the right tools (see the next section), go directly from camera to computer.

What about not quite flat art, like books? Your ideal solution is a large-sized flatbed scanner for page spreads (an option at some service bureaus and schools). But if you can't find one, taking photographs using a copy stand (see "Shooting 3D and oversized work") and some non-reflective glass is usually better than trying to graft two scanned pieces together in Photoshop.

I tossed a few images once I saw them on the website before it went live. We decided, "Oh, this doesn't look good large. This doesn't really read well, or it looks wimpy or it's too pale." Things that were sort of poster-ish read well on the screen.

—Nancy Hoefig

On the other hand, don't do a detail-for-detail comparison, or you'll never use any pre-digital work! Evaluate based on how you feel about presenting this material to someone who has never seen the original piece.

If there is any overriding theme, it's GIGO: Garbage In=Garbage Out. Keep each stage of your digitizing process as precise as possible. Start with the cleanest original material, and remember that bad quality can be introduced inadvertently at every stage of digitizing and cleanup.

And don't be afraid—or embarrassed—to look for help when you need it. It is better that your portfolio process be a learning process as well than to present a flawed finished product.

SHOOTING 3D AND OVERSIZED WORK

Digital art is flat; 3D art isn't. There's no perfect way of getting around this, but it shouldn't prevent you from showing your 3D work to good effect. Even traditional portfolios require artists and designers to use photography to transfer dimensional art into flat containers.

In fact, a digital portfolio is sometimes a better way to show a 3D piece than a 35mm slide. With a little skill, you can create the illusion of three dimensions in Photoshop once you have the artwork itself in digital form. Even without image editing, you can show multiple views of the same art or even just show a standard product shot but in glorious full-screen.

Unless you are handy with digital video, you'll need access to some of the standard tools of a photographer's trade: a camera, a copy stand and/or tripod, and some professional lighting. Some of the solutions I propose here are really workarounds that can give acceptable results when money is tight.

Choosing your camera

Because you'll be presenting your work on screen, not printing it, a digital camera will almost always give better results than using an analog camera, making slides, and then scanning the slides—that's too many generations. Plus, you can see at a glance in the digital display whether you've captured what you need and you can reshoot until you're satisfied.

As long as you are only shooting for your digital portfolio, you won't need a very expensive camera. The camera you choose must have optical (not just digital) zoom and a mounting hole in its base for a tripod. If you will be making PDFs or JPGs and want an image that will fill the screen, you'll need a 2-megapixel camera (or better). If you expect that you'll have to edit a higher resolution image, consider a camera that has a Raw or Tiff option, not just JPEG. (See Chapter 7, "Cleaning up," for more on image editing.)

One last thing—you'll enjoy shooting more if your digital camera has a display screen that pivots (like those in the Nikon Coolpix series), particularly if you'll be using a copy stand. That way, you won't have to crane your neck to see the display no matter how you've had to mount your camera.

Setting the stage

For books, mid-sized prints, or pieces with accordion folds or die-cuts, your best bet is usually a copy stand. A *copy stand* is a flat board with a camera attached above it and lights at an angle (usually 45 degrees) on two sides. The bulbs should be the same type and brightness to eliminate shadows. Ones with double copy-lights on each side and a large bed are best, but you can get a small stand, lights and all, for under $100. If you can't buy a copy stand, ask your friends and your professional network; libraries and art departments at schools and universities often have them.

We've set up a basic photo studio in the office, and sometimes we'll shoot pieces on white background, knock it out, and put the shadows back in. We shoot with a digital camera, adjust the images, and resize the work in Photoshop and optimize them with ImageReady.

—Michael Borofsky

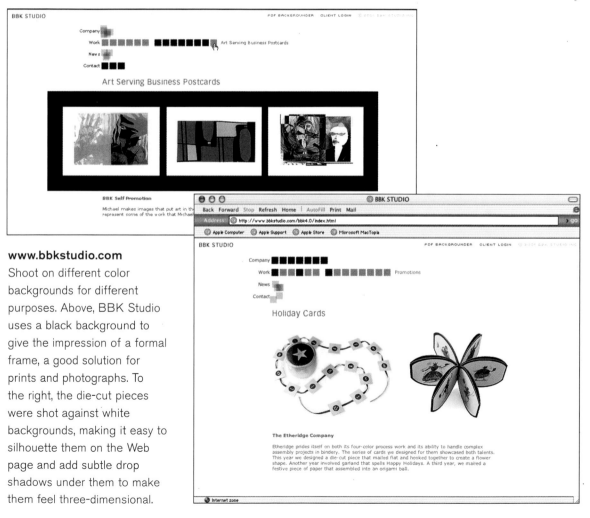

www.bbkstudio.com

Shoot on different color backgrounds for different purposes. Above, BBK Studio uses a black background to give the impression of a formal frame, a good solution for prints and photographs. To the right, the die-cut pieces were shot against white backgrounds, making it easy to silhouette them on the Web page and add subtle drop shadows under them to make them feel three-dimensional.

If you can't get access to a copy stand or your artwork is flat but too big to fit on the stand's base (like an architectural rendering or an etching), mount your artwork on posterboard with a large enough margin to create a uniform background for the art. Pin the mounted art on a wall in a large room. Attach your camera to a tripod and shoot away.

If your artwork is three-dimensional, you'll need a large, flat table as well as a wall. Photographers usually shoot against smooth, pure white matte backgrounds (often referred to as "seamless") to emphasize the object's dimensions and cast clean shadows. The background can be paper or fabric. Ideally, you should use a professional fabric, but if you can't, a white sheet can be a good stand-in. You can always clean up the results in Photoshop (see Chapter 7).

Resolution do's and don'ts

It would be nice to be able to scan everything at 72 ppi and not have to do a thing to the files, but you'll end up with much better results if you scan them in with more resolution and detail than you'll end up using. The trick is to know how much more you need, and when you're just wasting time and disk space.

If you expect to edit a photographic image, not just scale it, try scanning at 150 ppi. If you scan at too high a resolution, then downsample—resample the image at a lower resolution. Your image may soften so much that you will find the result unacceptable.

Your best rule of thumb is to scan so your pixel dimensions are roughly double what they'll end up on screen. If you want each image to end up about 400 pixels wide, scan at whatever resolution gives you approximately 800 pixels to work with. That may mean scanning in a business card at 300 ppi but a tabloid image at only 72 ppi.

Line art can get very jagged when scanned. You'll need to scan at high resolution and then clean up the art (see Chapter 7) before you scale it down.

Scanning printed work with great type design or sharp, flat art can drive you crazy because you're moving lovely vector art to rasters. Always scan such artwork at least double the resolution you'll need to show onscreen and then scale it to 50%. This will help to clean up the edges.

After you've chosen a resolution and made your scan, don't ever scale the work up. If you've miscalculated and scanned too small, rescan at the correct percentage.

If you have several pieces of the same type to scan, test first. Scan one, making whatever changes you think are necessary to bring it successfully to the size you'll show it in your portfolio. If you discover that you've scanned too high or too low, you have time to adjust before scanning the rest of the batch.

Worst-case scenario, find a clean, level floor. Again, put your artwork on a non-reflective background. Raise your tripod as high as you can, point the camera down, and shoot. Tripods that allow you to rotate the head mount so the camera points straight down will allow you to shoot flat art without angling or distortion.

The bigger your artwork, the harder it will be to shoot it. Try to avoid the temptation of a wide-angle lens. Many digital cameras have a panorama function that makes it relatively easy to shoot your images in visual "tiles" of overlapping segments. For very large images, you may need specialized panorama software that adjusts for distortions. (See Chapter 7 for more on stitching software.)

Lighting

Lighting is very important because it will determine the range of colors you shoot. The wrong type of light (like fluorescents) will shift all the colors to the blue or yellow end of the spectrum. It's possible to fix such problems in Photoshop (see Chapter 7), but it's better not to have them in the first place.

The way the lights are positioned is also critical. If you don't have a copy stand or a room with professional lights, try to locate a bright, day-lit room, and make sure that any lights in it are turned off. If your artwork is framed under glass or reflective plastic, take the frame apart. There's almost no good way to light a framed piece to avoid hot spots and reflections. Place your flat art so that no shadows are cast on it. (For 3D art, shadows behind or below are fine.) Whatever you do, don't use a flash. It will create hot spots and inappropriate shadows.

Another alternative if you don't have professional lighting available is to wait for a dry but overcast day. The light will be nicely diffuse.

There was a lot of trial and error to achieve our combination of high image quality and quick download. All the images are middle-to-high quality JPEGs. We got the best results by scanning in high resolution and bringing the images down to screen resolution later in Photoshop.

—Michael Bartalos

DIGITIZING FLAT ART

I encourage you to use a good-quality scanner for your digital portfolio, even though the cheapest scanner on the market today scans at an optical resolution better than you'll probably need for work you'll show onscreen.

Why? Color, features, and time. A good scanner will read and reproduce more colors than a cheap one—with more fidelity to the original art. It will have software with features that can save you lots of Photoshop work. In addition, on a cheap scanner, you'll wait for an image preview and even longer for the scan itself. The time difference isn't significant for one or two scans, but you'll come to dread it for a larger batch.

www.bartalos.com

Books are particularly hard to scan properly on a flatbed scanner because of distortions that can creep in. This scan by Michael Bartalos is notable for maintaining its crisp, clean look, even across the book's bound center.

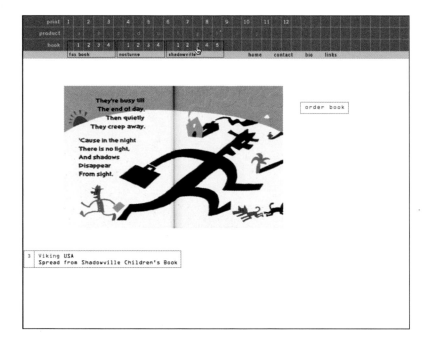

Flatbed scanning hints

There are several things you can do to improve the quality of your scans, some of which are very low-tech:

- **Clean the scanner.** Every speck will reproduce. Don't depend on scanner software that offers to clean up dust and scratches as you scan. It does a terrific job on the obvious places but can sometimes mistake a critical detail for a speck and eliminate it.
- **Square up your art.** In most cases, you'll want to square your artwork up, but all too frequently, it ends up just a little bit off. There's a quick and easy fix for that in Photoshop.

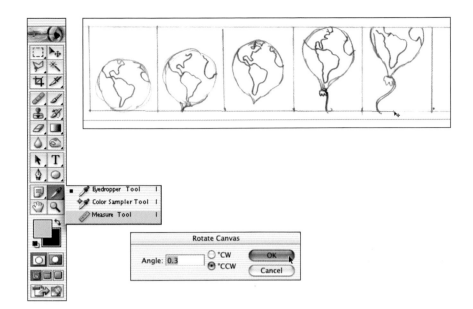

Select the Measure tool (an alternate of the Eyedropper) and draw a line with it along the angled edge of the tilted artwork. Go to Image > Rotate Canvas > Arbitrary, and the exact angle you need will appear in the dialog box. Click OK, and your scan is straight.

- **Watch for moiré.** You probably know that color printing depends on fine-screened overlays of dots to mimic continuous-tone color. Unfortunately, the dots are the product of screens, which do not have a one-to-one correspondence to pixels. When screens and pixels collide, you can get wavy, distracting patterns. Fortunately, most scanners now ship with software that includes a "Descreen" setting, which usually does a very good job on the problem. Sometimes moiré persists, or the scanner you're using is too old to have software that includes Descreen. If so, check out "Moiré," in Chapter 7.

These patterns are an example of particularly bad moiré. If you're still having problems understanding what moiré is and how it happens, visit **www.perspicuity.com/thatmoirtees.html**. The line drawing you'll find there is accurate, but the pun is priceless.

DIGITIZING SLIDES AND NEGATIVES

When you use a film scanner, you don't have to worry about screen moiré or lost dynamic range. Yet even with a slide scanner, your image quality can vary. Most of the unpleasant changes can be avoided by keeping some simple concepts in mind.

- **Clean your slides.** Spray your slides with canned air before you scan them. Dust can affect film just as easily as it can a printed piece.
- **Use film negatives.** If you have the choice between scanning a film negative and scanning a slide, use the negative. They're both films, but the slide is actually second generation art, just like a photo print. The negative contains more faithful color and a better quality image than the slide does.
- **Scan right side up.** If you scan with your slide or film wrong side up, you could end up with your image looking as if it was shot in a mirror. To avoid this, scan with the emulsion side of the film facing away from you (or down, depending on how you slide scanner is set up). To recognize which side is which, look carefully at the film. The emulsion side will look slightly textured, and often has the film logo printed on the holder. The other side will be much shinier and smoother.
- **Don't overscan.** Ordinarily, you need to scan a slide in at a very high resolution (2700 ppi isn't unusual) to use slide art for printing. (Slides are so very small—they need to go up about 900% to fill a letter-sized sheet.) But when you're heading for a screen resolution of 72 dpi, there isn't much point in creating a mammoth file. 400 ppi should easily give you a large enough image for the Web.

DIGITIZING VHS TAPES

One of the most frustrating realizations to a film and video person is that there is no digital video equivalent of the flatbed scanner. The process is time-consuming and often disappointing.

If you have already edited digital video using software like Adobe Premiere or Apple's FinalCut Pro, or if you have easy access to a professional digitizing studio, it may be worth your while to do your own digitizing. (Handling your own process is always preferable because you have more control over the final product.) But if you're a digital neophyte and you need a portfolio soon, your energies would be better spent learning the ins and outs of digital video and the above-mentioned software, while you pay to have your tapes digitized for you (see "Getting help" later in this chapter). Then all the clips you work with will be digital when you create your DVD.

Video versus computer, compressed

If you aren't a person with a video background, it can help to understand a little bit about video resolution before you attempt to digitize and edit videotape. What follows is an extremely stripped-down explanation.

Video resolution

Analog video and standard digital video are pretty low-resolution formats. They were created to be seen on a TV, not a computer. The TV broadcast standard is based on scan lines, not pixels as it is for a computer monitor. In the U.S., that standard is called National Television System Committee (NTSC), and it runs at 525 lines, at a rate of approximately 30 frames per second. In other countries, it's 625 lines, but only 25 frames per second. (The two formats are incompatible, and tape from one standard won't play in VCRs for the other standard.)

In both cases, the top and bottom rows of those horizontal lines are invisible, like a leader of black on a tape. They exist to make sure that the actual video broadcast will fill the TV screen. Once you subtract these extra lines, you end up with 483 lines in NTSC and 576 in Phase Alternation Line (PAL).

There isn't an exact correlation between lines and monitor resolution because monitors have square pixels and TVs have rectangular ones (this will come up again in creating a DVD, in Chapter 13, "Presenting your portfolio"). But effectively, any broadcast quality video won't fill a space larger than 720×480 (NTSC) or 720×576 (PAL). As you can see, you are already starting with a fairly coarse original compared with a computer image before you start to digitize.

Analog video formats and resolution

Although broadcast resolution could give you the above-mentioned 720×480 monitor window, that's not true for most of the video formats that you probably have archived. All consumer formats will be much, much smaller.

When your analog video was shot and on what type of camcorder will make a difference in its quality level, and the eventual window size you will be able to show it in. The original standard for VHS tape gave a resolution of only 250 scan lines, or effectively a 320×240 window on a computer. SVHS and Hi-8, which came out in the late 1980s, improved that number to 400 scan lines for a 480×330 window. So you should be prepared to keep your expectations moderate and your window dimensions small when you start to digitize.

Video digitizing hints

Some of the same issues in scanning flat art arise in bringing analog video to the computer. Alas, because of the added complexity of dealing with larger files, frame rate, and sound, they can be easy to miss until it's too late. Like scanning errors, the only way to remedy them is to redigitize.

- **Start with a good tape.** If the material you're working with has been processed twice—once when you edited pieces onto a demo tape and again when you made copies of the demo tape—you won't get a good quality digital result.
- **Transfer to DVD.** Moving from interlaced video at 30 frames per second (fps) to non-interlaced digital display can result in dropped frames and out-of-synch sound and video, and sound and video that don't always synch. Always make a DVD copy of your video, no matter how you intend to use it later. You'll need that quality. Unlike flat image files, you can't clean up your video by simply showing it in a smaller window.

• **Use the right tool.** Although you can use either consumer software such as iMovie or professional software like Premiere or Final Cut Pro to digitize your tape, there is a critical difference between them. Professional tools can edit uncompressed video; consumer tools can't. With a consumer tool, you will compress your video every time you edit and save it. Compression throws out visual information to save space. (See Chapter 8, "Repurposing and optimizing," for more about compression.) That's not a serious issue if you have shot digital video and are working in DV anyway. But with analog, the quality will suffer, sometimes tragically.

GETTING HELP

If you want to learn how to use the software for digitizing your specific type of artwork, I encourage you to buy the appropriate book in Peachpit Press's *Visual QuickStart Guide* series and to look for workshops in your local area for training on digitizing analog tapes. Scanning has to be done right, but it's drudgery, and it keeps you away from paying work. If you have an enormous backlog of work to digitize, some money to devote to the enterprise, or feel that you can handle some parts of the process but not others, there are viable alternatives.

Hiring students

If you live in or near a college or art school, inexpensive help might be close at hand. Most art and design students are well-versed in software technologies, particularly scanners and the basics of Photoshop. Many schools have clearing houses or bulletin boards (or more formal placement offices for part-time help, coops, interns, and so on) where you can post your needs. In some cases, you might find that hiring a creative student can help you produce a better portfolio, not just get your artwork on a flatbed.

Service bureaus

If you have negatives or slides, look for a place that advertises photo scanning. Ask them about their process and how they ensure quality for images that may need special handling to maintain color or dynamic range. Avoid service bureaus that specialize in document scanning. They make their money by putting standard-sized materials through scanners in batches with feeders.

DVD services

Most places that make video copies and transfer home movies now also have facilities to convert an analog tape to DVD-R. They're likely to charge by the hour, so you'll probably get the most cost-effective result if you have them transfer your original analog demo reel first (never one of the copies!), rather than whole project tapes.

Ask other film and video people in your area to recommend a service or another member of the community who does freelance work. If you can't get a recommendation, at least try to talk directly with the person who will do the conversion first, so they know what you'll need the film for and why its quality is important.

SPECIALIZED HELP: PARTNERING

By now, you may have skimmed forward in this book and felt a little overwhelmed by how much work your personal project will take. It might be time to ask yourself, "Do I need a partner?" There is no shame in concluding that you can successfully master some portions of designing and producing your digital portfolio, but not all.

Your partner may be a photographer who provides you with digital files of your projects. He may be a graphic designer who designs an interface for you. She may be a programmer who takes your graphic design and implements its interactive elements in Flash. Many times, partnerships are about bartering skills—a new business logo identity for one person, a photo shoot for another.

Your role in the partnership

Because the end product of a digital portfolio partnership is a creative work that will represent you, the last thing you want is a hired gun. Although you should trust whomever you work with to know their own area of expertise, come to the table prepared to explain who you are, what type of help you need, and how much autonomy your partner will have. If the areas you need help in are areas you should ultimately know and understand, use your partnership as a learning opportunity.

Handle as much of the process as you reasonably can. Know your target market and how you want to be seen. If you're working with a photographer, take some shots first from the right distance or angle, with your materials arranged as you'd like them. Decide what content goes into your portfolio and how you want your work grouped. If artwork needs to be processed and you don't do it yourself, you should at least quality control (QC) every piece before it enters the portfolio to make sure it represents you well. Last but not least, you should personally test the portfolio as it develops and before you post or send it.

What you need in a partner

A partner should complement your own expertise and be someone whose work you are familiar with and respect. Ideally, he or she should be someone you have worked with on another project, so you know what their strengths are and how you work together. Your portfolio is a very personal project, and the last thing you want is a partner who isn't prepared to support you and your vision.

Be prepared to give full credit for the partner's creative input. That probably means that you should not consider as a partner someone whose creative area overlaps yours. If you are an established print designer with no desire to enter new media, it's reasonable to partner with a new media specialist to write the program, create a database, and design the navigation. It's not reasonable to present yourself as multimedia designer if someone else has created the concept and implemented the site for you.

> I found a designer who was on the same page as I was. That was the very first thing: Can we understand each other? She was completely on board with me from the very beginning. Together, we outlined what content we were looking for and revised the outline until we got it to where we wanted it to be.
>
> —Jamey Stillings

PORTFOLIO HIGHLIGHT:
MICHAEL BARTALOS AND LILI ONG |
PARTNERING

www.bartalos.com

Online portfolios should ideally be as easy to 'flip through' as ring-binder portfolios are. Foregoing bells and whistles proved efficient to navigation and undistracting to the artwork.

—Lili Ong

Ideally, every illustrator would have the talent, skill, and time to design and produce his or her own website. But sometimes that lofty goal isn't possible. In illustrator Michael Bartalos' case, he had the basic knowledge to field his own site but lacked the time to do it right. He would have looked for a design partner to help him create his portfolio no matter what, but he had an ideal option near at hand—his collaborator and wife, designer Lili Ong. The partnership is clearly successful because every design decision respects and supports the artist's work.

From the opening graphic sequence to the last carefully optimized image, Bartalos' site is fast and streamlined. Many sites with similar stripped-down aesthetics reach that point through give-and-take processes between clients and designers. In this case, Bartalos was as much in favor of a Spartan approach as Ong, and both respected the other's talents. Bartalos specified that a fast site with minimal user interaction was his goal but was willing to leave the implementation in Ong's hands.

When you enter the site, you're struck with the balance between the playful graphic—light-hearted and cleanly designed—and the no-nonsense way it plays a functional role in the interface. On this first page, you know exactly whose work you'll see, the artist's style, and how to reach him. Every element is clear and very unobtrusive—a hint of what's to come.

Navigation and architecture

The site is very simply organized. The heart and soul of it is the grid. The grid explains visually exactly how much material is on the site and what category of work is represented. It is designed for expansion. Letters and numbers can be easily added, as can additional highlighted projects. Anchored at the top of the page, the grid offers one-click access to every piece on the site.

Ong has created the site with standard HTML frames, with only the image and its caption loading when a number or letter is clicked. That decision, combined with the relatively small file sizes, makes every image load extremely fast.

There is a "designed" aspect to much of Mike's illustration. I felt that the grid-motif menu complemented that graphic quality of his work and played off his artwork's shapes and elements nicely.

—Lili Ong

The site opens with a small, unfussy icon by Bartalos that distills his graphic, geometrically-driven style. Roll over the figure with his portfolio, and he "steps through" the door, telegraphing to the visitor that a click here will allow you to enter the site. Roll over the boxed email address and the bottom of the browser window tells you that it's a mailto link.

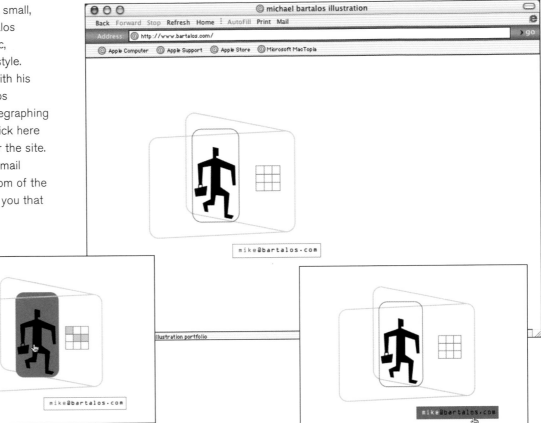

The layout practically defines the concept of "clean"—a grid and an open image area. Letters and numbers in the grid appear as identifiers in the caption of each image, so you never lose your connection to the grid. The interface color scheme is one that occurs frequently in Bartalos' art— neutral color fields rhythmically alternating with brightly saturated color.

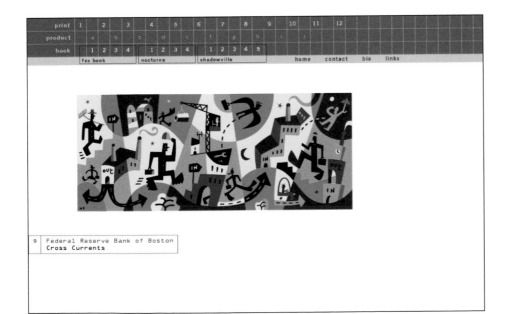

Each image is large and crisp—an important consideration given the graphic intricacy of Bartalos' style. Because his scanning process was so effective, digital and traditional work look equally good onscreen.

Content

A partnership requires more than a good understanding of the portfolio owner's needs. It also demands a clear process. In Bartalos and Ong's case, the design was collaborative, while other phases broke down according to each of their roles. Both worked on planning the site, as well as digitizing the traditional artwork and optimizing the digital art. Lili Ong built the website itself in addition to designing the interface.

Although Bartalos asked Ong's opinion about some images, essentially, he determined all of his site content, as well as the site map. He also specified exactly how additional links and contact information would be accessed—both on the home page and as a navigation link on the grid.

Product groupings are particularly important for an illustrator, and once again, his needs are served well by the simple elegance of the grid. You can tell at a glance that he is particularly strong in product design—not usually a major category for an illustrator.

> I felt it was important to represent the three major areas that my work covers. Project diversity within each category was important as well. I made sure to show as many different applications of my work as possible.
>
> —Michael Bartalos

Future plans

Although Bartalos occasionally replaces older work with new projects to keep the site fresh, it's clear that he is still happy with and proud of the current site. Ong's timeless, spare design gives him everything he wants and needs from a website portfolio: a place where prospective buyers can concentrate on his work and effortlessly sample the sharp, high-resolution images.

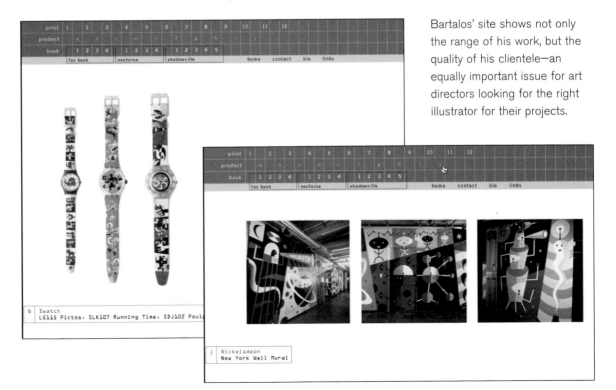

Bartalos' site shows not only the range of his work, but the quality of his clientele—an equally important issue for art directors looking for the right illustrator for their projects.

CHAPTER 7

Cleaning up

Even when you scan and photograph under optimal conditions, the result can be disappointing. The problem may be in the artwork itself. Pieces that have been damaged will be captured perfectly—warts and all. Or perhaps the art is so large or complicated that you've scanned it in pieces and need to put the pieces together. When you can't start over or substitute other work, it's time to pull out your software tools.

As anyone who edits digital files daily can tell you, full coverage of all the editing techniques you could use already fills dozens—perhaps hundreds—of computer books. To stay focused on portfolios, this chapter highlights the most frequently needed remedies.

WORKING PROCESS

Problems with digitized art boil down to a fairly short list:

- Tonal problems
- Combining and editing
- Size and resolution
- Sharpness

These issues occur with all types of digital art, both still and motion. In fact, video-editing software packages, particularly the simplest encoders like Windows Movie Maker and QuickTime, have many of the same filters and tools to affect multiple frames as you can find in image-editing software like Photoshop. The best adjustments are found in professional programs, like Adobe Premiere or Final Cut (Pro and Express). If you understand the concepts behind issues like tone, color, resolution, and sharpness, you can apply them equally well in any digital file.

It's critical to do your work on the right types of files, and in the right order. Follow this sequence:

1. Change your file type.
2. Adjust brightness, contrast, and color casts.
3. Clean up and retouch your art.
4. Save a copy of the image.
5. Adjust document size and resolution, if needed.
6. Sharpen, if needed.
7. Optimize and save in a compressed format. (This is covered in Chapter 8, "Repurposing and optimizing.")

The video-editing process has many of the same steps, although the size of files usually makes it necessary to edit before applying cleanup filters and effects.

CHOOSING A FILE TYPE

File types (formats) serve different purposes. You should select the format that best suits your purpose at each stage of your working process.

When you create a file, you work in a native file format—one "owned" by that application. Although some files open in other programs by the same software company, most of the time a native format is specific to the application that creates it.

When it's time to archive a file, move it into another application, or open it in a different OS, you should copy it to a universal format—one that many applications can read and edit. For photographic or continuous tone files, that format is usually TIF. For illustration and publishing, it's EPS. For onscreen moving image, AVI and MOV are the formats of choice. Good universal formats allow you to save and return to editing without quality loss.

For onscreen work that will be transmitted over the Internet or played back on a computer, your files must be compressed. Compression formats minimize file size in different ways. The most common image compression formats are GIF and JPEG. For publishing, PDF is the standard. Sound and moving image files can be compressed with many formats, such as the familiar MP3 sound files. Currently, the most common video compression formats are MPEG, DV, and WAV, but there are dozens of others, some of which may well become standards over time.

Never edit a JPEG...

...or an MPEG file, for that matter. These files are efficiently compressed. They can look as good as the original files, but they have lost information in the compression process. In fact, they continue to lose more information every time you open one, make an edit (no matter how small), and resave it. That's why some online artwork ends up so awful.

Compressed files should be the culmination of your editing process, not the working format. If you must edit a compressed file, resave it first into a non-compressed universal format. When you are finished, save a copy of the edited universal file in the compressed file format.

TONAL VALUES

Scanned or digitally photographed art can suffer from bad contrast or color shifts. As long as there is readable image information in an image's shadows highlights and color channels, it's possible to bring that information out, improving and preserving the artwork's details.

Many images that seem to have multiple problems really just need a tonal value adjustment. Briefly, an *image's tonal value* is its range from darkest to lightest areas.

What is a histogram?

A *histogram* is a chart of thin vertical lines that shows the distribution of brightness in an image, from 0 (black) to 255 (white). The taller the line, the more pixels the image has at that level of brightness. Darkest pixels are on the left, and brightest on the right.

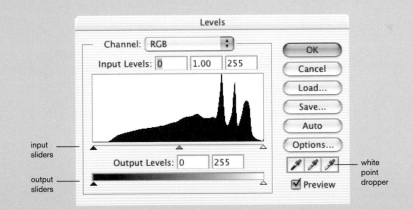

The input sliders regulate the distribution of brightness. The output sliders regulate how much contrast the image has. There are three small eyedropper boxes on the lower right. The one on the far right sets the white point, which is the brightest place on your image—pure white. The one on the far left sets the black point, the place of deepest shadow. Used together by clicking the whitest and darkest image areas, they treat an image's value range like a rubber band, stretching it out in both directions to use the entire value range.

Tonal problems respond best to a software program that generates histograms. Simple sliders for brightness and contrast will not do the trick. iMovie and consumer programs like it only offer linear adjustments. Professional editing programs (still and video) offer histograms and level tools, as well as brightness and contrast sliders. (Some programs also offer other tools, like Photoshop's Curves or Adobe After Effects' Levels and Channels. You're free to experiment with any of these options to find the ones that feel most intuitive to you.)

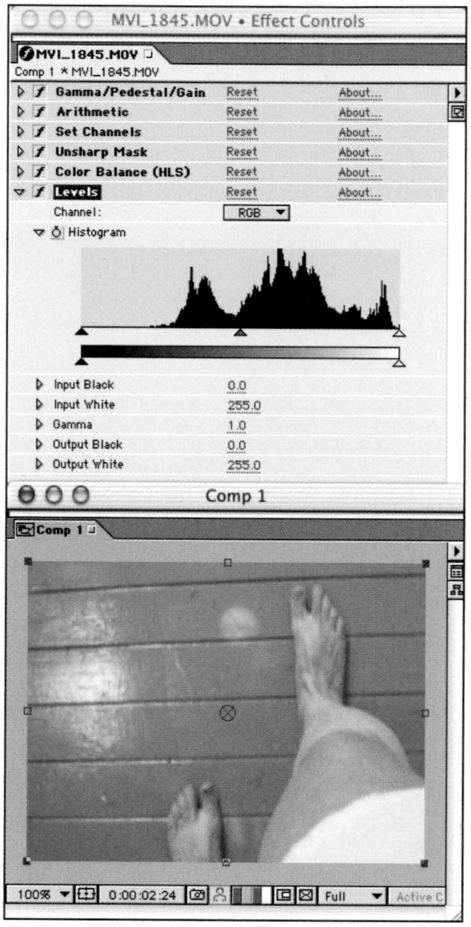

A professional's program, like Adobe After Effects, includes levels and channel tools.

Fixing brightness and contrast

Most image-editing software has an automatic levels function that can do a decent job on an image. For a portfolio, however, decent is not always good enough. (The figure below shows why.) The automatic function tends to increase contrast at the expense of maintaining detail—not a good feature for a photographer's portfolio, or for a designer whose work includes textures and subtle ink variations. Most of the time you should use the manual Levels function, which gives you much more control.

To fix the original image, I've tried Photoshop's autolevel function (Image > Adjustments > Autolevels).

Unfortunately, the image has some areas that are already as bright or dark as they should be. The motorcycle license plate is reflective white, and the buildings behind the arch in the back are in shadow. After autolevels, they bleed or disappear.

A

B

The histogram for the scan on the previous page shows a very dark image. When I move the midtone input slider left, it forces the image's brighter pixels to the right of the slider. The result is **A**: a much lighter image, but one that feels flat. By moving the black input slider a little to the right, I put the shadowed areas back at the end of the spectrum where they belong. That change creates image **B**, which is much truer to the original photograph.

Manually adjusting levels can be tedious, even to the initiated. One of the nice things about working in Photoshop is that I can create an Adjustment layer (Layer > New Adjustment Layer > Levels). It saves all of my changes in the file—without altering the original image—until I apply them.

Consider your audience

In many ways, the platform you use is irrelevant to designing and developing your portfolio. One of the times it becomes a factor is when you are setting values for your images. Windows machines are brighter than Macs. So, artwork created on a Mac will often look a little dark and muddy to a Windows person, and work created on a PC will look garish and harsh to a Mac user.

If you aren't certain that the people who count use the platform you do, look at your artwork in the other platform's color space before you adjust Levels. If you own Photoshop, you have a control panel called Adobe Gamma. (On Macs and PCs, you also have system-specific methods of setting gamma. Check your online help.) Use it to set your Mac to a gamma of 2.2 to see how a Windows user will see your work. Set it to 1.8 if you are a Windows user wanting to know what a Mac user will think.

Image-editing terms: A cheat sheet

Artifacts: Random image distortions, often introduced by too much compression, or by saving a file in the wrong format.

Channel: The portion of an image containing a single color's tonal information. For example, an RGB file has channels for each primary color: red, green, and blue.

Color cast: An overall shift in color, caused by unbalanced artificial light or an uncalibrated scanner.

Color space or color model: The range of colors that a device can recognize and reproduce. The same image will appear, scan, or print differently depending on the color space of the device that is outputting or displaying it.

Curves: A feature to fix color range problems. It allows you to change the amount of red, green, and blue pixels in an image, and their relative brightness.

Levels: A feature to fix value problems. It generates an interactive histogram so you can adjust the amount of pixels at each brightness level.

Mask: An electronic frisket, or defined area, that protects portions of an image from change, or determines by its level of opacity how much change will be applied. Masks can be created from selections, and saved for future use as a channel.

Color casts

Many photos are not taken under ideal conditions. For example, fluorescents (found in offices everywhere) tint everything blue-green. Scanners often shift the color toward magenta.

If the file has enough visual information, its color cast problems will respond to autolevels. However, if you try that and the colors are still off, experiment with Variations (Image > Adjustments > Variations). It is a useful "cheat-sheet" for helping you figure out your next move.

Although you can apply the choices you make in its dialog box, Variations is usually better as a diagnostic than it is as a solution. You can't apply variation changes through an adjustment layer, so anything you accept immediately becomes part of the file. Neither can you use the history palette to step backwards to a previous choice.

Instead, notice what improves in Variations, then fire up an adjustment layer and apply similar changes—non-destructively, and with more finesse. If Variations suggested that there was too little blue in the image, go to the pull-down menu in Levels and choose Blue. Moving the input sliders will change only that one color. If your image improved when you decreased saturation, find a good white point in your image and try the Levels eyedropper.

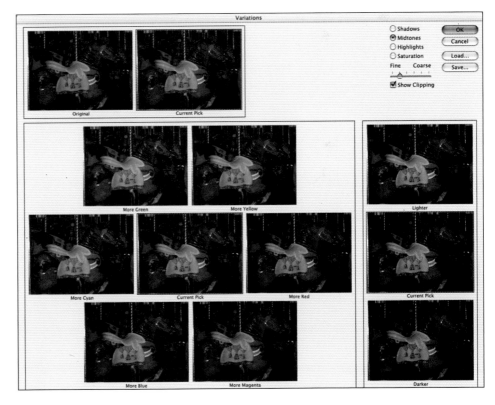

Variations shows the result if you add or subtract different variables. Be sure to check all four possibilities: shadows, midtones, highlights, and saturation.

STITCHING

Oversized printed material can be pinned and shot from a distance to capture it, but this strategy has two disadvantages. First, you can't see details, particularly if you're using a standard digital camera. Second, all sense of scale disappears. Murals, sculptures, and environmental design projects become indistinguishable from brochures.

The ideal is to shoot the artwork in pieces, and then reassemble them. But if you've ever tried it, you know that it's a lot easier in theory than it is in practice. When you overlay the photos, they don't quite match up. The closer you were to the artwork when you shot it, the worse the problem will be.

No solution is perfect, but there are two acceptable ways of merging material into one composite image.

With stitching software

Many digital camera models include a panorama function. It allows you to take several shots that can be merged into one image, usually with bundled software. Most frequently used for landscapes, it's also a good tool for shooting oversized artwork.

Because stitching software compensates for changes in shooting angle by slightly curving the individual shots, distortions in the composited image can occur if the artwork is very wide or tall.

> I've done a whole lot of scanning pieces and connecting them together. A fair amount of my work is hard to represent because it often has something that makes it special as an object.
>
> —Gunnar Swanson

To minimize distortion, shoot standing at the center of the work and use a tripod. Leave plenty of overlap—at least a third of each image should overlap the one before—so the software can figure out where to position each puzzle piece.

Even if your camera doesn't have a panorama function or bundled software, or you've used a scanner instead, you can still use stitching software. There are dozens of panorama stitching programs, ranging from the very basic to ones that create 3D virtual-reality effects.

By hand

Don't try merging multiple images by hand unless you are the type of person who engraves artwork on the heads of pins. On the other hand, it is possible to hand-stitch just two pieces with good success.

To get those pieces, use a flatbed scanner. It offers consistent lighting and a constant distance from the artwork. Even so, you may find that one side of the artwork is slightly brighter or darker than another side if the artwork doesn't lay completely flat. To guard against this, scan the work twice, the second time with the halves rotated 180 degrees. Try merging the left side of the first pass with the right side of the second, or vice versa.

Putting two pieces together manually requires a little delicacy and patience. First, use the hint on straightening scanned pieces from Chapter 6. Then put the two pieces on different layers. Invert the top one and change its opacity to about 40%. Inverting makes it easier to tell one half from the other as you adjust the two pieces. Imperfect match-ups will look blind-embossed. When you have the two pieces as perfect as you can get them, invert the top layer again, crop as needed, and flatten the image.

EDITING PROBLEMS AWAY

Whether the printing process has collided with scanning or you've made a design decision about your portfolio after your photo shoot, you may need to correct or adapt your material. The following issues are the most likely to cause you grief.

Moiré

As mentioned in Chapter 6, "Digitizing traditional work," moiré happens when the dot patterns of offset printing clash with the pixel grid. If you bring in an image and discover that it has moiré, the first thing you should do is try to scan it again. You can often eliminate or decrease moiré simply by finding a sweet spot—an angle where most of the screen dots don't create pixel patterns. Then a few simple tweaks in Photoshop can make your printed pieces sing again.

Place your artwork slightly off-kilter on the scanner. If you have a protractor, you'll find that a 6- to 8-degree angle works well. Scan the piece in at least double the ultimate screen ppi. Avoid a number that's evenly divisible by your final resolution, or the moiré could return when you scale your art back down. For example, 150 ppi works nicely for an image that will end up at 72 ppi.

Line art

Line art—pen and ink illustrations, marker or pencil sketches, and etchings—looks like it would be easy work to reproduce. In fact, it's the hardest. Because it only contains two elements (black and white), the lines break up into bitmaps. Diagonals develop stair-stepping, and crosshatching can look like jagged arrangements of dots.

In Chapter 6, I mentioned that you should scan line art at a much higher resolution than the screen quality you ultimately need (800 ppi is good). It's also a plus to have an original much larger than the final image needs to be. Scaling down line art always makes it look better, even with minimal correction.

A

B

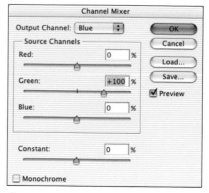

C

If the image still shows moiré (**A**), look at each color channel. You'll probably discover that one is in much worse shape than the others, like this blue channel (**B**). Create a Channel Mixer adjustment layer (**C**) and replace the image data of the really bad channel with the data from the best channel. The improvement can be enormous (**D**).

D

Be sure to scan in grayscale mode, not in bitmap. Otherwise, your result will look like the top image, rather than the bottom.

Then, adjust the Brightness/Contrast slider in Photoshop until you get the line thickness that most closely resembles your original art. Use the Sharpen Edges filter to reinforce the changes you made in your line weight and make the line edges feel crisper. When you're done, scale down the image to your preferred size.

Backgrounds

If you've followed the basic guidelines from Chapter 6 on photographing your artwork, you may not have to worry about backgrounds at all. A well-shot object can be cropped and shown in its own background.

An image background can need editing when you finalize the design of your site interface. Some people arrange several scanned objects together, adding a drop shadow to each object. Or they've shot a bright object against black for contrast, and then realize that they want to show the art against a different color Web page. If this strikes a chord for you, you'll need to separate the background from your image.

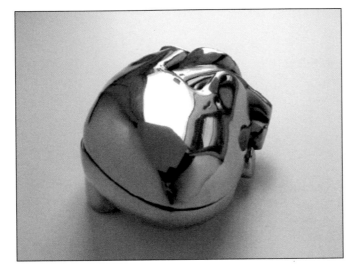

www.headsinc.com
So Takahashi's Terminator ashtray was beautifully shot on a neutral background. He simply cropped the shot, prepared it for the Web, and added it to his presentation.

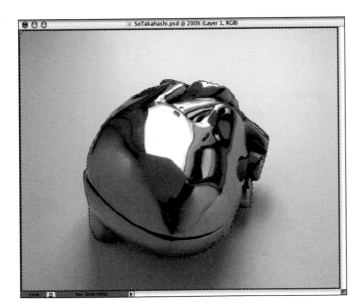

If Takahashi had needed to separate his background from the image, he could have done so by using the magic wand, but varying its tolerance level (how similar pixels must be to the one you clicked). Doing so minimizes the point-by-point clicking you need to do to describe the edge of an object, even one whose color is very similar to its background. This selection was created in two steps: by clicking on the background at a tolerance of 20, and then varying the tolerance between 10 and 20 to select the rest of the background.

Because you've shot your work sensibly, it's on a white or black background. That means it should be easy to select—probably much easier than trying to select the object in the picture. In Photoshop, once you've selected most of the object background with the magic wand, you can use the polygonal lasso tool for those places where the differences between the background and the object are too delicate for the magic wand to see, and to clean up areas where the magic wand hasn't given you a clean line.

CROPPING

If you've used a digital camera to shoot your images, they all appear to be at 72 dpi but have an enormous document size. Document size and resolution are two sides of a mathematical equation that describes how much information is in your file. If you crop your file before swapping document size for resolution, you are throwing away valuable information.

To be safe, before you crop or resize any file, save the file you've been editing and crop a copy. You may discover that you need more resolution after it's too late to get it back without redoing all of your adjustments and edits.

When you change the resolution and document size of a digital camera file, always deselect Resample. Doing this locks the ratio between width, height, and resolution, and prevents Photoshop from throwing out useful picture information.

Image Size

Pixel Dimensions: 9M

Width:	1536	pixels
Height:	2048	pixels

OK
Cancel
Auto...

Document Size:

Width:	21.333	inches
Height:	28.444	inches
Resolution:	72	pixels/inch

☑ Constrain Proportions
☐ Resample Image: Bicubic

Changing resolution and resizing

Eventually, you'll downsize your files to fit your portfolio design. When you downsize, you are asking the software to resample the file. The program will throw away information, downsampling to reach the smaller size. Downsampling is like doubling your resolution while shrinking the onscreen size. It makes some art look much better, although somewhat softer. Never upsize your scan. That's called interpolation, and results in the computer creating pixels by mathematical guesswork and adding them to your file—very bad for a portfolio piece.

It's better to resample only once, since files can require a little sharpening if they come down more than 30 percent. Each time you sharpen, you coarsen your image, potentially introducing artifacts. Resize and sharpen more than once, and your artwork deteriorates. If you have Photoshop, Image Ready, or another application that offers a Save for Web function, use it to handle your resizing at the same time that you optimize (see Chapter 8). It will offer a better result than resizing by hand.

SHARPENING

Only sharpen images that really need it, and then use the least amount of sharpening to get your result. Avoid the standard Sharpen filter: It's a blunt instrument for a surgical task.

The correct solution to soften images is the "Unsharp Mask" filter, one of Sharpen's alternates. The filter's strange name describes how it works. It takes a blurred copy of the image and uses it as a pixel mask. The filter compares each pixel with its blurred mask. Pixels without changes (because they are not at the edges of areas) are untouched, or masked out. The filter only notices areas where abrupt color or value changes indicate visual edges. It then does some complicated math to determine what to change and how much.

If you have images that develop outlined edges even when you use Unsharp Mask, try working on each channel of the image separately, sharpening the noisiest channel (usually blue) least, and the cleanest channel (usually green) the most. But be careful. Sharpening one channel at a much higher percentage than the others can lead to color shifts.

Make sharpening the last thing you do before you save a file in a compressed format. You should never sharpen a file that is already compressed (like a JPEG). Return to a universal file format and make your changes there, then resave the file for the Web.

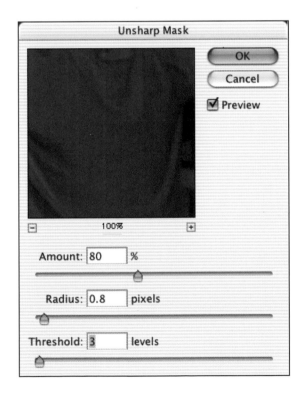

These are typical settings in Unsharp Mask for a 72-ppi image that needs sharpening.

Radius and Amount should increase with your resolution. At 72ppi, Radius should be between .3 and 1.0 pixels, with .5 to .8 usually giving optimal results without over-sharpening. For Amount, I start at a default of 75% and move up to 175%, watching for harsh lines that warn I've gone too far.

Threshold should decrease as resolution increases. A Threshold of 3 to 5 will take care of a normal sharpening need at screen resolution.

PORTFOLIO HIGHLIGHT:
ELEVEN, INC. | COMMUNICATION AND CLARITY

www.eleveninc.com

Most philosophies tend to run together, and there's only so many ways to present your "unique" process. If a creative process works or a strategy is truly unique, it will show up in the work.

—Michael Borosky

Most Flash intros are superfluous. Monuments to design hubris, they take too long to load and usually say nothing that you couldn't get more quickly by reading the home page. For busy users, the designer usually provides a "skip intro" link, making the hours of work the intro represents almost a guaranteed waste of time. San Francisco agency Eleven, Inc.'s intro surprises because it falls into none of these traps.

The first thing that appears onscreen is the site navigation, but the intro begins so quickly that you hesitate…and remain. Spare and purely typographic, it telegraphs that this firm can deliver content with elegance and a sure command of technology.

Scrolling down the window is a row of nonsense letters. Fading in as they drop, they fade out as words—eleven, branding, design, strategy, advertising, and interactive—appear. Each word breaks up and fades in turn, leaving one letter (in this case, the "r") to touch the row of falling gibberish and become part of the next word. In seconds, the animation identifies the company, tells what it does, and visually introduces its business philosophy—integrated services and clarity brought from noise.

The intro's message is reinforced by Eleven's highly legible portfolio images and their clean and simple navigation. At any time during the animation, you can select Portfolio from the navigation on the left. It brings you to their portfolio's opening page, where a grid of icons illustrates examples of each project category.

Both the nav bar and the pictures are live. Roll over a picture, and it confirms its category name. Click, and you move to a page with a large version of the previous page's thumbnail image. It's a medium-quality JPEG that loads quickly on the page.

In a typical portfolio, you'll go through three spreads and all of a sudden you're into packaging, or something entirely different. Those things can just sort of run together. That's why in our case studies, things are organized by client. We attempted to structurally illustrate that we're best if you use us for a number of things.

—Michael Borosky

Navigation and architecture

Eleven's navigation has two parts: the vertical text bar on the left of the page and the pull-down menu below the section title. Navigation on the left is category-based. Topics are explored with branches, and the branches are linear in nature. You can move forward and back through the work with simple arrows.

The right pull-down menu is below the category heading because here the clients are a subcategory of the type of work. This placement reinforces the connection and organization of Eleven's case studies. Potential clients like the ability to jump to the case studies and find out more about how Eleven works.

The two menus provide an interlocking and extremely flexible way to approach the portfolio. Combined, they do a good job of orienting viewers without making them work to find their way around.

Navigation cues are simple. Each category has a unique color that displays when you are in it, and appears on roll-over. Subcategories highlight in their category color. Colors are consistent between the left navigation bar and the right client pull-down menu. (The KODAK logo is a registered trademark of Eastman Kodak and is reproduced with permission of the Eastman Kodak Company.)

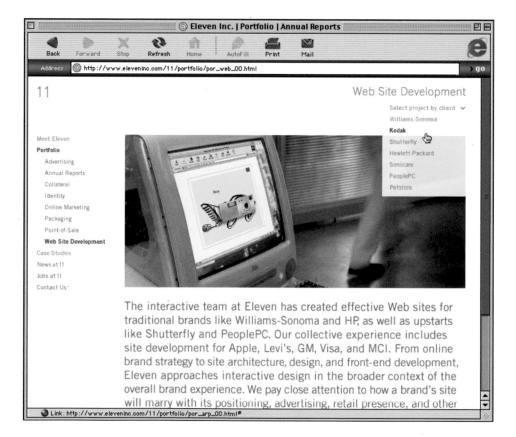

Although not under the portfolio section of the site, Eleven's case studies are a second portfolio with additional work organized by category for specific clients. The pages of work are laid out essentially the same as the standard portfolio pages, but they allow you to see how Eleven approaches design and branding for a single client in many different campaigns. (The KODAK logo is a registered trademark of Eastman Kodak and is reproduced with permission of the Eastman Kodak Company.)

Content

Eleven's portfolio, like its opening animation, is a professional delight. All content is shown large enough to truly represent the work and its nuances, but comes up onscreen without hesitation. Along with each portfolio image is a concise narrative of the project's development.

Although this is a very large portfolio site, at no point does the work feel overwhelming. By organizing the content into categories, keeping the pages clean and open, and avoiding any need to squint, Eleven makes it easy to stay longer—one of the hardest things to accomplish online.

Small content decisions add to the site's ease of use. For example, little visual cues tell you how many pages of each project you'll see, and where you are in the series. They also prompt you to notice when you're leaving a client's work or a section.

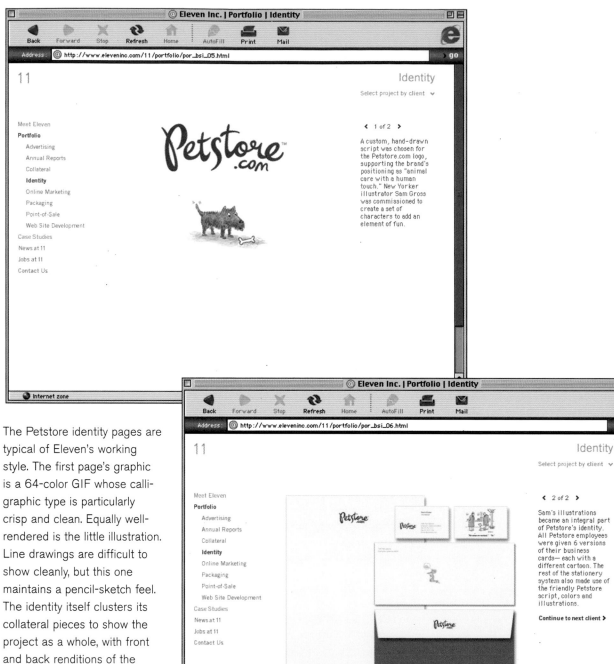

The Petstore identity pages are typical of Eleven's working style. The first page's graphic is a 64-color GIF whose calligraphic type is particularly crisp and clean. Equally well-rendered is the little illustration. Line drawings are difficult to show cleanly, but this one maintains a pencil-sketch feel. The identity itself clusters its collateral pieces to show the project as a whole, with front and back renditions of the envelope and business card.

Future plans

Even a well-designed site eventually needs freshening and rethinking. Although they update their site periodically, new ideas are afoot. As a collaborative firm in action as well as in words, their current site was the product of many creative minds, even though Michael Borosky, Eleven's vice president and creative director, was responsible for working out the navigation. Their next version of the site is already under internal discussion. Borosky feels that the new navigation will be simpler, and will likely focus on their predominant disciplines of advertising, design, and interactive.

The fact that we're an integrated agency is spread out over the site. It's more of a "dim-sum" approach; lots to choose from. In the next redesign, we're moving toward a more directed approach and simpler navigation. We plan to offer a more focused range of work in categories that better reflect our approach to brand integration.

—Michael Borosky

CHAPTER 8

Repurposing
and optimizing

Most of us who work on the computer view our finished, printed art as the final step in a long creative process. When we gather our work for a portfolio, it's natural for us to think of that physical artifact as the work we should show. After scanning, shooting, and agonizing over lost details, it can suddenly dawn on us that the best art is the original version—the file forgotten on the disk.

Returning to your original work is sometimes your only choice. When you freelance, or leave a company while a project is still in production, you may never receive a copy of the final work. Then there are the times when you create something you're particularly proud of, only to see the final, produced work and groan. The printer erred, or the client decided to make last-minute changes against your better judgment. Templates are particularly dangerous. After they're out of your hands, anyone with technical competence and no taste can "improve" your best decisions.

You're much more removed from the print work in a digital portfolio. Many of the subtle production choices that can make or break a great piece are simply lost in a 72-dpi image. Paper weight, finish, size, scale, varnish, binding—all those cues are lost in the digital world. The only things you have left are shape, color, and imagery. I've seen pieces online that don't even begin to resemble or represent the real thing.

—Michael Borosky

You can return to your original file, but you can almost never use it exactly as it is. Working files are too big, and in the wrong file format. This chapter provides some suggestions for repurposing and optimizing your existing artwork for your portfolio.

FILE ADAPTATION STRATEGIES

Designers do more than create onscreen. They choose colors and types of ink, select paper, and specify die-cuts. Sometimes those choices are the ones that make a project great. Unfortunately, finesse can be hard to capture in a scan, and even harder to see at the size work is presented in a digital portfolio. You can accept the scan's limited representation, and bring samples of special work to interviews. But doing that with too many pieces negates the point of a digital portfolio. And if the pieces are part of your best work, not showing them hurts your marketability.

Repurposing is particularly attractive for oversized work that has no special paper stock, like a poster, but it can work in lots of other situations. Here are a few suggestions to illustrate possible solutions:

- If you have an original file and a paper sample, scan in the latter and use it as a texture with the original file.
- If the paper sample you chose is transparent or translucent, you can mock up the finished piece and use transparency to let a background slightly show through.
- Using animation, you can show a piece at various stages of opacity if it was printed both front and back, or create the effect of turning pages to show a transparent overlay.
- Shooting an oversized book can leave shadows in the gutter, obscuring details. You can take a two-page spread into Photoshop, and use a displacement map to give the "book" a curve and a slight, non-destructive shadow in the center.
- A metallic ink often just looks like a flat color when scanned. Try suggesting graphic metallics in Photoshop, or with a mesh in Illustrator.
- Embossing is impossible to capture in a scan. Bring the file to Photoshop, select the embossed element, and then sharpen its edges. Run a light brush over the insides where the sharpening effect is too obvious.

The things that I bring to my print work are often hard to photograph. If I've done a piece that has metallic inks on it, it might have this mysterious glow in person, but when it's printed in an annual or turned into a JPEG on a website, the shimmer is gone, and the ink just looks lifeless.

—Gunnar Swanson

www.gunnarswanson.com
If used tastefully, animation can be a good tool for indicating a special effect. Here, Gunnar Swanson uses animation to simulate the twinkle of gloss varnish on matte paper.

REPURPOSING WITH PDFs

One of the best ways to repurpose published work is to create a PDF. It can be a good way of presenting a file that was originally created in a page layout or illustration program, or to bring together multiple image files in a coherent single file.

Screen-based PDFs are pretty easy to make, but they deserve just as much attention as larger, more complete presentations. They can often be the key to winning an interview.

A PDF is more flexible. It's like showing boards, because you can put pieces on different pages and they can be various sizes.

—Yang Kim

You owe it to the people who'll receive your files to create your PDFs correctly, and in a format they'll find easy to view. Many applications allow you to save your files directly as PDFs. However, a full version of Acrobat will allow you to create an integrated portfolio, not just a loose affiliation of files. That can be a critical difference. Many people quickly print a PDF and take it with them in paper form for review. They won't want to fuss with settings, or multiple files.

Here are tips for creating good PDFs:

- **Avoid scrolling.** Create letter-sized pages, so viewers can view and print them out easily. Set up your PDF in landscape format to fit better onscreen.
- **Shoot original files.** Always return to your original file for your PDF material if you can. For example, Flash-based websites can be shot from the .FLA file, not from a browser window.
- **Use TIF files.** If you're creating screen shots, shoot them as TIF, not JPEG, files. You are certain to end up needing to scale them as you lay out your pages, and scaled JPEGs quickly lose quality.

- **Optimize JPEGs.** Once you know the size of your JPEG on your designed PDF page, optimize your images (see below). Maximum-quality JPEGs in a PDF just bloat file sizes.
- **For a fast attachment, merge your PDFs.** If you have several individual PDF files from different projects, it's easy to combine them into one PDF file.

To make one PDF out of many, open all the PDFs at once, then open each of their Thumbnail palettes. Drag all the thumbnails to one document. You can reorder them as you like in the final document's thumbnail palette.

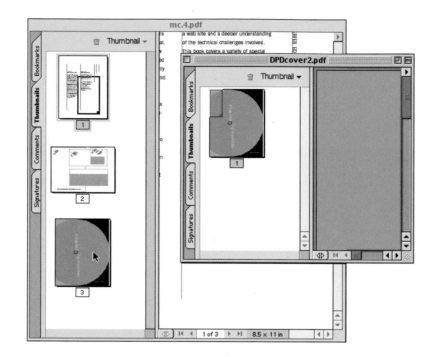

- **Make your PDF a project.** A graphic designer should have a designed PDF, with a redesigned resume as part of the package. It's often useful to export your Quark files in EPS format, and then lay out selected sample pages in Illustrator. They become very easy to scale, retain their crispness, and remain editable if you need to tweak them. When you're done, you can save the Illustrator file as an EPS, then drop the file back into Quark as one piece of artwork.

My preference is not to get an email with twenty PDFs attached to it. I don't want to have to hop around to open them all up. If I can't get one PDF file, I'd rather have a URL that directs me to a website.

—Cynthia Rabun

- **Create a cover page.** If you have a multiple-page PDF, create a cover page with your contact info as the first page, then place your name and the page number as a header or footer on each subsequent page. If your work is printed, the pages will still be identifiably yours, and remain together.
- **Watch your file sizes.** Even in these days of cable modems and DSL lines, no PDF should exceed 1 MB. Many recipients who have fast connections still have limited storage space on a mail server.
- **Label your artwork.** Just as you would on a website or disk, your artwork should include captions that identify it.

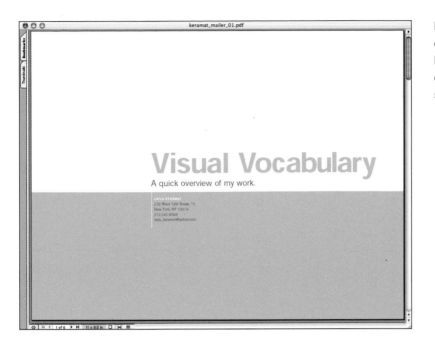

Layla Keramat provides a well-designed cover page for her PDF portfolio that will print equally well in color or on a standard laser printer.

- **Name your PDF sensibly.** Don't call it "mywork" or "myportfolio." Use your full name in the file label. If you must send more than one PDF, name the files similarly, so they'll appear together when sorted.
- **No headshots.** Unless you're a performing artist, don't ever put a picture of yourself in your PDF. You're not entering a beauty contest, nor are you a member of a corporate sales force. Creative directors and placement agencies target you as clueless as soon as they see the photo.

OPTIMIZING IMAGE FILES

All your files will eventually need to be optimized—altered to fit the requirements of transmission. Websites, emailed images, and those dropped into PDFs will need the most shrinking. CDs and DVDs have less stringent requirements, but optimized files will take less time to load.

A well-optimized file looks good onscreen, but takes up very little file space. The smaller the file space, the faster the file. With the exception of your creativity, nothing will have more bearing on how your portfolio is perceived than how much time the viewer must invest to see it.

Designers who are designing in an office don't always remember that not everyone has DSL or cable access. So your design may be wonderful, but if it takes way too long to load, I need to move on.

—Cynthia Rabun

About slicing

Slicing is a way to break up large images and interfaces into small, bite-sized elements that load more quickly than a single image would. Many applications, including Photoshop, offer a slicing feature that helps you to slice an image before you optimize it. But slicing is often an unpleasant distraction. Unless you have a good visual place to break the file (like in the center of a two-page spread), it's better to use optimizing techniques to have the file load progressively, or simply keep your file sizes down.

Optimizing basics

Optimizing is a delicate balance of four elements: color, image quality, image size, and file size.

The ratio among these four elements shifts as technology improves. Browser limitations and platform differences still compromise color (see "Color profiles and JPEG files" later in the chapter), but good image quality is finally attainable. So is a decent onscreen image size. Unless you have a very budget-conscious client base, you can optimize for 16 million colors displayed on a 17-inch monitor. No more 216-color non-dithering palette and postage stamp-sized projects.

We all know connection speeds have improved. The rule used to be that no web page should take more than 30 seconds to load on a 28.8 modem. That's no longer the case. Most users are working with at least 56k modems, and in many urban markets, the minimum standard crests at 128k, often with cable modem connections. But that doesn't give you the license to throw anything you'd like into a portfolio. Image sizes are cumulative on a page, and even as our options have

This type design has been optimized as a GIF. The original file appears at the top for comparison. Although the two images look very similar, the GIF is a minute fraction of the file size of the original.

increased, viewer expectations have too. No one will actually wait 30 seconds to watch a portfolio page render. And during really high-traffic times or in the middle of a worm attack, even a cable modem connection can slow to a crawl. Every .5kb saved in optimizing will still be appreciated.

You'll need to optimize before you begin actual production on your portfolio, but you'd be wise to already have sketched out a layout for a typical portfolio page before you optimize. It's always possible to downsize art in HTML or Flash, but the closer you are to optimizing your work at 100% of the size it will be onscreen, the happier you'll be with the results.

The number-one killer on a website is the speed. Corporate clients will run out of patience. They have high-speed connections, and they're not used to waiting. We try to keep to a certain number file size. We're always hovering just below what we think might break people's patience.

—Yang Kim

OPTIMIZING PROCESS

There are some specialized tools for optimizing, like Debabelizer, but the easiest and most common method is to bring the file into either Photoshop/ImageReady or Fireworks. Both programs have similar optimizing windows and offer the same range of variables.

In either software, you can choose between optimizing the file as a JPEG or as a graphics file, usually GIF. The standard rule of thumb is that photographic images are optimized as JPEGs and graphic images are optimized as GIFs. This rule can be bent, especially for portfolio pieces, as what works best varies based on the nature of the file.

Optimizing applications provide presets as jumping off points. Many people who don't know much about optimization select one of these presets and just apply it globally to their images. That's better than not optimizing it all, but it usually leads to files that load too slowly, or are significantly smaller onscreen than they need to be.

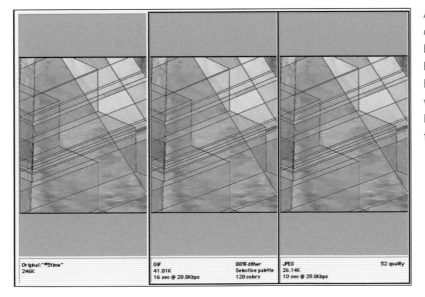

Original: "#5time"
246K

GIF
41.81K
16 sec @ 28.8Kbps

88% dither
Selective palette
128 colors

JPEG
26.14K
10 sec @ 28.8Kbps

52 quality

A graphic image with a mixture of flat areas and smooth blends should be tested as both GIF and JPEG to find the best combination. Here, either version has reasonable quality, but the JPEG is much smaller than the GIF.

Optimizing hints

Let's examine some of the ways optimizing can improve your portfolio and impress your target audience. There's one set for GIFs, and another for JPEGs.

> No matter how slick the presentation is, it won't make mediocre work better. I sometimes wonder if the reason people keep their work so small is to hide the funky details.
>
> —Michael Borosky

To begin, set a goal for each page's download. For a standard, non-animated portfolio, a good goal is eight seconds, based on a 56.6kb modem or ISDN. If your images are photographs, you can set it a second or two higher. Assume that your portfolio image can represent the bulk of that time, since it's the focus of your site. Then change the setting in your software's preview menu to reflect your target access speed.

You can process files in bulk, using a standardized optimization setting and the software's automation menu. I don't recommend it. Although we've come a long way since the days when everything had to be coded manually, optimizing still requires a commitment to examine every image individually.

GIFs

It's not a problem to get acceptable-looking GIF files. The difficulty is to shave little bits of file size from them without making any dismal changes in the appearance of the finished file.

Photographic files

There are fewer elements to consider when creating JPEGs. The most important thing to remember is the difference between the general categories—Low, Medium, High, and Maximum—and the quality gradations within each category. You continue to have a high quality at any setting between 60 and 79, but the file size you generate can be radically different at these settings.

One extremely useful option is the Progressive setting. The larger your JPEG is, the longer it will take to load. If you choose Progressive, your JPEG will begin to load immediately at low quality, improving as it goes until it is completed. Progressive loading gives the viewer a sense that something is happening.

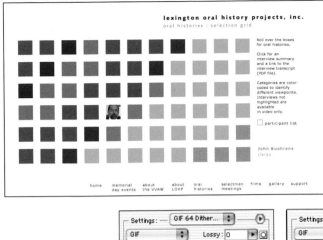

There's more than one way to optimize a file. This image is the result of creating custom settings (the dialog box on the right, below) instead of accepting a preset (like the dialog box to the left, below).

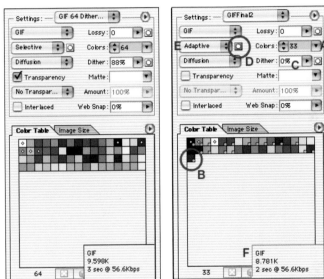

A. Minimize the number of colors. Starting with a 64-color preset, I've dropped colors from the palette one by one until I reached the minimum acceptable for the image.

B. Several colors dropped too soon. I stepped backwards, selected the most important colors to preserve, and locked them. Locked colors can't be dropped as colors decrease.

C. This image is mostly made up of flat color and type. Through experimentation, I've found that I need no dither at this size. In fact, the type is crisper without it.

D. It was important to hold some details in the face icon when decreasing the number of colors. I created a mask of that box and saved it. Then I enabled the mask by selecting the mask button next to the palette type and protected this small detail from being posterized. This strategy is called "weighted optimization" and it works for both GIFs and JPEGs.

E. There are different methods of selecting colors for a palette. Adaptive palettes are determined by the most common colors in the image—good for pieces with lots of flat color.

F. As a result, the final optimized image will take a full second less to load. That doesn't seem like much, but when the goal for your entire page is five seconds, one second is 20% of the time.

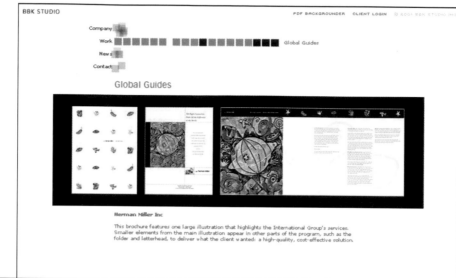

www.bbkstudio.com
The JPEG portfolio image on this page takes up a lot of screen real estate, and appears to be a high-quality image. Yet, it was saved at Medium, tweaked upward to a quality level of 40. When you zoom it up to 300%, you can see that some areas are surprisingly well defined, while others (like the type) are barely gestures. As with GIFs, you can use a mask to weight the quality in the areas that are most important, allowing less critical areas to slide. The result is a much smaller JPEG.

Color profiles and JPEG files

A *color profile* holds information about the color space of an image or a device. If every device you use is calibrated and has a color profile, the computer can translate color between the devices so you will always see the same range of colors no matter where your file is.

Photoshop allows you to embed a color profile to an image, which is invaluable for most graphic and art purposes.

Unfortunately, most browsers don't yet read these profiles. They just show all artwork in sRGB. If you want to have an accurate assessment of what colors will look like in a browser, prepare your files in sRGB, and bring them to a browser window before you create your portfolio.

These are exactly the same JPEG file, with the same ICC profile, captured on the same monitor and operating system.

The top image is color corrected. The bottom image is how it appears in a browser.

Optimizing video

After editing a video file in a non-linear editing program—cutting, splicing, adding effects, and cleaning it up—you encode it: Save it in a different, compressed format. Your major decision is to figure out what format or formats you should use to create your new file. From there, you select settings that determine the final quality and file size of your clip.

There is no standard format for video, which is a tremendous headache for portfolio creators and viewers alike. Each format is optimized to be viewed from within its own player (see the next section, "Encoders and players"). Some players allow you to view other formats, but the quality is often compromised. Unless you are quite certain of your target audience's platform and technology, you'll have to output in more than one format.

Video optimization terminology

Aspect ratio is the proportion of the horizontal to the vertical dimensions of an image. The computer/standard TV ratio is 4:3. Film/HDTV (the new standard, and the ratio of Apple Cinema Displays) runs at 16:9.

Codecs are algorithms that are built into software. They are converters that **co**mpress and **dec**ompress digital data, particularly video files. There are dozens of video codecs, including DV, MPEG-4, and Cinepak. Some are better for your purposes than others.

Fast Start is pseudo-streaming. When you play QuickTime and Windows Media Player files from a regular web server, the file downloads to the viewer's computer at the best speed for its connection and begins to play while the download is still taking place.

Hint Tracks tell a streaming server how to prepare video clip data for successful streaming. Without a hint track, the video will not stream. Hint tracks aren't needed for downloading or pseudo-streaming.

Streaming is the process of sending data to a computer in real time. The viewer doesn't have to wait for the clip to download before they can see it.

ENCODERS AND PLAYERS

To see encoded video, the viewer needs a player in your format. The "best" player format for you is one that is already installed on your viewer's computer. Because you can't always predict what that will be, you'll need to create files for more than one player. The players mentioned below are the most popular ones.

If you are creating movies for both Mac and PC users, save your edited files in at least two formats—AVI (for Windows users) and MOV (for Mac users). Even though both movie types can be played on both platforms, very few Mac users have Windows Media Player. Conversely, although a reasonable number of Windows users have QuickTime, all have WMP.

- **QuickTime.** QuickTime is Apple's cross-platform video software. It imports many other file formats, including .AVI and output to a variety of codecs. Windows users of IE5.5 and later need to download a special Active-X file to be able to see QuickTime content.

www.cefaratti.com

Like Mike Cefaratti, most graphic designers who show video in their portfolio use QuickTime as their format.

- **Windows Media.** Windows Media is installed on all Windows computers, making it the single-most popular player. The player is cross-platform, but must be downloaded by Mac users and does not support some competing formats.
- **RealOne.** RealNetworks is a provider of a codec for streaming video. Because the company's codec is used to deliver music and video content files by large corporations, the Real player has good coverage on Windows and Mac computers alike. Only the Real player can read and play a Real-encoded file.

There are two additional ways of encoding and/or playing audio and video on the Web or on a disk. Each of them relies on one of the main technologies listed previously, but requires an additional player or software on the user's computer:

- **Flash.** Macromedia Flash allows you to import video from other sources and add an interactive layer to it. You can output files in Flash's own .SWF format, or as a QuickTime or Windows Media file.
- **DivX.** DivX is a popular codec with 3D animators and DV enthusiasts. It offers high-quality, large window sizes and fast performance. It uses the Windows Media Player in Windows, and QuickTime on the Mac side.

www.deluxepaint.net

Animators like Cemre Ozkurt consider DivX a requirement for serving 3D animation over the Web.

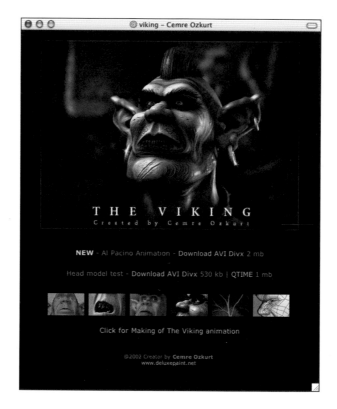

You can't offer too many formats, but you absolutely can offer too few. You can include a player on a CD or ask a viewer to download one, but most people find that extra step extremely irritating…if they are willing to do it at all.

ENCODING SETTINGS

After you've determined what format or formats best meet your needs, your next step is to select the settings that will determine the final quality and file size of your clip. Rule number one is that the more you compress, the smaller your file is and the faster it will download and play, but the worse it will look. You can maintain more quality by keeping your window playback size small.

Rule number two is that no setting is perfect for every clip. You'll want different settings for two clips in a Web-based portfolio if one is a full-motion video and another is a 2D typographic animation. Also, every person's eye and tolerance is a little different.

Window size

Everyone wants to show their work as large as possible, but unless your Web portfolio will reside on a streaming server, you'll have to compromise. If your movie is just a slide show or simple animation, you might be able to get as large as 320×240, because the still images or those with a static background will compress efficiently. Although standards are always improving, it's safest to display motion video in a small window, usually 160×120. If you really want to upsize to take advantage of better technology, create two window sizes and allow your viewers to choose.

Work on CD can be somewhat larger, with 320×240 being a good starting point. DVD is usually designed for a full TV screen, although you can use it to show smaller clips.

Compression type

There are too many compression types to choose from, and it can be bewildering to see the list of codecs in a typical export menu. In fact, most of them are completely useless for your portfolio. Some are for videoconferencing, for example, and others are actually almost obsolete. Even more frustrating is the list of audio codecs. Unless you have high-quality music as part of your video, you won't want to compress audio at all. Compressed audio sounds really bad, and you don't even get the benefit of smaller file sizes.

After you eliminate all the unnecessary complications, you're left with two preferred compression codecs: Sorenson and Cinepak. Cinepak is a better choice for cross-platform video clips. Sorenson is wonderful for Macintosh movies, but it isn't supported consistently enough on Windows machines to make it a safe bet for every clip. You can, however, create your .AVI files with Cinepak and your .MOV ones with Sorensen.

Always place a black or white leader—a few frames of empty background—at the beginning and at the end of a video clip. That gives the person a chance to find the video's open window and focus on it before the action begins. iMovie allows you to set this in a dialog box.

Frame speed

A higher frame rate per second gives a smoother look to your clip, but adds size to the file. Over the Web, you should probably stick with 10–15 fps. Moving up to 15–20 fps on a CD should be fine.

Key frame rate

Encoders can determine how much a movie changes from a reference frame (called a *key frame*). To make movies smaller, they only send information about the things that change in the frames that follow. The more key frames, the smoother the movie will appear, but the larger it will be. Too few key frames, and the movie will be small but jerky. I recommend 5–7 key frames for a CD. Web settings should be tested, depending on how much actual movement takes place in the clip. A setting of 15 ensures an update every second if your movie is playing at 15 frames per second.

File naming

It is very important to name your files with the correct extensions. Be careful not to delete these extensions by mistake, or they will not be recognized properly by their players. QuickTime uses .MOV, Windows Media uses .AVI, and RealOne uses .RM.

The settings for this QuickTime movie have been set assuming cross-platform delivery. They are a compromise to allow someone on a 56kb modem to see the work at reasonable quality. Your mileage will vary.

A. Color depth. Select the highest option available.

B. Quality. For the Web, start with Medium, and test. For a CD, start with High.

C. Not all encoders let you set a data rate. If you can do so, keep the number above 30Kbps.

D. Sound. These are standard settings for portfolio audio. Set the Channels for Mono (one channel). If your video is accompanied by high-quality audio, select Qdesign on a Mac and MP3 for Windows.

E. Even if you are downloading, not really streaming, you must check this box for Internet delivery.

AFTER THE ARTWORK

Repurposing and optimizing will frequently represent the single-most intense amount of time in preparing your portfolio. Like most production work, it can feel like an obstacle in the way of the fun, creative part of portfolio development. But when you're finished, you'll be able to reuse most of it again and again as your portfolio requires.

PORTFOLIO HIGHLIGHT:
MICHAEL CEFARATTI | EXQUISITE DETAIL

cefaratti.com

The best technology appears effortless. If you do everything right—repurpose, optimize, design—nothing will pull attention away from your work. Of course, if you are also someone whose favorite projects involve manipulating bleeding-edge combinations of media, anyone who needs your talents will pay as close attention to how you do your work as to how elegantly it is designed. Mike Cefaratti's portfolio holds up to both types of scrutiny.

> I am challenged by opportunities where I can create fully immersive, interactive experiences that draw upon new technologies.
>
> —Mike Cefaratti

Like most savvy interface designers, Cefaratti knows that you can't take anyone's technology for granted. Although his home page should pop up only a moment later, on the opening page he offers contingencies. There are directions, as well as every link his viewers might need to see his site. One very savvy detail: He puts his contact link right on this first page. If someone is just looking to get in touch with him, they don't have to wade through an interface to find it.

An accomplished interface designer in New York, Cefaratti works full-time in his own freelance design firm. Although he also considers his peers in the mix, his primary target audience is his clients. They're people who want to see his work as quickly as possible. Knowing their needs, he keeps distractions to a minimum: Every element serves a purpose, and there is not a single wasted gesture or word.

Cefaratti's presentation may be very straightforward, but it doesn't come across as stark or cold. Design choices and details make the pages feel rich and visually satisfying.

> I refrained from using complicated navigation and animation that might detract from the overall user experience. A good user experience allows the work to suggest a voice that doesn't "shout" at the user.
>
> —Mike Cefaratti

The site's predominant color is a cool teal, with a soft photographic image providing texture. Hairline rules define the portfolio display area, and combine with transparent overlays to define page architecture. His crisp white text is small but highly legible.

Front and center are the main portfolio branches, including the highlighted link to his most recent projects. This link is set off by color and positioning to make it the most prominent one on the page.

Navigation and architecture

Cefaratti is a good host. He's given a lot of thought to what brings a prospective client to his site, and what they expect to find when they arrive. First, they'll want to know what he's done lately, to see that he is active and to scope out his current clientele. Then they'll want to see some examples of prior work, to examine his capabilities. If they have time, they'll look deeper, but most won't click past the first few projects in each sequence.

Knowing what they want, Cefaratti streamlined his navigation and architecture. Everything is immediately accessible and intelligently organized. His linear groupings aren't arranged by something arbitrary like chronology or alphabet. His best projects come up first. This strategy also ensures that if they're in a hurry, prospective clients will only see the projects he thinks are his best.

It's very important to choose work that best describes you as a designer and is also appropriate for your audience. I strategically placed some of my strongest work at the beginning of each section for ease of reference.

—Mike Cefaratti

The bulk of Cefaratti's professional work can be reached from the interactive and motion branches. Roll over the other project links, and color-coded brackets that echo his logo appear around them. The colors dominate the interface design for each distinct area.

Although Cefaratti's architecture is meant to be experienced linearly, his navigation offers viewers many opportunities to take control if they wish. They can view projects out of planned order, jump to one of the other main portfolio sections, or explore some projects in more depth. The site is an excellent compromise between the designer's need to control and the user's desire for choices.

Content

As you enter each portfolio section, Cefaratti presents a short introduction to the type of work it includes and his share of the projects. Doing this upfront lets you know that he is capable of playing multiple roles. Every page that follows is specific as to what he did and the client brief he met. There is no guessing about what his responsibilities might have been—a problem that can readily crop up in collaborative projects.

A second set of links appears in the upper-right corner of the page, separated cleanly by a horizontal bar that defines the portfolio display area. These persist throughout the main portfolio sections. Instead of brackets, a thin plum underline appears on rollover. This color change reinforces the distinction between the portfolio and the person behind it.

Below the display area is a new set of links: a numbered sequence. The links make it easiest for you to view the work in Cefaratti's preferred order, but don't prevent you from jumping around. To keep you oriented, the page you are on is highlighted with a circle, and the client name appears with the navigation.

At any time, a click on the logo above the bar returns the viewer to the home page.

All too frequently, work online is small and typographic details are non-existent. Most of Cefaratti's images can actually still be read, and his typographic aesthetic understood. His optimizing in both still images and video clips is impressive.

Not unexpectedly, Cefaratti's content appears with blinding speed. What is extraordinary is how beautiful it looks. There is almost no *posterization*, or the jpeg artifacts that often appear when the quality level is too low. Cefaratti maintains image quality and achieves good download times by using Equilibrium's Debabelizer to create custom palettes and experiment with compression settings. No potential client will ever be surprised by the difference between what they think they've seen online and what the project actually is.

Savvy content choices extend beyond accomplished repurposing. In interactive work, you often have several screens that represent different levels in a site. Showing too many examples could bore some viewers, while others might be genuinely interested in seeing how an entire project was handled. Cefaratti's solution serves both needs. Some projects have additional links that allow the viewer to explore a project in depth.

When a project has additional examples, a forward arrow appears and blinks discretely, accompanied by explanatory text. The arrows become back and forward arrows as the sequence unfolds.

Future plans

Cefaratti's ultimate goals are to combine his interactive talents with his interests in broadcast design and music in kiosk or tradeshow installations. To ensure that people will be aware of these interests, his portfolio currently includes separate sections for motion and music composition. The recent projects section is fairly new. In the future, it will allow him to keep his existing site intact while building a small subset of new projects that he can add to as they are completed—a clever solution to the update problem.

I highlighted one or two visually strong images for each project, and then gave the user the choice of either seeing more examples of that project or moving on. This also worked better on a visual level. I had more real estate and was able to maintain an uncluttered interface.

—Mike Cefaratti

CHAPTER 9

Creating

written content

"Someone showing their art should at least pretend they're competent," I heard a student sneer while surfing a site. That was harsh, but it's easy to criticize when you know the difference between good and bad work. Writing is no different. Whether you're dyslexic or just hate writing, you can't afford to be embarrassed publicly.

The easiest way to avoid the issue is to design a portfolio with no written content—just your contact information. This risky strategy can work for some disciplines (animation comes to mind) but is deadly for most design areas. Too much of what makes a good designer is in the decisions. For those, viewers need some context.

Fortunately, you don't have to be a brilliant author to write competently. What you absolutely need to know can be learned, and most of what's left can be handled by a combination of software and patience.

This chapter will help you figure out how much text your portfolio needs, prevent you from making the very worst writing errors, and help you keep the visual and verbal elements of your portfolio in synch.

WHAT TO WRITE AND WHY

You choose your samples carefully and attempt to craft a seamless presentation. What you write is equally important. People often want to know about your career or education, what you contributed to a project, and how you solve visual problems. They need a sense of who you are. The right text in the right place can help them do that.

Some types of text are more important in your portfolio than others, so if you don't write well, you can concentrate on these critical elements. In order of necessity, you will write to:

- Identify your work.
- Introduce yourself.
- Explain your ideas and process.
- Speak directly to your audience.

IDENTIFYING YOUR WORK

Even a minimalist portfolio includes captions keyed to the work. Your captions should include the client and a short title. Either the title or another line of the caption should specify what role you played in the project (art direction, illustrations, or programming, for example). The title can be descriptive ("graphics and art direction for") or a formal work title ("Beyorn identity package").

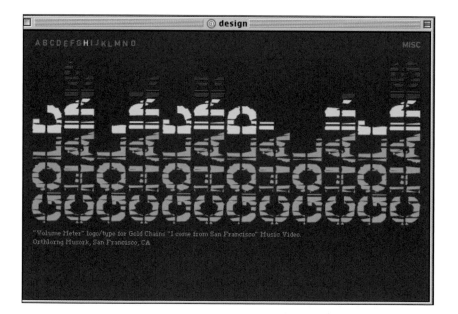

jon@commonspace.fm

If you are mixing different types of work in your captions, give people a visual cue that tells them which it is. Jon Santos uses simple quote marks to distinguish a description from a simple title, but initial capital letters, a typeface, or formatting change will work as well.

Distinguish between these captions and the descriptions of the work. Captions are not the place to explain your design ideas and process.

Check your facts…don't depend on your memory for titles, names, and spelling. Don't use abbreviations for the client name unless it is so well known that everyone will recognize it.

Portfolios in second languages

Creativity is international. It's possible that you are now working in a different country from where you started. If so, you might not be as solid a writer in your adopted language as in your native one. To a point, potential employers or clients will accept imperfections in your writing if they know that you are working in your second language, particularly if you present yourself well in person.

That doesn't give you carte blanche to butcher your adopted language in print. In fact, if you are looking for a job where you are likely to be working with text, not just image, it is extremely important that you convey your ability to maneuver in your second language. If you don't, people could wonder if you will misunderstand instructions or make expensive or embarrassing errors under deadline pressure.

You should not only follow the guidelines in this chapter for proofing your work—you should take them one step further. If at all possible, have a native speaker read your text before you post it.

INTRODUCING YOURSELF

Your portfolio presentation must include some personal information. You provide that with some text about yourself—a résumé, bio, or cover letter.

The résumé

The classic professional writing requirement is the résumé. There are scads of books and workshops on creating effective résumés. None of them are worth squat to a creative. With the exception of academic vitae, the résumé is secondary to your portfolio. It could get you in the door at a large company's human resources department, but it will never get you a job. It can, in fact, have the opposite effect. A sloppy résumé can be the tipping point when a company is having a tough time choosing among a short list of candidates.

The best advice anyone can give you about writing a résumé is: Keep it clean, visually and verbally. Then make sure that it contains no errors (see "The telltale signs of bad writing" section that follows). Send it through a spell checker every time you edit it. Get other people to read it— the more eyes, the better.

Clean also means spare. Few résumés need to be longer than one page, even if you've already had a long career. Older experience tends to become less relevant as time passes and can be cut or radically condensed. Education is an example. It's important when you've just graduated, but after you've had even one job in the real world, it belongs at the bottom of the page. By the time you're heading for your second job, details (such as your grade point average) should disappear as well.

Another "delete me" is the Objective that management gurus tell you to put at the top of your résumé. The only time you might find one useful is if you've had an unusual career. When you've done a variety of work that you need to tie together or you're making a radical change (from exhibit designer to interactive designer, for example), an objective can help you explain the transition: "My objective is to leverage my experience with wayfinding in physical space to designing for the virtual environment."

Brevity is a creative blessing. Text-heavy résumés written by and for creatives simply don't get read. No paragraph should be longer than four sentences, and no sentence should run longer than four lines, assuming about 30 picas a line and ten point type. Shorter is even better. Stick to your responsibilities, range of work, and most significant accomplishments. Or simply take a sentence to explain what you did and then list the clients you did it for. You can always elaborate in person.

A résumé is best written and designed to be printed and read offline. That means it should not include anything that will slow the download and tempt someone to break the connection. No placed art of any kind. And use your name as the file title, not "résumé." How will anyone remember whom your PDF belongs to otherwise?

Your résumé and your portfolio

When you send email, of course you'll include your résumé with your samples. You'll also include it on a CD or DVD. But these portfolio forms are most useful when you have a personal contact or know of a specific hiring opportunity. With an online digital portfolio, you can choose either to include your résumé or replace it with short descriptive text and contact information. Some people deal with the résumé question by creating a download link to their PDFs. There's nothing wrong with this approach, and it has many positive results. It ensures that your name will find its way into a paper file and encourages viewers to find out more about you while your portfolio is still fresh in their minds.

In some situations, you might want to use the bio plus contact approach. Separating your résumé from your portfolio can be useful for three reasons:

- **Confidentiality.** When you put your résumé on a standard Web page, its text will be searchable in engines such as Google. Although this might seem to be a good thing, remember that few people will search on your name. Instead, your site will come up most frequently when they look for information on your prior—or current—place of employment. If you are actively looking for a new job while you're still employed or have had issues with a former employer that might come up in an interview, this information might be better left less accessible.

www.cefaratti.com

Mike Cefaratti doesn't include a bio on his site, but he makes it easy to view his résumé. Like most designers, he prefers that people read his PDF because he has designed it. But he makes no assumptions about the technology of his potential clientele. You can read his résumé online in a Web page or even download a Word file (Mac or PC formatted).

- **Contact.** Handing out your résumé without requiring any contact takes a possible point of control away from you. After all, your résumé is only important to a company if they are already intrigued by your work. If they email to request the résumé, you have instantaneous feedback on your site. You also have an opportunity to present yourself in a less formal, more personal way—and gain a contact name for future mailings.

- **Customizing.** Waiting to send your résumé on request also allows you to customize it slightly to each query. You can create one or two alternate résumés to keep on hand for different situations, sending the most appropriate one when asked. Or you can use it as an opportunity to gain points. After you know who wants your résumé, you can visit their site to find out more about them. If you've done a project that's directly relevant to their clientele but isn't in your digital portfolio, a PDF along with the résumé can show not only what a good fit you'd be, but that you think fast.

The bio

People don't always need your full story. A good compromise is a short bio or note that describes your experience and expertise. An online bio, like most Web text, should be as short as you can make it while still hitting what you feel are your most important points. If you are looking for clients instead of employment, your bio should emphasize your capabilities or the type of work you do.

Remember that your text introduction is not a résumé replacement. It's a centering device to give a reader a way to look at your work.

The telltale signs of bad writing

As someone who sees lots of student résumés, I've been treated to many remarkable writing errors in portfolios and résumés. They don't make the potential employer feel confident, although they can brighten up a tense day at the sender's expense. My personal favorites...the one who claimed proficiency in "Adope Photoshot" and the person who misspelled his own name.

L ouis Etudiantia   9975 55th Street, San Dorito, CA 90335
Phone: 415 9939999
Email: clariEtudi99@aol.com

O bjective: To tap my creative potential while utilizing my technical
and design skills in a position that allows me to develop
both personally and professionally.

S chooling: 1997
BFA in Graphic Design, College of the Arts,
University of Erewhon, Boston, MA.

E xperience: Etudianta Associates
October '01 to present

Web design, print and identity packages for small
to medium-sized businesses and indivdduals.
Responsible for managing freelance illustrators and
production assistants, handled billing and client services.

Web Designer, Megaproductions Unlimited
June '98 - October '01

Created site maps, designed interface and managed
production of over 25 major Website rollouts.
Clients included NetEd.com, BristleWorks.com,
Petcetera.com, Freezerworks Limited, and Animationworks.

Graphic Designer, Fairweather Studios
June 98 - June '99

Print and identity design and production for San Dorito's
award-winning "Save the Wheels" campaign. Designed
book covers for Grapefruit Publications. Responsible for ten
covers per week on topics ranging from corporate ethics to pet care.

R eferences: Will be furnished upon request.

Sometimes you get so wrapped up in your work that you miss something truly mortifying. Look carefully at the graphic device of these initial caps. What do they spell?

Want to look bad in print? Here are a few ways to do it.

Lousy spelling

In the age of spell checkers, there is no excuse for misspelled words. They tell people that you are sloppy. Spell check even if you think you are good at spelling. Everyone has some words they consistently spell incorrectly, and everyone makes typographical errors.

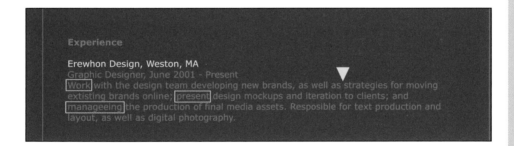

This is an excerpt from a real online résumé, replicated with its identifying information eliminated or altered to protect its maker. The résumé itself is very nicely designed but has a remarkable amount of errors for one short paragraph.

The highlighted words in the copy are all misspelled or mistyped.

This is the same paragraph as the previous one. Besides its misspellings, it has two major grammatical problems. The yellow triangle indicates a place where a word is missing. The person might have thought that the word "developing" in the first part of the sentence didn't need to be repeated in the next phrase. The verbs "work," "present," and "managing" should all be in the same form. "Manageeing" should have been simply "manage."

continues

continued

Bad grammar

If you don't spell well, chances are your grammar isn't perfect either. Grammatical errors are trickier to catch than spelling errors but can lead to real embarrassment when they make their way into your portfolio.

Microsoft Word can be irritating, but it does a pretty good job of preventing the worst grammatical goofs. In it, you can select Tools>Spelling and Grammar at any point and check your document for errors. Of course, that means you have to remember to run a check when you write or make changes. If you don't mind interruptions as you work, set Word to prompt you. To do this, go to File>Preferences (Windows and Mac Classic OS)/Word>Preferences (Mac OS X). In the dialog box, you can choose to have Word highlight spelling and grammar errors as you type, so you can fix problems as they arise.

Fractured headlines

One little-known fact about spell checkers is that they don't check words in all capital letters unless you tell them to. You are less likely to notice mistakes in all cap words because they are usually headlines or captions. Allowing Word to check uppercase words is usually worth the added hassle of false positives.

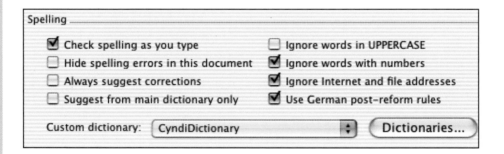

After you've unchecked the default "Ignore words in uppercase," Word will stop you on every acronym it doesn't know. To avoid this problem, create a custom dictionary. In the Word preferences dialog box, there's a spelling and grammar section. Select it, then click Dictionaries. In the next dialog box, you can add a personal dictionary. (I like to put mine in the Office folder where Word's default dictionary lives.) The first time Word stops you on an acronym such as AIGA, add it to your custom dictionary. Not only will Word stop bothering you, but it will alert you when you mistype the acronym in the future.

Photoshop blindspots

You can type text into every art and design program. Unless you are a good typist and speller, don't do it. Write everything in a text program that has a spell-check function and then cut and paste the text into whatever image or development program you're using.

▲ Top | 🖶 Print this page | Home | Company | Services | Concepts | Porfolio | Contact | Login

Photoshop and many other design and illustration programs don't have a spell-check function. This is an example of a common error.

Verbal diarrhea

Strange but true—people who hate to write almost always write too much once they start. Just as minimalist design is the art of deleting until you get it right, the trick to good writing is good cutting.

Too many "and"s

Don't use the word "and" unless it's in a series of things. "Books, periodicals, *and* annual reports" is fine. "This project was created to serve the needs of the client who wanted to focus their brand *and* they planned to use it for future online projects," is incorrect. It's actually two sentences glued together. Run-on sentences, besides being bad writing, are hard to read and understand onscreen.

Capital objects

In general, you should only capitalize words that begin a sentence, are proper names, or are initials (such as UI for user interface). Excessive capitalization puts emphasis where emphasis doesn't belong. Be particularly alert for this problem if English is your second language.

Experience

Briana's 18 years of Design and management experience cover a broad arena, including developing UI solutions for Finance, Banking, Business Portals, B2B, ERP, CRM, Manufacturing, and Cultural organizations.

Prior to entering the Internet and Software arenas, Briana was involved in Environmental Graphic Desi...

Experience

Briana's 18 years of design and management experience cover a broad arena, including developing UI solutions for finance, banking, business portals, B2B, ERP, CRM, manufacturing, and cultural organizations.

Prior to entering the Internet and software arenas, Briana was involved in environmental graphic design...

Two versions of the same portfolio Web text. The one on the right only capitalizes those words that require capitalization.

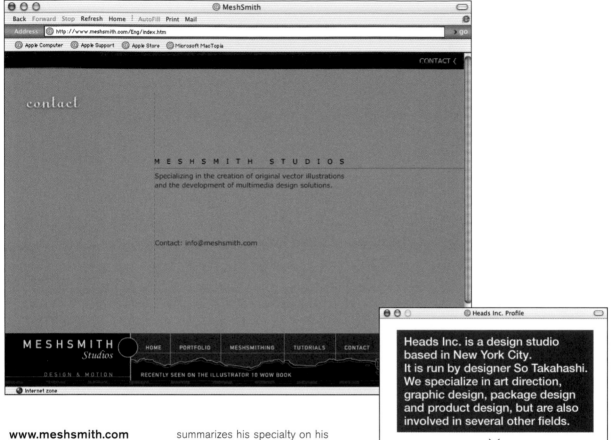

www.meshsmith.com
www.headsinc.com
Two examples of client-oriented portfolios encourage the viewer to make human contact. Ivan Torres (left) summarizes his specialty on his contact page. So Takahashi (right) briefly lists his capabilities to put his work in context. Neither provides any personal information.

Cover letters

When you send a portfolio or samples, you'll need a cover letter to accompany them. You'll also need to respond if someone sees your website or contacts you from some other connection.

Whether that letter is tangible or virtual, you should compose as much of it as possible in advance—a particularly important step if you are not comfortable with any writing beyond messaging. A cover letter should include a standard salutation, a short reference to who you are and why you are sending your material, and a thank you (in advance) for their interest in your work.

EXPLAINING YOUR CREATIVE THINKING

Your portfolio doesn't have to include a written commentary on your projects. Many artists and designers prefer to wait until they present their portfolio, particularly if they are more articulate in personal interviews. But some form of explanation can be a valuable asset in your portfolio.

Not all disciplines take the same approach to commenting on their work or adhere to the same standards. Fine artists, for example, write artist statements, which generally speak about a recent body of work and its inspirations. It is a big plus to have a statement that is both personal and well-written, but content is far more important than form. No fine artist has ever had their work rejected because of fuzzy thinking or typographic errors in his or her statement.

Design professionals are at the opposite end of the spectrum. To fully appreciate the design, it helps to know something about the commission. Many designers include a short descriptive comment about their client's activities and purpose in the work's caption. At its briefest, the comment provides useful context for a design project. At its most expansive, it becomes a case study.

> Copy is one of the many tools that can be effectively used to engage the viewer/consumer. We utilize it whenever possible to create the link between our client's message and their customer's needs.
>
> —Rick Braithwaite

wrecked.nu
Gabe Rubin provides context for this project by telling the viewer something about his client, the Music Farm.

Design brief

Because design work is done in response to a set of requirements and constraints—usually called a design brief—it can be very useful to take the extended captioning one step further by including the brief, so the viewer can better understand the route you traveled. Design briefs can be short and minimal—a capsule overview of the client and their project—or they can be more complete explanations of the project and its criteria. Just remember that in a digital portfolio, "brief" is the operative term.

www.cefaratti.com
Mike Cefaratti provides a classic thumbnail design brief for each of his portfolio projects. He lists the client, decribes the design brief under the PROJECT heading, and then explains in the DETAILS section exactly what his role was in the project.

Case study

If you decide to share a full analysis of the design problem and its solution, you are writing a case study. Case studies should not be undertaken lightly because they require good writing and analytical skills. Because they are usually at least a full page of text, you should give the viewer the choice to opt in. Put the case study in its own window or frame or separate it out entirely by making it a downloadable PDF (see BBK Studio's portfolio highlight in Chapter 2, "Adaptation").

Process comments

In disciplines where work evolves in stages, it can be enormously useful not only to show examples of your process, but to annotate your sketches with comments. What led you to your final color choices? What inspired the form for your product design? Here, as in most other writing, avoid duplicating in words information that a viewer can get by looking at the sketches themselves. Process comments can usually be treated like captions—short, direct phrases are good.

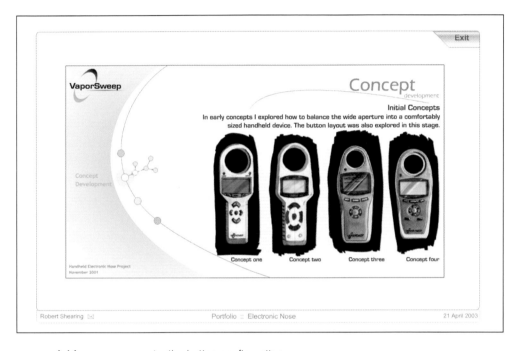

www.rob.id.au
Industrial designer Robert Shearing provides annotations for his process sketches. Although the viewer would have eventually figured out that the button configuration was the most relevant design challenge, Shearing's brief note focuses attention immediately.

Philosophy

Do people sit at your feet and hang on your every word? Do you turn down the opportunity to judge at award ceremonies because you're just too busy advising the UN? I'm betting on "no." If I'm correct, write about your design philosophy, by all means, but leave it off of your portfolio. Your work itself should address how you think and what you believe about your profession. It's not necessary, or advisable, to include it in a digital portfolio. Most people won't read it, and some could be actively put off by it.

WRITING TO YOUR AUDIENCE

In Chapter 2, "Adaptation," I emphasized how important it is to know who will be viewing your portfolio and what they'll be looking for. That guiding principle applies to writing your portfolio text. Whether you are writing to CEOs, small design studios, or to a highly-focused niche audience, your vocabulary and style should adapt as needed. Generational slang, niche culture references, and other elements that might make the text hard for your target audience to understand should be stripped away.

One of the easiest ways to check your tone is to hand your writing to someone who is similar to your audience. For example, if you're young, enlist a mentor or older relative. If you can't find the right reader, go in the other direction and read what your target audience writes. You don't have to imitate it, but you should be sensitive to the differences.

Obviously, the more like your target audience you are, the easier it can be to write appropriate text and the more of your true personality you can expose. But even if you are quite different from your audience, it can be an enormous plus to be able to project a little of yourself into your writing. Light humor (see the "Humor" sidebar), a friendly tone, or a brief anecdote about a project can all help to get the reader on your side.

> Humor is one of the ways that we make people like us. In its simplest form, you smile at somebody; in its more complex form, you say something that makes a person laugh and enjoy the contact between two individuals. I think in a portfolio, it works exactly the same way. What you're trying to do in a portfolio is make a friend on the other side of the table, and humor is a wonderful way to do it.
>
> —Stan Richards

Humor

Nothing is more valuable—or trickier—than adding humor to your portfolio. Humor is a great leveler. If someone makes us laugh, we instinctively warm to them and often to their work.

Unless you are as good at writing as you are visually, the best way to add humor to a portfolio is to show it. A project that includes humor can be valuable in a portfolio filled with serious, restrained work. Don't grab just any funny project, though. Avoid any humor that relies on putting down others. You never know the sex, religion, age, or ethnicity of a potential employer or client. And gross-out humor is just as likely to alienate as amuse.

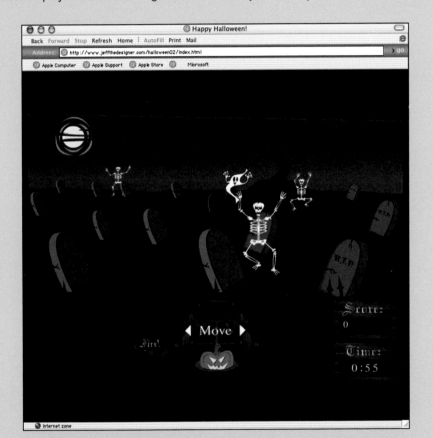

www.jeffthedesigner.com

Jeff Kaphingst's Halloween game is an example of "safe" humor. The game object is to throw pumpkins at spooky creatures with a catapult. Its portfolio purpose is to showcase his illustration and Flash programming skills.

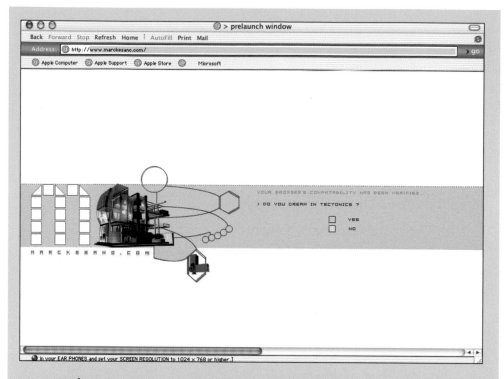

www.marckesano.com
Architect Patrick Marckesano uses quirky visual and verbal humor to set the tone for his portfolio site. This pair of images is from his site's prelaunch page. If you answer Yes to any one of his series of questions, you get rewarded with an animation and an upbeat musical phrase as his site launches. If you answer no, you get another question and a downbeat tonal sequence.

If you don't have any projects that allow you to show your clever side, you can add some playful elements to your interface. Your portfolio presentation is a perfect oppoortunity to let people peek under the curtain and see what you can do without client constraints.

Most importantly, consider your audience. If you are primarily targeting small studios and other creatives, you can probably be a little looser than if you are attempting to speak to the corporate market. Until you are established and can afford to break the mold, humor in the business world is best left to personal encounters, not incorporated into your personal sales tool.

PORTFOLIO HIGHLIGHT:
SANDSTROM DESIGN |
GETTING YOUR WORDS-WORTH

www.sandstromdesign.com

To build a design portfolio on text and humor, you must be one of two things: crazy or very, very good. Rick Braithwaite, the president of Sandstrom Design in Portland, Oregon, is probably both. Fortunately, being slightly crazed in a creative profession can be a selling point. In an environment where so many sites seem to look the same and share the same phrase-book, Sandstrom stands out as a company that really knows how to use the power of the word to sell design. Their portfolio is undeniably unique.

An underlying goal of any portfolio site is to separate from the crowd. Sandstrom Design's site doesn't just cross the street, it packs its bags and moves to the Bermuda triangle, circa 1960. Here, all type has big serifs, all icons are cheesy, and the aesthetic is about as different from today's image complexity as you can get. Yet it is perfectly designed on its own terms: simple, clear, and everything precisely placed.

It's also a nicely implemented Flash site. There is no need for preloads, and none of the time you "waste" is spent waiting: the site is extremely fast and responsive. A nice, user-friendly touch: Sandstrom's window can be scaled as you wish, and the type remains legible. Most Flash design sites are programmed to minimize—or eliminate—the visitor's ability to resize because to do so might break the layout.

Based upon our website, I guess you might think we are seeking clients who like to be abused and waste a few precious hours in useless pursuit of a cheap laugh. Actually, that is correct, but we also are hoping that some of them might be insightful enough to realize that effective communication can be unpredictable, engaging, and bold. We've found that prospects who love the site make for great clients and usually avoid creative shootouts.

—Rick Braithwaite

The Sandstrom opening screen is a simple block of justified serif text on post-it blue. The single interface element: the bold word "enter," which becomes bold italic when moused over and launches the home page when clicked.

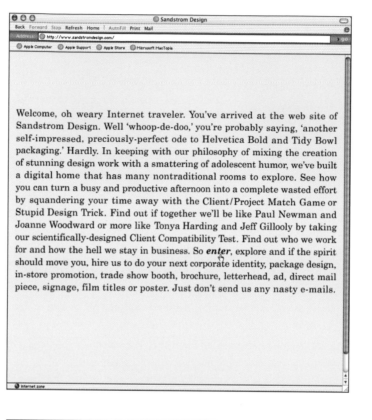

All the site pages have backgrounds the color of old NCR and office paper colors: blue, pink, green, and classic yellow.

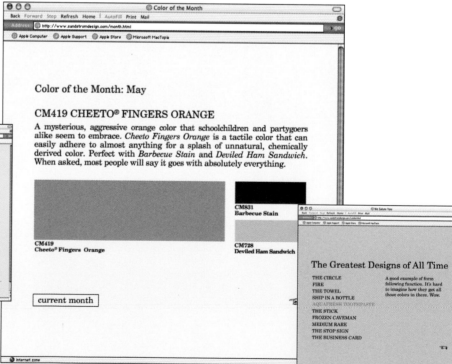

Navigation and architecture

If good design is knowing what to throw out, then Sandstrom Design has the ultimate navigation scheme. The only consistent navigation tool is the back button, a pointing hand. All of the other interactions you have on the site are specifically tied to the themes of each section.

The site architecture is a set of branches, none of which are formally called "portfolio." After you're in a branch, you can sometimes back out to the home page, but you can't hop into a different branch. Each branch must be explored in order—a necessary requirement for a site full of punchlines. The firm makes sure that each visitor sticks to the site like an insect to flypaper.

The home page is a real menu, not a computer drop-down list. Roll over boxes next to the options and a checkmark lets you know these are links. To visit any of the site areas, you click the box.

Inside the browser window:

Official Information
Client Compatibility Test
Client/Project Match Game
Logo Clinic
A Salute to the Greatest
Color of the Month
Stupid Design Trick
The Answers
What's in the Fridge?

Look for this symbol in each section to return home.

Most of the navigation is based on very simple click-throughs that cycle within an area. These are two examples from the case-study section, titled Logo Clinic. On the left is the logo clinic six-step process. Explanations of each step appear in the right column. On the right is one of the case studies, accessed through a simple Previous|Next click-through sequence.

Logo Clinic

Back Forward Stop Refresh Home | AutoFill Print Mail

Address http://www.sandstromdesign.com/logo.html

Apple Computer   Apple Support   Apple Store   Microsoft MacTopia

❏ Step 1
Testing and Evaluation

❏ Step 2
Deconstruction

❏ Step 3
Rebuilding and Assimilation

❏ Step 4
Advanced Training

☑ Step 5
Pre-Introduction

❏ Step 6
Public Introduction

❏ Case Studies

PRE-INTRODUCTION
In a controlled environment consisting of designers, account people, and clients your logo is subjected to a salvo of difficult questions regarding both hypothetical and real-life situations. For example, how well would your logo represent your company lying in a giant heap of post-apocalyptic rubble?

Internet zone

Back Forward Stop Refresh Home | AutoFill Print Mail

Address http://www.sandstromdesign.com/logo.html

Apple Computer   Apple Support   Apple Store   Microsoft Ma

Logo Clinic, Reprogramming:

Case Study No. 10047-ML   Previous | Next

Before   After

Internet zone

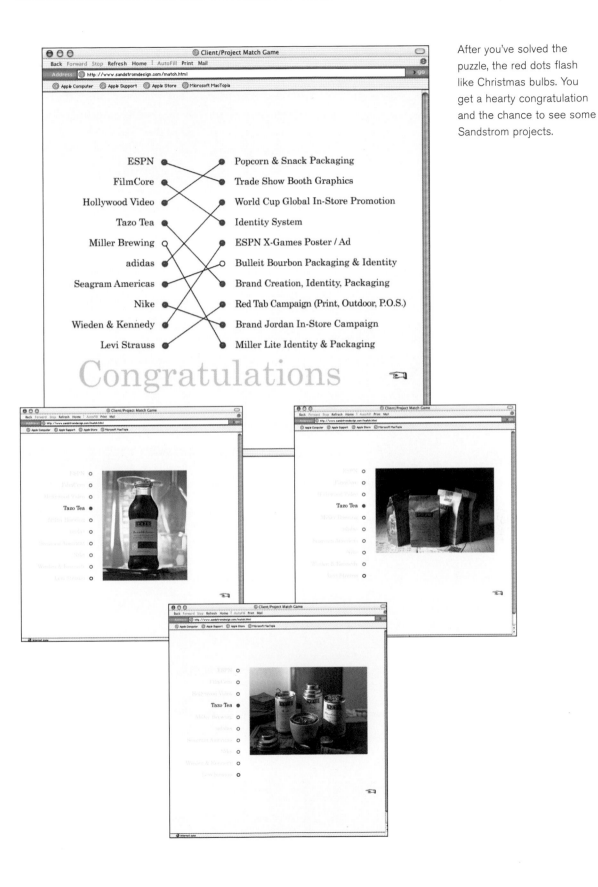

After you've solved the puzzle, the red dots flash like Christmas bulbs. You get a hearty congratulation and the chance to see some Sandstrom projects.

We felt we would be better represented by the complete avoidance of terms like "strategic planning," "brand experience," and "results-oriented," not because we are weak in these areas, but because they offer no point of differentiation.

—Rick Braithwaite

Content

This is not a minimalist site, even if the interface is unfussy. Braithwaite promises hours of wasted time, which is only a slight exaggeration. You can find the Sandstrom client list, portfolio samples, and "case studies" but only if you spend time exploring the site.

All the site content has a purpose, even the Stupid Design Trick (try it and see), but the purpose isn't always clear until you've made your way through each section. The boldest decision was the Client/Project Match Game. You have to match all ten clients with a major project to win…and finally see examples of the Sandstrom portfolio. However, nothing tells you in advance that the game is your gateway to the work. But most people are suckers for a game, and once you're in, it seems natural to want to see what these people actually do, especially because the client list is extensive and prestigious.

At the end, there's What's in the Fridge? A break from the clever text, it's the last thing you find if you make your way through the site menu in order. The line seems like a complete throwaway, but when you visit that branch, you find a gleaming refrigerator packed with award statues. Message delivered.

Future plans

Although Sandstrom has added "new, time-wasting pages" since the site went up, no major redesign has taken place for the past couple of years. The company has begun discussions about a change but hasn't made a major decision. With too much good feedback on the current site and too many prospects responding positively to it, the only reason to change the site would be to prove that they could top it.

One thing I know for sure, our site will never, never, never look, talk, act, or smell like all of the other design firms' sites out there.

—Rick Braithwaite

Part III

Production

Chapter 10

Development basics

You've brought all your work onto the computer and transferred it to an appropriate file format. You've written sparkling text. You know who you want to impress, and why. Now, finally, you want to get your work into a portfolio. Should you start creating buttons and laying out a page?

Not so fast. In order for your interface to be appropriate and effective—and not distract badly from your wonderful work—it needs a foundation. The foundation is the skeleton that your artwork relies on to stand up to scrutiny.

A portfolio foundation requires three things: an appropriate technology, a structure, and a visual concept for your interface. You need to consider all three before you make a single decision about graphics or page content. All of these ingredients affect one another, and should be impacted in turn by your work.

The chapter begins by exploring the types of portfolio you can design, and how much knowledge each one requires. It connects concept and technology, and introduces the metaphor as a development tool. By the end of this chapter, you should understand the choices that will define your portfolio, and be ready to create a site map and begin interface design and production.

CHOOSING THE DELIVERY FORMAT

> Being able to bookmark pages is always super-important, especially if you're giving a recommendation to somebody. If it's a Flash site, there's no way to bookmark things and say, "I really thought this person was good because of this particular project."
>
> —Layla Keramat

Technology has a big effect on design, particularly at the beginning, when you are looking at how much time your project will take and how you are planning your time and figuring out how to optimize your work. (See Chapter 8, "Repurposing and optimizing," for an explanation of optimizing.) It will certainly act as a constraint on your design decisions, perhaps making it difficult to implement some of them. So you'll need to understand the limitations before you allow your creativity to go wild. The following survey goes in order from least- to most-technically demanding.

Everyone seems to approach digital portfolios thinking that theirs must be an interactive masterpiece. Unquestionably, a person in Web development is expected to display his or her creative and technical knowledge. But for people whose métier is more traditional, it's often the wrong move. What is important is to show your work in a favorable light.

Software basics

If you're designing a Web portfolio, you'll at least need Microsoft's Front Page to create a simple website. For more creative control, you'll want a web publishing program like Adobe GoLive or Macromedia Dreamweaver. To create a self-contained portfolio player, you'll need Macromedia Flash.

If you're designing a CD-ROM or DVD portfolio, you can use many of the same tools. But for CDs, invest in software that creates *hybrid disks*—disks that can be read in both Mac OS and in Windows. To make a DVD, you'll need Photoshop to create the interface, and DVD-creation software to make your interactive DVD menu and link your work to it. On the Mac, that means iDVD (free with OS X) or DVD Studio Pro. In Windows, DVDit! is a fairly simple program to learn and use.

If your portfolio will be a straightforward slideshow, you have many application options, but you should only use the ones that create a self-contained file—one that doesn't require your viewer to own any software. Anything made with one (or both) of the standard video players—QuickTime and Windows Media Player—will work fine. One cautionary note: avoid PowerPoint. This is a business application. Most pros in the world of art and design will snicker if you show up with a portfolio in PowerPoint.

Instant portfolios

An instant portfolio can be a life-saving stopgap while you either find a partner or get comfortable with Web design and production. Some services, like Yahoo GeoCities and .Mac, provide website templates in a variety of styles. In Chapter 4, "Format," I go over some quick-and-dirty options.

Besides using Web tools for a CD or DVD portfolio, you can use software that creates slideshows. Adobe Acrobat allows you to make beautiful PDFs that you can show page by page. Web layout programs (like Dreamweaver or GoLive) make it relatively easy to combine linear navigation with an image-focused presentation. A simple video editor like QuickTime will also allow you to create a non-interactive slideshow that can play on your website, a CD, or a DVD. A program like iMovie makes the process easy for a disk presentation. You will only need to determine the order of play, how long each image waits on the page, and (if the software supports it) transition effects between images.

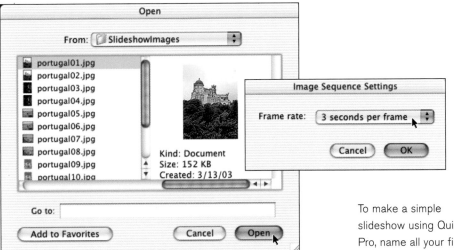

To make a simple slideshow using QuickTime Pro, name all your files sequentially (iView Media Pro can batch rename for you). Go to File > Open Image Sequence, select the first file in the sequence, and set your frame rate. When you save the file, be sure to make the movie self-contained.

For both email distribution and CDs, you can make PDFs (see Chapter 8 for more about PDFs). But PDFs are really most useful for designers who are adept with print but uncomfortable with producing material for the Web. Besides, PDFs still require a design concept to be effective. Otherwise, they don't do anything that couldn't be done just as well, and with smaller files, by simply loading several images into one JPG file.

Static pages

A *static page* is a simple Web page that doesn't contain any interactive elements. Static pages can have text links and links from thumbnails to larger renditions of images, so they do have simple navigation. Static pages are one step up from an instant portfolio, because you can design them. They're also very easy to use as a base for continual upgrading and tweaking once they're in place.

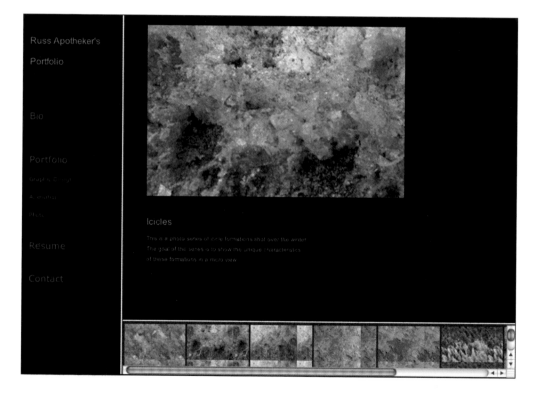

This static page uses frames to provide some layout variety, but is really very simple to create. The Dreamweaver template used to create this page can be applied to the rest of the site.

Simple motion or interaction

With a program like Dreamweaver, moving from a static page to one with standard interface interaction is a relatively small step. Good web layout programs write the Javascript that runs interactivity for you. As a result, you can either design site navigation from scratch, or add interaction to a static website.

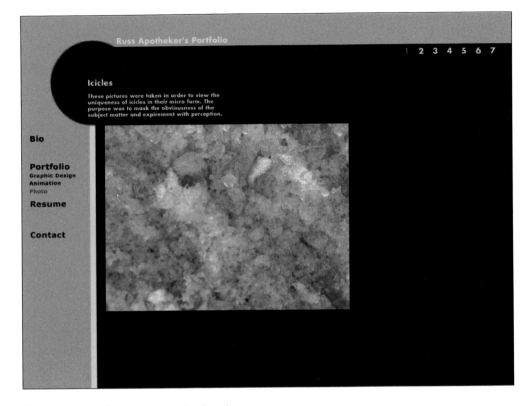

The previous static page has been cleaned up and redesigned to use a simple interactive scheme. The graphic elements allow the viewer to jump to different portfolio topics, or to view the work sequentially.

Complex movement and interaction

It is a big step to go from a simple layout to one that takes advantage of HTML's power. If you want a website that includes animated elements, plays video inside the page, uses unusual or customized navigation, or simply protects your code and images from being downloaded, you'll either have to master Javascript, or use Macromedia Flash. Flash is not a trivial program. It has recipes for frequently used interactive elements, but you'll still need to learn a little Actionscript (Macromedia's programming language). On the other hand, there is almost no limit to the things you can do once you've mastered Flash.

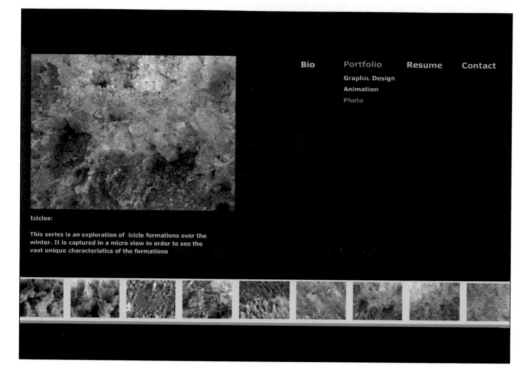

The content is the same, but this site has been planned and executed in Macromedia Flash. The thumbnails at the bottom scroll left and right, and can be displayed larger when clicked.

WEB VERSUS PORTABLE PORTFOLIO

Once you've decided on your basic technology, should you put it on the Web or on a disk? You can have both. If you create your CD portfolio to work within a standard browser, you can maintain the same design for both versions. Don't just copy from one format to the other, though. It doesn't make much sense to send a CD if you can point to your URL. Adjust the CD portfolio version to provide full-screen renditions of your video and animation, increase the size and quality of your still images, and provide extra material for personal presentations.

If you are dealing primarily with video or animation, you'll probably have to separate the Web and disk portfolios. Although your design concepts for the two should be related, the contents for each will be optimized differently, and may even run at a different aspect ratio. Although you could create a CD, you'll probably be better served by a DVD.

THINKING ABOUT STRUCTURE

You will face technology decisions every day as you design and produce your portfolio. But once you gather your materials and whatever software you'll need, your focus should shift. If you are creating anything beyond an instant portfolio, you'll need to find the ideal way to sequence and group your work, and then the very best way to "wrap" it. As you'll see in Chapter 11, you should always start with grouping and arranging, because the way you create your categories can and should influence your design concept.

SELECTING A METAPHOR

A metaphor is a way of thinking about your portfolio structure. Metaphors are powerful. They allow you to visualize your digital portfolio—a hazy, virtual collection of megabytes— as a concrete form. A metaphor says that your portfolio is organized in a certain way, and is like something we know and are familiar with in the real world. It helps you to create an appropriate organization and interface for your portfolio. Later, it helps the viewer to understand and interact with your format.

> We look for work that begins with an idea, is developed deeply and with a deft touch, and that is presented simply and with honesty.
>
> —Rick Braithwaite

Terminology for portfolio metaphors is not precise, because it's not possible to exactly mimic a real-world format in an electronic one. Nor would you want to, because doing so would artificially limit you to real-world constraints. Even so, most portfolios adhere to at least one of the following basic metaphorical concepts:

- Gallery
- Spec sheet/brochure
- Outreach
- Narrative
- Diary
- Experience

Gallery

The museum or gallery metaphor is that of a formal space where you come to see work. When you use this metaphor, you say, "This is my work. Draw your own conclusions."

Gallery sites can be as simple as an intimate room, or they may inhabit a number of differentiated spaces. Some explicitly mimic a museum space, with frames and captions, but you can easily have a gallery site without these standard forms. Gallery sites are usually linear, or linear within sections. In a gallery portfolio, the interface itself is very understated, to emphasize the image. Gallery portfolios can be implemented with very little technical knowledge.

www.sharpeonline.com

The Sharpe + Associates site is a classic gallery presentation. Each artist has his or her own "room," where their own artistic visions are presented with representative images. Here photographer Robert Kent is in the spotlight.

Spec sheet/brochure

Spec sheets and brochures provide business information. The brochure does so in generalities; the spec sheet provides functional details. In portfolio terms, this is a capabilities metaphor. When you use this metaphor, you say, "Here is what I can do."

The portfolio demonstrates, through work and through portfolio interface, your talents and specialties. It organizes material around work categories. Capabilities portfolios are usually Web-based, and at least minimally interactive.

Outreach

An outreach portfolio is client-centric. It can superficially look like a capabilities portfolio, but it differs from the spec sheet concept, by offering integrated services rather than skills. It says, "This is what I can do for you."

www.bbkstudio.com
Like most full-service design firms with branding expertise, BBKStudio and Eleven has designed a client-centric portfolio. They're easy to recognize because of their cross-pollinated navigation, and their emphasis on case studies.

The client-centric portfolio is almost never sequential. Work is organized by relationships. The portfolio is usually distinguished by fairly complex navigational linking. Client-centric portfolios reflect the target audience more than the portfolio maker, and are frequently (though certainly not always) visually conservative and technically sophisticated. They make it as easy as possible for the viewer to navigate the space.

Narrative

In a narrative portfolio, the portfolio tells a story through its sequence and organization. Narratives are not usually stories in the sense that they have a plot, but they do have a clear order. They may even have a formal beginning, middle, and end. A narrative portfolio says, "My work is about something specific."

Narrative portfolios usually contain a few very carefully chosen works, because it's important that the viewer experience the entire portfolio. A large narrative portfolio only works if the narrative is contained in "chapters." These chapters, like case studies, can be experienced as individual modules. No particular format is required for a narrative portfolio, although Flash presentations lend themselves to this metaphor because they allow more control of page access.

> What do I look for in a portfolio? Good organization and, even more important, good storytelling.
> —Michael Borofsky

www.dialogbox.com
Britt Funderburk provides a
carefully selected cross section
of his work in an interface that
makes a bold statement about
his visual sensibilities.

Diary

A diary portfolio is intensely personal, created more for the portfolio maker than for any client or prospective employer. This format is good for an artist, or for someone who wants to explore new ideas without having to wait until a project comes around to pay for it. They say, "This is my work and my work is me."

In one respect, they can end up being very effective marketing tools, because they can become capabilities-oriented without the formal, programmed feel. Diary portfolios are almost by definition Web-based, because they require frequent updates. As a result, they either require a strong command of technology or a lot of free time. Because of their personal nature, they are often less hierarchical and organized than other portfolios.

Experience

Experience portfolios take you for a ride. They differ from diary portfolios by their emphasis on entertainment. These portfolios are almost always visually or technologically rich, and frequently are a humorous outlet for the portfolio maker. Always interactive, they say, "Play with me."

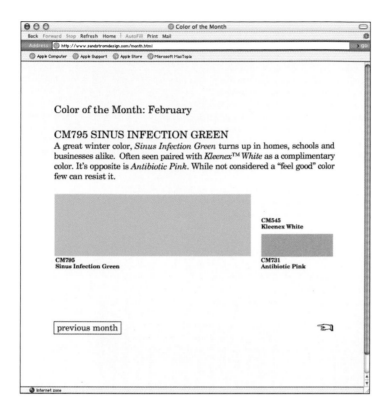

Sandstrom Design knows that the longer you're compelled to stay on their entertaining site, the more likely you are to remember them.

Although brilliantly memorable when handled with a sure hand, this is an extremely difficult portfolio metaphor to carry off successfully (see the section, "Concept versus style," later in the chapter). It can just as easily put people off as suck them in. Experience portfolios sometimes have experimental interfaces and are frequently complicated to create. They lend themselves to Flash presentations.

How you use a metaphor

A metaphor can be applied literally ("Welcome to my gallery") or simply be a way to think about your portfolio site map. For example, a capabilities portfolio requires you to think about which of your projects best demonstrates your skills. Perhaps you'd highlight a project and show how you applied your knowledge through process sketches.

You are not limited to a single metaphor. These ideas are flexible enough that some can overlap. For example, large studios frequently combine the spec sheet with outreach. However, you should mix and match with care. Don't combine metaphors with radically different objectives. Outreach and diary simply don't mix, and will leave you ping-ponging between pleasing yourself and pleasing others—ultimately pleasing no one.

PORTFOLIO HIGHLIGHT:
SO TAKAHASHI | SLIDESHOW METAPHOR

www.headsinc.com

If you would rather not tackle interactivity, consider the slideshow. Product and packaging designer So Takahashi's portfolio site demonstrates that the slideshow can be a viable professional alternative to a three-ring circus of Flash interactivity. Like his work, it represents him in high style.

What does my website say about me and my work? Simplicity with impact.

—So Takahashi

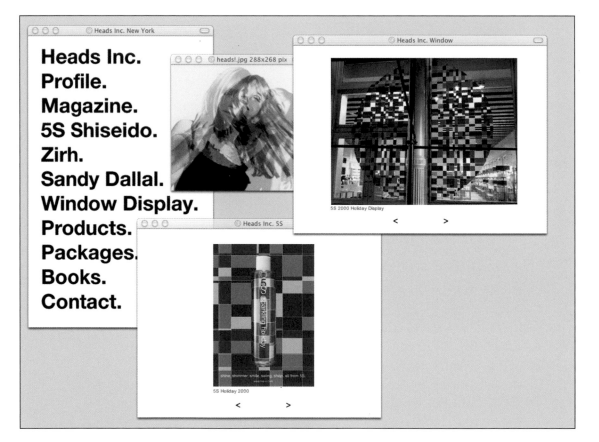

The Heads Inc. interface opens a window with an uncomplicated column of text links. Each one, when selected, opens a new slideshow window. It's very easy to browse through—open a window, and click through the small groupings. The interface within each window is only the two arrows needed to move through each window.

Takahashi's 3D design material is particularly effective, since so much of it boasts bold color and crisp geometric form—ideal for onscreen viewing.

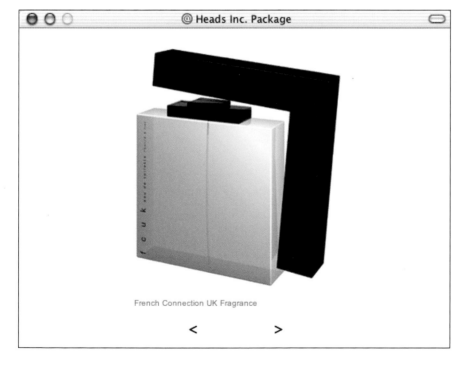

Navigation and architecture

Takahashi stayed true to his original intent: The site's architecture is simple and modular. The categories are mixed. Some represent work for done for a specific client, and others contain work for a variety of clients within a category. In most sites, this mixing of main categories (clients and work types) could lead to confusion. But So's interface is so accessible—no levels, no layers—that the extra layer of organization seems unnecessary.

Takahashi deals with the most potentially problematic interface decision—what to do with all the open windows—by closing each one when you reach the end of its sequence.

> I wanted to make my site as simple as possible, yet not boring. I wanted it to be different from the typical Flash-y site. And I wanted to build it with HTML only so everyone can view it without plug-ins or upgrades.
>
> —So Takahashi

Content

Takahashi's strong style and bold images provide ideal content for a slideshow format. By grouping his material by client—even within the project categories—the viewer sees Takahashi's ideas expressed as little sequences. The impression is of someone who sees the unique attributes of a brand, but maintains a strong personal style.

Takahashi's files are fairly large because they don't have to fight for download speed with an elaborate interface. Text is equally spare. Captions are labels, not briefs or explanations.

Future plans

Takahashi has been happy with the site's performance, but is considering weeding it down to a digital teaser. This could be a good move, because his work is the end product of design processes that can easily take months to move from concept to completion. Because the site is modular and unfussy, any changes he makes will be easy to implement.

CONCEPT

A metaphor is also useful to start you thinking about your concept—and to keep you from mixing too many ideas. But it is only a starting point—the good bones that you flesh out with a concept. The concept is the visual way you express how you think about your work.

A concept is much more than figuring out whether your buttons are green or blue. It is the reason you make that decision in the first place. At the very least, the design concept should not get in the way of the work. It is much better to create a very simple, barely noticeable interface design than to create an interface that overwhelms your projects. At best, the design concept should enhance your work, so the two engage in a pleasant visual conversation.

A good concept is clear to anyone with Internet experience. It works with your work, not against it. It emphasizes the things that you do best. It is consistent on all pages. Navigation is easy to find, and easy to figure out. When you go to a site with a consistent concept, elements are related to each other visually and functionally. You should be able to tell the difference if you move from one designer's concept to another, and to recognize the look and feel of each concept when you return.

> I think the worst thing is a site that works against you and becomes annoying. If I have to look for hidden corners to click and reveal a concealed menu that doesn't explain what and where I can find things, that browser window could get shut just as quickly as it was opened.
>
> —Layla Keramat

Concept versus style

Don't confuse concept with style. Concept is an idea that you apply consistently because it fits your work and your site's architecture. Style, on the other hand, is a collection of attributes that create a surface look. For most people, style is what's hot. If you find yourself thinking of your interface in terms of using a cool effect or type treatment you've seen in an annual, you're letting a style dictate your concept, not the other way around.

> When you start looking a little deeper, you realize that a lot of the portfolios look similar, and the work really isn't that strong. They all have similar surfaces—this quasi-Wired noise factor.
>
> —Bill Cahan

It's not easy to develop a really terrific concept for your portfolio, even if you are a graphic designer. But it is easy to avoid the very worst sins.

Classic concept blunders

What can go wrong in a concept? Plenty. Here are some that even well-schooled designers occasionally fall into:

- **I'm too sexy for your job.** Avoid a portfolio interface that is so intricate, it feels like you've forgotten its purpose for existence—your projects.

- **Hide and seek.** Lots of really interesting work is being done on experimental interfaces. Unless you are an interface god, don't experiment on your portfolio. Make your navigation easy to find.

- **Low contrast.** Because of the difference between Macs and PCs, two colors that may seem quite different on a Mac may be perilously close to each other on a PC—both will be very dark. Check your color combinations before you commit to them.

- **Glass ceiling.** All portfolio designs should be modular from the beginning—easy to update and replace. Don't design work that cannot be changed without breaking the page. Ask yourself, "What if I had to add three things here?" before you finalize your concept.

- **In-jokes.** Something may be very cool to a small number of people in the know, and totally pointless or even ugly to those who are not. Show anything you're not sure of to your mother (or someone like her).

- **It's all about sex.** Well, it isn't. Unless you want to work for porn sites, avoid suggestive comments or images in your concept.

PUTTING IT ALL TOGETHER

It's not easy to develop a really brilliant portfolio design, but almost anyone can manage a decent one. Don't be afraid to look at portfolios by other people. In fact, look at as many as you can, so you won't be tempted to copy anything specific. Ask yourself what makes some of them really memorable and attractive to you. If you select a technology you can master, choose an organization scheme that fits your work, and design an interface that keeps the viewer interested and focused on what you do, the portfolio that results will be one you are proud of.

PORTFOLIO HIGHLIGHT:
JON SANTOS | CREATIVE : CONTROL

jon@commonspace.fm

Memorable portfolios are a rare treat, although they come in a variety of forms. Some are polished marketing tools. You admire their focus, drive, and flair. Some are client-centric, models of clarity and clean presentation. They're designed to inform, communicate, and interact. Others are creative statements. The last group can be fascinating but are often self-absorbed. Their interfaces overwhelm the work presented, which almost always turns out to be too small or too slow. It's a relief to find one where the interface is understated but the work speaks strongly.

Jon Santos' Web portfolio is one of these few. Designed for potential clients, as well as for friends and his own pleasure, it respects the work and makes it easy to view it. It's also a website constantly in the middle of a reinvention, knitting all of his creative interests into an unconventional but coherent whole.

The Common Space home page sets the tone. The picture is one of a series of images John refers to as sketches, accessed from the left pull-down menu. The images are unpredictable. Some are pure illustrations; others are composites. Like graffiti art on the walls of a building, they give you a sense of the neighborhood.

> There are differences between what we can call graphic design and fine art and illustration. I think that the distinction that I make between what I think is my art work and my graphic design work is always changing based on who I'm working with. But, I think the way that you present your work can define how you are perceived.
>
> —Jon Santos

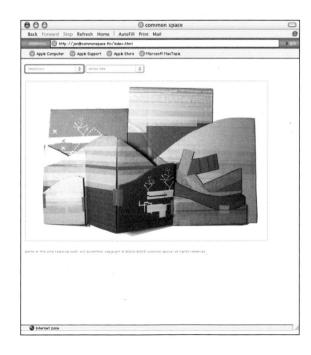

When in doubt, people tend to select the left of two links, making it likely that someone new to the site will use the first drop-down menu to see Jon's sketches before checking out the menu on the right and entering Jon's main site.

Navigation and architecture

There are a limited number of directions to travel in this site, and most of them are self-contained. Navigation elements are a combination of an unconventional hand-lettered navigation bar and pull-down menus.

> I've always been interested in discovering new ways of working and different ways of presenting my work. It's appropriate to put sketches and works in progress on my website. It gives a little bit of context to people who are meeting me for the first time.
>
> —Jon Santos

The portfolio portion of Common Space has a shallow architecture. Jon designed the site to be completely modular—easy to add to or subtract from without disrupting links or connections. Because no project is dependent on or linked to any other in a hierarchy, updating anything on the site is a speedy process. As soon as work has been repurposed or optimized, it's ready to upload. This strategy would not work in a more traditional portfolio site with complex branches or a sequential structure. It sacrifices organization for speed and flexibility.

Selecting any of the links in the project list will launch a new window. With one exception, that window remains the viewing space for other projects when they are selected. The design slideshow that opens from the graphics link operates independently from the other projects.

Navigation is provided by a small cluster of styled words bracketed at the top of each page. Roll over a live link in the cluster, or below it in the project list, and it highlights in the same gold as the brackets.

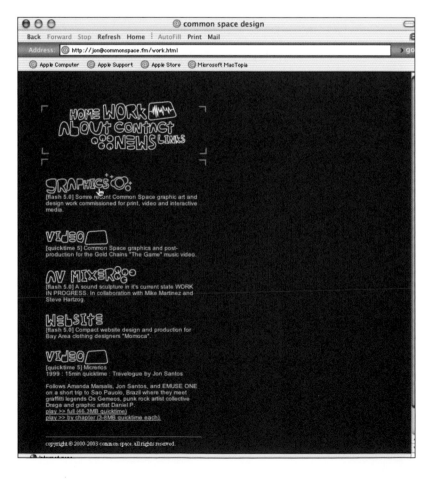

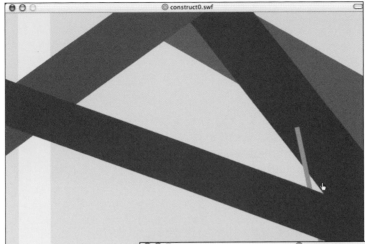

Once launched, each video or interactive project downloads immediately and begins to play. Control is limited to exploring the work itself or closing the window. You can also replace the work with another project by selecting it from the project page, which remains open onscreen.

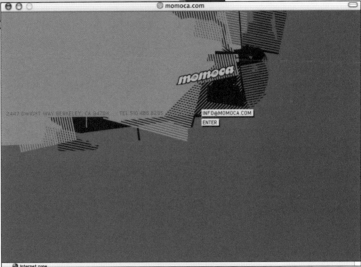

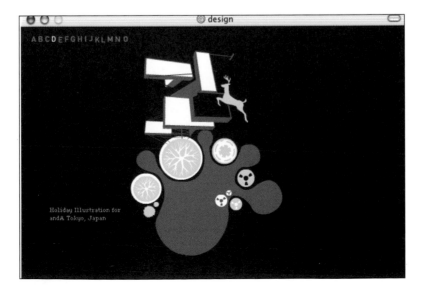

Roll over a letter in the slideshow and it highlights. Because the alphabetical letters have no meaning other than sequence, the slideshow is very fluid. Work can be added with another letter, or artwork can be decommissioned and replaced with something else just by updating a Flash symbol object.

This music video shows how Jon's design and illustration talents connect to his work in video and interactivity. The video, originally shot in MiniDV with a 16:9 aspect ratio, plays in a downloaded window.

Jon's background illustrations, created after the original video footage was shot, take the artist and his date through a series of imaginary settings around the world. Collaborating with LA director Reuben Fleisher, he handled the art direction, illustrations, and post-production in Adobe After Effects.

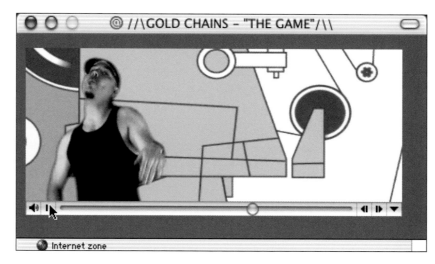

Content

Jon Santos is a West Coast transplant to New York City who is accustomed to doing a little of everything. Although he maintains a traditional print design portfolio to show breadth, his Web portfolio exists to create his future. It includes only the type of work he wants to do more of, not all the types of work he can and has handled successfully. A mixture of many portfolio media, the work is held together by a common aesthetic.

The website content has grown organically. Starting with the spare interface and an illustration slideshow, over a period of weeks it expanded into video and interactive to show his full creative range. Although there are only a few projects on the site, the work feels substantive. It includes a travelogue (the oldest, and only "historical" piece on the site), a music video, a website, and a virtual installation that explores color and form in an interactive Flash animation.

> My work is an ongoing dialogue. If I can have a good interaction with whomever I'm working with and be a part of the art direction as well as the design, that to me is fun. And if it's meaningful to the intended audience or market—even better.
>
> —Jon Santos

Future plans

The only reasonable prediction on future plans for the Common Space portfolio is that its content will mutate as Santos' body of work shifts. Because Santos has the technical virtuosity to repurpose his content seemingly at a moment's notice, the site will probably have been refreshed and updated between the writing of this book and its publication. The overall design "wrapper" will probably remain intact for as long as the flat architecture remains useful—functional, but in a supporting role.

> I think that websites in and of themselves are not resolved. Many are always changing like mine.
>
> —Jon Santos

CHAPTER 11

Designing a

portfolio interface

Chapter 10 provided a conceptual framework for thinking about your interface and how it's organized. This chapter is all about process—what you need to know to move from concept to implementation on a portfolio interface. What follows is critical if you've never made an interface before—or have only done so by the seat of your pants.

Process can sound boring, especially when you think you have a brilliant idea for the way your interface should look. In fact, a good, honest process can be the reason why a brilliant idea remains sparkling when it's finished. Without it, your interface can turn into an unattractive, haphazard, or frustrating experience.

Interface design is a specialized discipline that is still changing rapidly. Even seasoned graphic designers learn new skills and ways of thinking to master it. To build an exceptional interface, you must study user interaction, have a special talent for organizing data, and be a good visualizer. You must also know a lot about complex technology and adhere to many arcane rules so the largest possible audience can access your material.

Fortunately, your portfolio, having a very specific and limited purpose, requires a subset of interface design. You don't have to know everything to create an interface you'll be proud of.

THE SCREEN IS NOT A BOOK

One of the first things we learn about Internet or disk presentations is that each file or screen is a "page." There is only one tiny problem—it's not a very accurate metaphor. Unless the book is purely for reference—like a dictionary or encyclopedia—you experience it sequentially.

This distinction is not just a detail. If you design your interface the way you would a book, you will drive your audience berserk. We need different metaphors to think about a portfolio interface.

How is your portfolio "page" not a book page?

- **Multiple entryways.** Reading a book is like walking down a hallway. You start at one end, and finish at the other. Experiencing an interface is like walking into an atrium, with multiple doors around the walls, the floor, and the ceiling.
- **Linear versus dimensional thinking.** It's possible to dip into a book, read a chapter that interests you, and skip another that doesn't. But once you're in a chapter, you read page by page. An interface is more like a deck of cards. Depending on the game you're playing, each card can mean something different, and be more or less valuable.
- **Control.** When you design a book, you make decisions about everything. When you design an interface, there are many contingencies you can't control. You can't know your audience's monitor size or resolution, their type of computer, or their browsers or plug-ins.

INTERFACE DESIGN PROCESS

For your audience to see your work in the most optimal way, you need to figure out what pathways serve your portfolio best. Like many other stages in the portfolio design process, planning and organization are key, and are just as much part of "design" as layout and graphics are. The interface design process can be summed up in four stages:

- Group
- Map
- Schematic
- Look-and-feel

It's impossible for a visual person to ignore the layout and design stages while working on the first two. (That's like being told not to think about pink elephants.) But self-control will save you time and much reworking later.

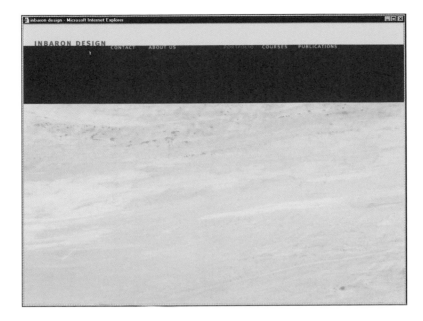

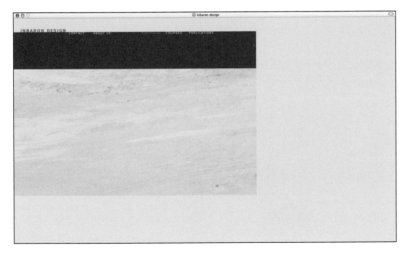

Some Flash sites are designed so that their windows automatically fill the screen, and remain locked at full size. That might be justified on a 15-inch monitor, because all that space is needed to see the portfolio. But what about people who use large monitors, or own an Apple Cinema Display? People in the art and design professions are much more likely than the average web surfer to have a large screen. Because the portfolio interface is never designed with enough content to take up such a large screen, the window just fills with the background color. The result: wasted space and an irritated viewer, who can't see anything else on his computer while the portfolio is onscreen.

To avoid this, don't set the width and height dimensions of a portfolio to 100%. Either set the percentage to something that will still leave desktop space (like 80%), or set the exact pixel dimensions of your design—then design for a width of 700 pixels or less.

PORTFOLIO HIGHLIGHT:
LAYLA KERAMAT | THE MASTER PLAN

The best way to understand the interface design process is to watch someone who is a master of that process step through it. Layla Keramat is a senior designer at frog design, inc. and an adjunct professor at the School of Visual Arts (SVA) in New York City. For years, she's kept a traditional print book of samples. She added a PDF component so she could email examples of her work, but realized that it was time to finally design a digital version of her book.

Why am I creating a digital portfolio now? For my students to understand the scope of my experience and for potential clients. And for my own desire to start documenting.

—Layla Keramat

Layla Keramat's traditional book emphasizes the individual brands she has designed during her career. She provided a timeline with each brand in its chronological position, and then showed individual projects tied to that timeline.

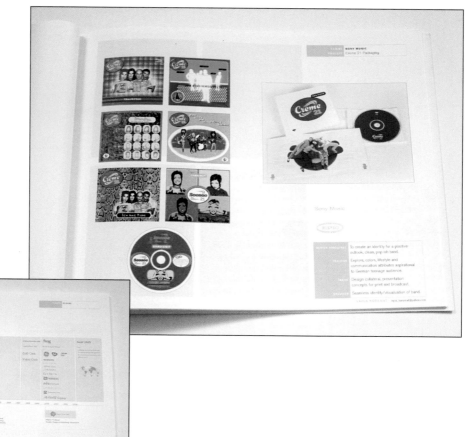

Her digital portfolio needed to meet some rigorous criteria. It had to be visually consistent with her existing materials, but work effectively in a different medium. It had to reflect some new thinking she'd been doing about her work and her career. And it had to be exemplary, because she would be showing it, when completed, to her own students.

Throughout the bulk of this chapter, we'll see Keramat's portfolio take shape, as she talks about her decisions and design thinking.

Group

The first stage in the development process is grouping. It is where some of your organizing from Chapter 5 comes into play. How have you naturally organized your work? If the way you've chosen to organize your archive feels right, it might be the best way to organize your portfolio interface.

Many people select a project grouping by tossing a coin. But there are dozens of ways to arrange your work to show it off optimally. Here are a few to get you started.

Group by:
- Date/employment history
- Discipline/area (design, illustration, photo)
- Category (collateral, packaging, editorial)
- Technology (print, interactive, moving image)
- Medium (traditional, computer, 2D, 3D)
- Process (sketches, modeling, character animation)
- Client
- Client industry/market
- Difficulty/size of project
- Visual interest

> You need to have an understanding of the practicality of your pages. Not categorizing your projects or having too many categories can be frustrating. People shouldn't have to guess which category to choose.
>
> —Layla Keramat

Look at the work you've chosen through each of these filters to see where it fits. Or find your own. How you think about your work, and what type of work it is, should drive the groups you choose. For example, Layla Keramat began to notice that she had made a major change in how she approached design. In her opinion, it was so striking that it was a better way to group her work than by brand or simple chronology.

If you need help to decide, make a spreadsheet with the name of the project along the left and each possible category at the top. Put checks next to a project when it fits a possible category.

Look at the spreadsheet for patterns. Is there a cluster of checks under one category and very few in others within the grouping scheme? If so, those categories are bad ones to use for your portfolio. The thin ones will telegraph that you don't have enough experience. The fat ones are fat because you haven't found the right grouping for them, or haven't written down enough elements with the group.

> My first ten years of design experience were driven by intuition. I still subscribe to the enthusiasm of those early days and I want to preserve that in the impression that I communicate. But I also enjoy understanding a client's corporate communication needs. That's when I understood that I could categorize these two features in my portfolio as "designed by intuition" and "designed by process."
>
> —Layla Keramat

You may look at these groups and discover that you could organize your portfolio equally well in more than one way. That's wonderful! It means you can offer alternative paths for people to experience your work.

Map

Once you have groups, you're ready to impose a hierarchy on them. Will you go directly from the home page to your work, or will you have a second level of pages for each group? Will all the work in a group be equally available, or will you want people to see pieces in a specific sequence? These are big decisions. That's why you need a site map.

A *site map* is a flow chart representing every page in your portfolio. This chart will enable you to recognize links that belong within your pages, or out to other sites. It will also help you to organize your ideas logically, so visitors to your site won't feel lost as they explore it.

A good site map shows three things at a glance:

• **Grouping:** How you've broken out your work.
• **Hierarchy:** Where each page fits within the site.
• **Connections:** What links from each page.

There is no standard form for this chart. A small site can start as a sketch on paper or with Post-its, and then become an Illustrator file as it solidifies. Flow-charting software can make the process easier, particularly if you anticipate a complex site. I can recommend Inspiration (**www.inspiration.com**), which is cross-platform, inexpensive, and easy to learn.

No matter what physical form your site map takes, make sure that you leave enough room on it to insert items. You may discover as you work that you need to move things around, or add a major project that develops while you're still designing your portfolio.

What will your chart contain? A home page, of course, and perhaps an opening page for each group. Every group should branch from one of these types of pages. Remember to account for single pages that aren't part of your work groupings.

> People often forget the importance of persistent elements. Just a few days ago, a friend of mine was showing me his site. After the home page, there was no link to email him.
>
> —Layla Keramat

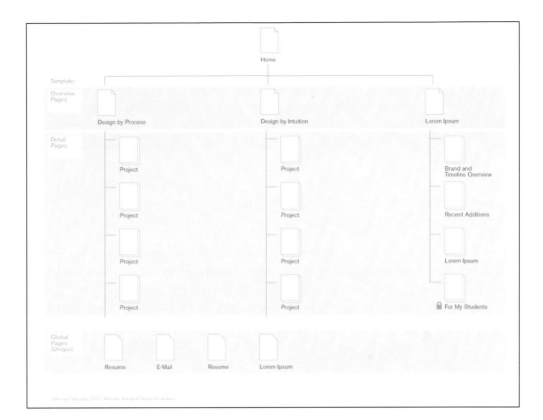

Keramat determined that, in addition to her main categories of Design by Process and Design by Intuition, she needed a branch that fit neither of those categories.

The flow-chart site map clearly shows her hierarchy, with the home page at the top, her categories at the next level, and the projects and other items linking to the main categories. Note also that there is an additional block of pages that do not link specifically to any branch. These are global pages, which will be accessible on every page.

After you've accounted for every page, move them around to make sure that you've got their hierarchy correct. Pages that are only accessible from a main page should be drawn beneath that page. With your pages in position, draw lines to document your planned links. Remember to consider outside links too. For example, if you have a link to a client's site, document that.

If you have created any video or animations, they qualify as links as well. On a website, you'll want to provide links to any plug-ins they require, and consider how people will see them. Will you open a new window for your clips? Will they play in a frame inside your portfolio window?

Keep your chart on or near your computer, so you'll be able to name your actual files and directories to match your documentation. Don't rename files or move them. If you do, you'll break the links you've made to them. Troubleshooting broken links is frustrating, and avoidable.

Modularity

Designing a good portfolio is such a major project that it's hard to contemplate doing it again. Eventually, you'll have to redesign, but it would be nice to put that day off and just update. Unfortunately, many portfolio sites that simply need updating don't get it, because doing so would be almost as much work as creating the original. Try to approach every step of the master plan with the word "module" at the top of your mind. It's particularly important to think of modules when designing a Flash site. If you are not yet an expert, you can fail to group interface elements together in timeline layers, or make one-off objects instead of creating reusable symbols. Your site may look great and run fine, but it's frozen—out of date before its time because you can't add a new link to your main nav bar.

Schematic

You'll have a feeling of accomplishment after you have a completed site map. Seeing the bones of your portfolio will make it feel more real. Next, step down one level and do the same kind of planning for your pages by creating a schematic.

A *schematic* is basically a page layout grid. You create one for each level of your site map hierarchy. On it, you determine where you'll place repeating material, different types of navigation, and variable content.

Choose a page size

How big should your web page be? Consider your target audience. Will you be showing your work on a laptop, where the screen will be smaller than most desktops? If so, design conservatively, keeping your window small. It is always better to allow a viewer to enlarge a window than force a person on a smaller screen to scroll vertically.

A conservative design maintains a maximum size that fits comfortably in an Internet Explorer page on a 17" monitor. Most people specify a screen size at 800x600, but in fact, all those pesky icons and taskbars at the top and bottom of the browser window decrease that size—sometimes considerably. To be safe, use a maximum of 730x400. That will leave enough wiggle room for every browser variation, and allow someone working in the smallest window to still click on the desktop if they need to.

Outline a grid

Some people deal with varying content by creating radically different page layouts for it. That's a mistake. When you carry a traditional portfolio, you arrange everything so it fits in the case, upsizing the case or downsizing the artwork. You use the same type of matte board for mounting, and the same rules for positioning work on your boards or in sleeves.

You present a better impression if your page architecture is equally compact. If possible, every page should be the same size, or at least the same width. Every page's content should reflect an underlying grid. Images should appear in the same area, even if their dimensions vary.

This image of two overlaid schematics shows how Layla Keramat originally used two grids to reflect her site map. I've used thin red lines to show how her page was divided into four columns, and thick gold ones to show the division of the work display area.

After you have dimensions in mind, divide the page into equal-sized columns. Use these columns to help you position your elements, and to make sure that they all line up. Use combinations of these columns to help you determine how much space to allow for each type of thing.

LAYOUT FOLLOWS CONTENT

A portfolio site usually contains three types of material: unique page content (images, captions, explanatory text), navigation (links to main groups, secondary navigation to get you around inside a group), and global information (branding, contact info). Your portfolio might also include tutorials, news, a section for experimental work, or a portfolio highlight. You'll want to account for all of it.

Keramat's schematic layouts for her home page and category page use color to identify her three types of content and indicate her thinking about placement for different types of information.

Home Page Schematic

Keramat / I.D.

| Design by Process | Design by Intuition | Nav Item 3 |

Welcome Message

| Content from "Recent Additions" | Project Image/Text | Project Image/Text | Project Image/Text |

| Resume | E-mail | Lorem Ipsum |

■ Navigation
■ Content Area
■ Global Component

Category Overview Page Schematic

Keramat / I.D.

| Design by Process | Design by Intuition | Nav Item 3 |

Project Item 1
Project Item 2
Project Item 3
Project Item 4
Project Item 5
Project Item 6
Project Item 7
Project Item 8

Design by Process
Lorem ipsum dolor sit amet, consectetuer adipiscing elit, sed diem nonummy nibh euismod tincidunt lacreet dolore magna aliguam erat volutpat. Lorem ipsum dolor sit amet, consectetuer adipiscing elit, sed diem nonummy nibh euismod tincidunt lacreet dolore magna aliguam erat volutpat. Lorem ipsum dolor sit amet, consectetuer adipiscing elit, sed diem nonummy nibh euismod tincidunt lacreet dolore magna aliguam erat volutpat. Lorem ipsum dolor sit amet, consectetuer adipiscing elit, sed diem nonummy nibh euismod tincidunt lacreet dolore magna aliguam erat volutpat.

| Project Image/Text | Project Image/Text | Project Image/Text | Project Image/Text | Project Image/Text |

| Resume | E-mail | Lorem Ipsum |

■ Navigation
■ Content Area
■ Global Component

When you actually start to design, use actual content instead of *greeking* (gibberish place-holder text). Find your largest image, your longest caption, your deepest description. Draw outline boxes representing the image dimensions and the approximate text block size.

LINKING DECISIONS

Before you can lay out your navigation, return to your grouping decisions. If you were able to see a method of grouping your work in more than one way, your navigation and linking will be affected. In most cases, you can't combine the two groupings in the same nav bar area. Maybe one version should be reflected in your main nav bar, and the other available as links from a separate page.

Make it easy to back up a level in your hierarchy, and jump between branches. Visitors shouldn't have to hit their browser's Back button to return to the beginning of a section.

NAVIGATION LAYOUT

Use the same strategy for planning your navigation space as you do for your content. Account for all navigation levels so they won't extend into the portfolio content.

Roughly sketch out how your navigation will be arranged when it's at its most expanded state. Try both vertical and horizontal orientations. You'll discover that one will probably work better than the other.

> The process is understanding how the elements snap to a grid, have a folio, have a pagination. I'm trying to develop the grid, perhaps putting the navigation on the left-hand side to have more area around it.
>
> —Layla Keramat

Detail Page Schematic

Keramat / I.D.

Design by Process | Design by Intuition | Nav Item 3

Project Item 1
Project Item 2
Project Item 3
Project Item 4
Project Item 5
Project Item 6
Project Item 7
Project Item 8

Project Name
Task/Goals:
Lorem ipsum dolor sit amet, consectetuer adipiscing elit, sed diem nonummy nibh euismod tincidunt ut lacreet dolore magna aliguam erat. Lorem ipsum dolor sit amet, consectetuer adipiscing elit, sed diem nonummy nibh euismod tincidunt ut lacreet dolore magna aliguam erat

Client:

View:

Item 1 (Front)
Item 2 (Inside)
Item 3 (Details)
Item 4 (More details)

Image

Resume | E-mail | Lorem Ipsum

Navigation
Content Area
Global Component

On the detail page, horizontal navigation is reserved for main categories and global links. Access to individual projects, as well as separate views of these projects, use vertical navigation. In general, horizontal navigation works better when there are fewer items to navigate through. Vertical is more efficient when there are more items and their specific number may be variable.

Thinking about type

If you've had some formal design training, you know that typography is an important element. In fact, many people think it is the single most important factor for how they judge a design portfolio. Although non-design portfolios don't have to meet as rigorous a standard, truly bad type usage can reflect poorly on good illustration and art.

Here are a few suggestions tailored to the needs of a portfolio interface. These suggestions are no substitute for true knowledge, but they will keep you from making the most obvious typographic mistakes:

1. **Legibility is everything.** If you can't read the information, you might as well not put it in. Type is not necessarily more legible when it's bigger. If the font you've chosen seems hard to read, change the font before you upsize it.

2. **Use CSS style sheets.** No matter how you design your text, style sheets will keep your decisions consistent. If you define your type with pixels, not point sizes, you will gain the most consistent type size across platforms and browsers.

3. **Audience age matters.** Type can be slightly smaller for young eyes, but should be slightly larger for older ones.

4. **Don't type in all capital letters.** That goes for headlines, too. Unless you space them properly, words in all caps are hard to read.

5. **Avoid horsy type.** Most people make headlines too big, and then end up with text that's also too large. Really bold and large type doesn't communicate—it screams.

6. **The smaller your typeface, the narrower the column.** Don't run captions the full length of your window. Specify an area for text in a Web layout program, and use the HTML tag **<blockquote>** to limit your line widths. For short caption text, break lines manually.

7. **Don't center headlines. Ever.**

8. **Avoid Times Roman.** It was designed for newspapers, not computer screens. If you need a serif typeface, try Georgia.

9. **Don't use italic, at any size.** Because of the way a computer monitor displays, italic fonts can break up or get jagged in a browser.

Interested in knowing more about type? You'll find that *Stop Stealing Sheep & Find Out How Type Works*, by Erik Spiekermann, is a very good, and very visual, introduction.

Look and feel

By considering your content and creating quick sketches of your page and its elements, you've started designing the look and feel of your portfolio. Your sketches should be suggesting to you the size of your navigation elements and their placement. Now you have to think about what style or theme you'll use, as well as how people will interact with your design decisions.

Even if you are using the wrapper as a portfolio project, it shouldn't be fighting with your other work for attention. That doesn't mean that your interface can't be visually arresting. It means that it should be appropriate to who you are, who your audience is, and what your work is about.

When you're just hatched as a designer, a lot of times you're more concerned with the entertaining factors of your site. The level of excitement is usually geared toward an opening sequence. You don't always understand that your navigation behavior should be consistent, and you should have a very good idea on how your pages are intertwined.

—Layla Keramat

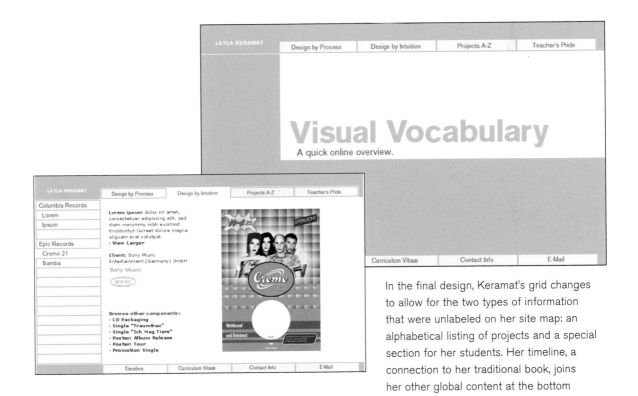

In the final design, Keramat's grid changes to allow for the two types of information that were unlabeled on her site map: an alphabetical listing of projects and a special section for her students. Her timeline, a connection to her traditional book, joins her other global content at the bottom of the page.

Simplicity rules in Layla Keramat's final design for her digital portfolio. Her buttons are text-based elements. Visually, they become part of the same layer as the detail page content when you are in the section and project that they represent. With her design in place, she is ready to produce her portfolio and complete her triad of presentation tools: traditional book, email PDF, and sophisticated website.

AVOID DISTRACTIONS

Once you start thinking about your look and feel, it's easy to forget the rigorous way you've approached your process and give way to some well-known portfolio excesses. If you still adhere to your basis schematics, the portfolio will still function well. But you want a portfolio that is both functional and visually satisfying. To ensure that....

Remember to KISS

KISS stands for Keep It Simple, Seriously.

Simplicity really is the most important virtue in portfolio design.

It's not easy to develop a really terrific interface for your portfolio. But it is easy to avoid the very worst sins:

- **Look for an idea that will be easy to create.** If you will have to spend hours making your buttons, they are probably too eye-catching for a portfolio.
- **Keep animated actions small and discrete.** Even better, limit your actions to ones that happen when a mouse rolls over a button. There is nothing more distracting than buttons that flash or change color or shape when a visitor hasn't done anything to activate them.
- **Limit your color palette.** Especially if you don't have a lot of experience in design, select two colors plus black and white. Make all your interface elements variations of one color. (Start with the pure color at rest, make a brighter version on roll-over, and a darker version when you click.)
- **Don't put a texture or a picture on your background.** Stick with a solid color, preferably black or white if you're new to interface design.
- **Don't fight with your artwork.** It's the reason you're making a portfolio, isn't it? Keep it the focus of each page.
- **Don't fill up the page.** For a portfolio, you almost can't have too much white space. You can have too much stuff on a page, however.
- **Limit your page size.** A portfolio viewer should never have to scroll to see artwork. Use a horizontal format (they're easier to control) and keep your page size consistent.
- **Arrange your ideas in groups.** Keep all your navigation together. Put any captions and other text all together in one place. Always show your work in the same place on the page.

Heather Hampton photos

resume

contact

portfolio

 product

 portrait

 landscape

  heartland

  winter series

  portugal

   Oporto

   Lisbon

Algarve photos: 1 2 3   5 6 7

Praca da Vao, commissioned for Nuevas Portugal magazine, 2002

heather hampton : photos   ☐ resume ☐ contact

product
portrait
landscape
 heartland
 winter series
 portugal
  oporto
  lisbon
 algarve

Praca da Vao.
Commissioned for
Nuevas Portugal
magazine, 2002.

☐ ☐ ☐ ■ ☐ ☐ ☐

Here are two versions of a portfolio page. They contain exactly the same amount of material, but the first one feels cramped and busy, while the second one is spacious. In the second, you can focus on the art.

PORTFOLIO HIGHLIGHT:
BRITT FUNDERBURK |
HOMAGE TO THE SQUARE

dialogbox.com

I like to have significant input into the architecture and organization of content as well as visual form. Interactivity can be enhanced by thoughtful graphic design, but a well-conceived foundation is essential. These design components are often treated as separate problems, but in my experience they are inextricably linked.

—Britt Funderburk

If it's hard to conceive of a beautiful, knock-out interface coming out of problem-solving, talk to graphic designer Britt Funderburk. He adheres to the same principles of focus and simplicity that Layla Keramat does, but expresses them in ways unique to his own aesthetic and needs. His portfolio is strikingly different from the average presentation, and is a perfect example of concept connected to—and enhanced by—the development process.

The first thing you notice when the home page appears is its visual punch: A site in stark black and white truly jumps off the page. The window can be resized to any dimension, but the interface itself is the simple white square.

The minimalist design is very functional. Everything on the home page is an active link. There are no graphic devices, logos, or content except the interface itself. The geometry reflects Funderburk's Dialogbox logo: the black square in quotes in the upper left.

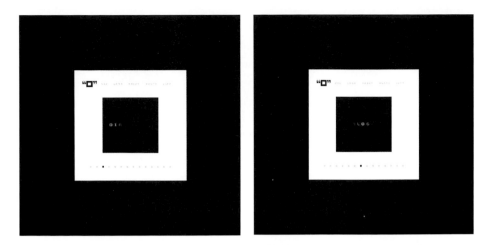

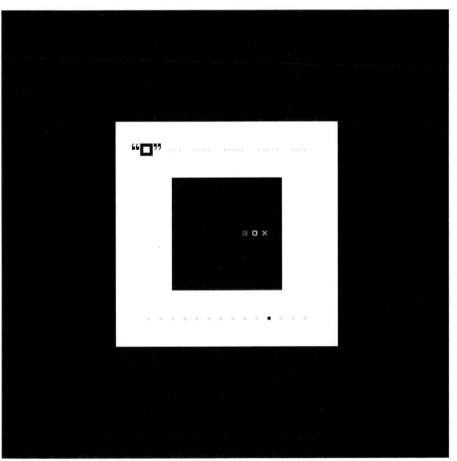

Roll over the small gray squares at the bottom of the interface. The site name appears like a sign illuminated by a moving flashlight. This little animation is like a flipbook: The viewer controls the speed, and can enter or leave the animation at any frame.

Navigation and architecture

People versed in modern art can't help but smile as they begin to explore the interface. Click a group link, and what was a stark black and white composition becomes a color study—and a tip of the design hat to Johannes Itten and Josef Albers, two masters of color theory. (To see an example of Funderburk's inspiration and to learn more about color, search for Itten's *The Art of Color* on Amazon.com.)

> Many designers today use elaborate, complex layouts and try to push technological boundaries with their sites. I wanted to create a simple container that was visually distinctive without overwhelming the work.
>
> —Britt Funderburk

Funderburk manages to do two seemingly different things at once: define his groupings and use them as navigation, and make a statement about his concept at the same time. This interface idea may look simple, but is in fact a very complicated and precise grid of color overlaid on his main groups. Such an economy of idea would be impossible without his having first worked through the grouping and mapping of his content and allowing that process to affect his layout and design.

This is Funderburk's working grid of his groupings and color combinations. Every color variation has been documented and applied to each hierarchy level.

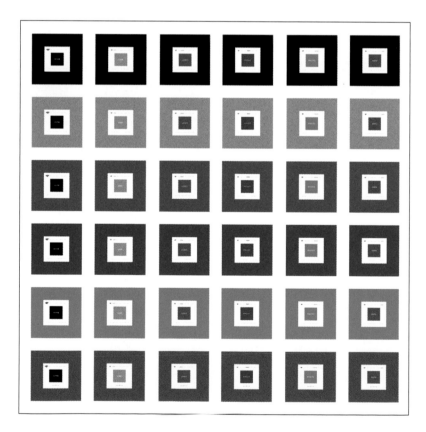

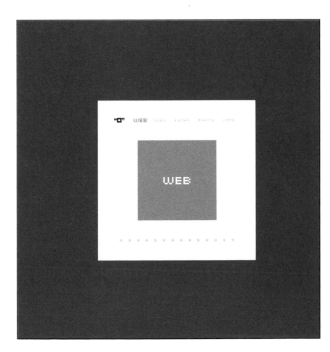

Mouse over the gray text at the top of the box, and the black interior square becomes a brilliant flat color. Select a group branch and the background color changes to match the link and the interior box. Roll over another branch and the center box color changes, creating elegant combinations of color.

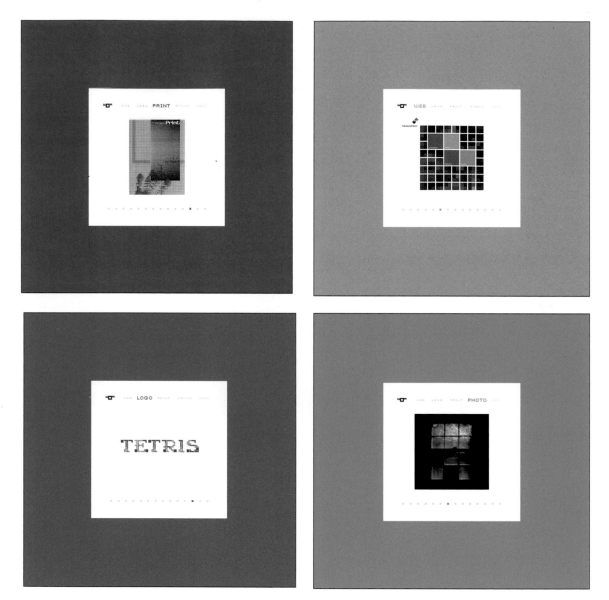

The gray boxes from the home page become secondary navigation when you are in a category. Each one represents a project, and takes on the color of the grouping when selected.

When Active, the navigation type changes from descrete anti-aliased outline to colorful bitmaps, as Funderburk plays with the idea of text brought from print to the screen.

I wanted to counteract the information overload that characterizes much of the web today and allow the work to speak for itself. To achieve maximum visual impact, I decided that the inclusion of captions would be more of a distraction than a benefit.

—Britt Funderburk

Content

The colors Funderburk has chosen for his group categories are also very effective foils for his artwork. Pulling colors from work he's previously done emphasizes that his content and portfolio interface are complementary.

Many of Funderburk's print pieces are very rich, typographically sophisticated, and textured. To show them in larger sizes would not only break the elegance of his interface, but would probably not do them justice. By choosing to keep his images recognizable but small, he maintains some print projects that are intriguing, but best seen in person.

Future plans

Dialogbox is a fairly recent design that gets very favorable reviews from its target audience: busy professionals. They like its highly distinctive look and minimalist approach. As Funderburk's only portfolio—he abandoned his suitcase in 1997, but retains a small book of printed pieces for customized personal presentations—it is sure to be updated for new projects, but will retain its striking presentation for the immediate future.

MOVING TO PRODUCTION

After you've finished your design, you're ready to create your website, CD, or DVD. Although production will take time, it will fly by compared with the hours you've spent in preparation to this point.

Because there is no one right application to build your portfolio, and every application handles the process differently, it makes more sense for you to reference a good hands-on, step-by-step book for this next stage. In Appendix A, you'll find resources covering each of the major software methods of producing your portfolio.

Marketing

CHAPTER 12

Copyright & portfolio

Not too long ago, it was easier to call an artist and ask for permission to use their work than it was to appropriate it. Now that so many projects are digital, there is a smorgasbord of ways to borrow, sample, copy, alter, and out-and-out steal creative work. It is also harder to stay within the law, even when your intentions are honorable.

How does this impact your portfolio? In more ways than you might imagine.

A few examples: the website you designed may be copyrighted by the company that paid your fee. The photos from the royalty-free CD you used may have reverted to the copyright of their original creator. A print project that's perfectly legitimate to display in a traditional portfolio might get you into trouble if you put it on a website because your contract says that you can show, but not distribute, the work. It's also easy for you to be the victim of a copyright violation. Your work could turn up in someone else's portfolio—with another person claiming credit for it.

You can't cover every possibility without becoming too paranoid to show any work digitally. This chapter will help you become more aware of your rights and responsibilities, suggest ways to minimize your risk, and prevent you from making assumptions that could get you into trouble later.

Terms of ownership

Intellectual property: A unique or new intangible asset created by the human mind.

Copyright: Exclusive rights to an identifiable expression of intellectual property, as defined specifically by the government that grants the copyright.

Trademark: Something that visually and/or verbally distinguishes one individual or organization's product from their competitors. A trademark can be a logo, an advertising phrase, a symbol, a brand name, a design, or some combination.

Fair use: The doctrine that some forms of expression that use another's copyrighted intellectual property do not infringe the copyright.

Infringement: The improper use of a legally recognized piece of intellectual property. Trademark infringement is limited to the misuse of an identifying symbol, like incorporating Mickey Mouse ears into a logo for a company called Mouseworks Design. Copyright infringement is broader, since copyright protects most original artistic and intellectual expression.

Cease and desist order: A legal order that forces a copyright infringer to immediately stop using infringed art, or pay fees, which are usually steep and accumulate daily.

UNDERSTANDING FAIR USE

Most copyright problems arise from a misunderstanding about fair use. Whether your use qualifies as fair use is determined by a combination of subjective factors. Issues like intent, type of work, and the profit motive are all considered. In all cases, interpretation is key.

What is the work you're planning to use? Just as some nudity is protected under the idea of "redeeming social value," some source material—like a Matisse—is considered more worthy of protection than a less socially or creatively valuable item—like a mass-produced velvet painting.

Why are you using the work? Fair use frequently protects free speech, like when an artist excerpts a piece to make a political or social statement. Relevance won't protect you, however, if you use the copyrighted work of another artist whose work has nothing to do with your intended target. (See the section, "Collage," later in the chapter.)

What about work that you've used "just a little"? The law considers the percentage of the piece you're using, and how critical that piece is to the original.

Whether you intend to profit from the use makes an enormous difference. Violating copyright of a commercial item for non-profit or educational purposes is generally seen as less serious than if the violator profited handsomely (or at least hoped to) as a result.

Finally, will the owner of the copyrighted piece lose money, or the ability to market the original piece, if you use it? If your work could prevent someone from buying the original—or even a reproduction of the original—you could be in trouble.

Note that there is a big difference between copying an actual artistic creation and using the idea behind it. Neither ideas nor facts can be copyrighted—only the specific way that they are expressed.

One final consideration: Even when your piece meets all the legal tests for fair use, you can find yourself challenged in court by a company with a large legal department if the piece moves to the wide visibility of a website. Even if you win, it could be an expensive victory. When in doubt, don't do it.

When you borrow a generic piece of sky from a photograph, it's likely that no one will notice, even though you have still violated the photographer's rights. But if you use an image like this one, the sky is central to the concept, and your violation will be clear to everyone.

RESPECTING OTHERS' RIGHTS

Portfolio assets that aren't yours can get you into trouble. The creative community is small enough that, eventually, people who fail to respect the rights of others feel the consequences. And it's worth considering: A person who is willing to borrow or appropriate the work of others shouldn't be surprised if someone else returns the compliment.

"Orphan" projects

An orphan project is one where the client no longer exists. There is little chance that the client is going to rise from the dead, grasping for rights with its mummified hands. But photographs or other artwork in these projects may have been purchased for limited or one-time use. Showing such work on a disk or at high resolution might be chancy.

Design comps

It isn't ethical to use another person's work in a comp without requesting permission, but it's accepted professional practice to do so if you end up hiring the artist for the project or paying their licensing fee.

But what if you didn't end up hiring the artist? Sometimes, a designer develops a concept, but their idea isn't the one the client picks. Unfortunately, if the comp artwork wasn't licensed, you can't show it in most digital ways. What if the work is clearly presented as a comp, the artwork was already online at low resolution at a stock site and you don't show it at a usable size? No one's likely to break down your door. But that's not because it's okay; it's because the Internet is too massive for most people to track down the infringement.

Clip art

Most download sites state their usage policy explicitly. Usually, your rights are limited to online or home use. Completely copyright-free sites provide very small, screen-resolution images meant for web page backgrounds and clickable buttons. This is low-quality art, and it shouldn't find its way into a creative professional's work. The general rule: If it's good enough for you to want to use it, it's probably copyrighted.

> People come into the industry having done very well in school, but they don't know how to draw. If they had some reasonable level of drawing skills, they could have put down an idea in less than a minute. Instead they spend hours going through found photography, trying to find precisely the right photograph. I don't think that's healthy for our industry.
>
> —Stan Richards

Collage

Collage involves not just the collection of images, but their careful extraction, composition, and alteration. It doesn't seem fair that practicing a respected form of art could get you in hot water. But even without the added complication of a digital image, collage can run afoul of copyright laws.

For example, in 1991, Robert Rauschenberg incorporated a photo of a car from an old *Time* magazine into a collage, and was sued by the commercial photographer who took the photo. Mistakenly, he viewed the decades-old work as "found" material. Students often do the same, scanning elements from magazines and books. The sources frequently are an important element in their composition. Anyone who appropriates materials from magazines and design annuals could someday present their portfolio to the very person who created the source art.

Derivative art

"Derivative" art is work that is based on someone else's creative output. The Copyright Act clearly states that only the original work's copyright owner can copy, duplicate, reprint, alter, or adapt it.

What about the "gray area," where you think you've altered the piece to such a degree that it qualifies as new art? The law takes a commonsense approach to these actions. If you pluck a person off the street and show her both images, would she recognize them as being similar? If so, no matter how you've changed the work, you have violated the law.

Sometimes the medium you select for your derivative art affects its usage. Many artists return to historical art classics for inspiration, or even as a starting point to comment or satirize the work. When appearing in a painting or other one-of-a-kind work, the use can be perfectly legitimate. But a reproduction of the same artwork that could be downloaded and printed—like a piece of your online portfolio—might fail the rights test.

Derivative style

There is a big difference between adapting an existing artwork and working in the style of another artist. Working in someone else's style can be an homage, particularly if the artist has historical relevance and the work is not a copy of any existing work. It can also be a way to get the superficial benefit of a distinctive look without having to pay the original creator. Copyright law has no way of protecting the original artist or designer in either case.

For example, one of the best known graphic posters from the late '60s is Milton Glaser's Bob Dylan poster. If you scan a copy of his poster, change the colors in the hair design, and straighten Dylan's nose, you have done more than use an idea. You have created a work to replace the original and have violated Glaser's copyright.

On the other hand, if you came across Glaser's work and it inspired you to create a totally new graphic combining a solid color form and strips of curved, stylized lines, a savvy viewer might recognize that you are working in Glaser's style, but you are in the clear legally.

I hired a designer who had been designing and art-directing for multi-platinum–selling artists. About six months later, a book was sent over to me. I zeroed in on one project that was also in this woman's book. I finally said, "You know, we hired so-and-so, and that same project is in her portfolio. She says she did it." He was defiant, but his body language told me that he was lying. He was good, but I did not put him forward to the creative director.

—Cynthia Rabun

ROLES AND LARGE PROJECTS

It can be very exciting, when you have worked on a project for a well-known brand or took part in a major campaign, to include the project in your portfolio. Before you do, be honest with yourself about your share in the work. Were you a junior designer, or the art director? Did you develop the concept, or only execute the production?

It's always better to present your share of the project honestly. Everyone knows that major projects are the work of many minds and hands. If a project is great, taking credit for only your share will reflect well on you. Giving credit to those who earned it will prevent confusion when more than one team member applies to one firm or deals with the same placement agency. Not only will you be better prepared to speak about the portion of the project that you know intimately, but you will be spared the embarrassment of being confronted with any gap between reality and your presentation.

OWNING YOUR WORK

In a surprisingly large number of cases, even when you create all your own material, you don't own the copyright to it. The circumstances under which a work was created determines who owns and gets to license it. This can have profound implications for a digital portfolio, which by its very nature involves copying and adaptation. It has particular implications for illustrators and photographers. If you maintain rights to your work, you can recycle an image into the stock market, making your portfolio a potential income stream.

If you have created an image on your own time, for your own purposes, it remains yours to duplicate or change. Even if you sell the original artwork, you can retain the right to show copies of it in your portfolio, no matter what form that portfolio might take. If you choose to make a series of unique images in the same style, on the same theme, or with elements from the original, you are still free to do so.

On the other hand, work you do might conceivably belong instead to your employer, your client, yourself in combination with one of the above, or a third party entirely. The key to this distinction is your working relationship to the other parties.

Employee or independent?

Were you an employee when you created the work? Did you do the work while having taxes deducted? Did you have a supervisor? If so, the work belongs, and will continue to belong, to your employer. You can certainly claim that you did the work, and probably show a printed copy of it, assuming that trade or non-disclosure contracts are not in effect. But you can't copy it, sell it to someone else, or adapt it for a freelance job. If you want to use the work in a digital portfolio, you will need to get permission in writing from your employer to do so.

A freelancer is considered an independent contractor if you use your own materials and computer, work at home (or not regularly at the client's office), set your own hours, and get paid by the project, not by the hour. Unless there is a contract stating otherwise, the freelancer retains copyright on the artwork, and the client simply has rights to use it. The nature of that use (how extensive and broad) should be negotiated at the beginning of the project. The independent contractor has every right to reproduce this type of work in portfolio form.

You (or your employer or client) can't have it both ways. If you want to retain rights to the work, you can't also get the benefits of employment—sick days, health insurance, overtime, and so on. Conversely, your employer can't deny you these benefits by calling you an independent contractor unless they also let you retain your copyright.

Work-for-hire

Unfortunately, lots of visual work changes hands in a land in between. In a contract where you have agreed to work-for-hire, an independent consultant is paid to design, create, or produce something for a fixed sum, selling their rights to the work to the person or company who pays them.

This contract clearly states that the artist is selling the rights to their work.

Consultant Contract

This Agreement is made between Serif & Sans, Inc. (client), 400 Causeway Street, Boston, MA and Brian D'Donnell (contractor), 47 Trowbridge Lane, Sudbury, MA.

Consulting Services
The contractor agrees to perform the services described in Exhibit A, attached to this Agreement, with deadlines and responsibilities as indicated there.

Payment
In consideration of services to be performed by the contractor, the client agrees to pay the contractor $5,000, according to the terms set out below.

Independent Contractor Status
The contractor is an independent contractor, not the client's employee. The contractor and client agree to the following rights consistent with an independent contractor relationship.
The contractor has the right to perform services for others during the term of this Agreement.
The contractor has the sole right to control and direct the means, manner and method by which the services required by this Agreement will be performed.
The contractor can perform the services required by this Agreement at any place, location or time.
The contractor shall perform the services required by this Agreement; the client shall not hire, supervise or pay any assistants to help contractor.
The contractor is responsible for all applicable income taxes. The client will not withhold FICA and other taxes from the contractor's payments, or make state or federal unemployment compensation contributions on the contractor's behalf.

Intellectual Property Ownership
To the extent that the work performed by the contractor under this Agreement includes any work of authorship entitled to protection under the copyright laws, the parties agree to the following provisions.
The contractor's work shall be deemed a commissioned work and a work made for hire to the greatest extent permitted by law.
The contractor's work has been specially ordered and commissioned by the client as a contribution to a collective work, eligible to be treated as a work made for hire under the United States Copyright Act.
The client shall be the sole author of the contractor's work and any work embodying the contractor's work according to the United States Copyright Act.
To the extent that the contractor's work is not properly characterized as a work made for hire, the contractor grants to the client all right, title and interest in the contractor's work, including all copyright rights, in perpetuity and throughout the world.
The contractor shall help prepare any papers the client considers necessary to secure any copyrights, patents, trademarks or intellectual property rights at no charge to theh client. However, the client shall reimburse the contractor for reasonable out-of-pocket expenses incurred.

contractor _____   client _____

By _____   By _____
contractor's signature   authorized signature

date _____   date _____

Work-for-hire is a growing problem for creatives, who can end up with large chunks of their creative output belonging to someone else. An old-fashioned portfolio situation, where one copy of a finished work was carried around, shown, and returned to its case almost never resulted in a legal action. The existence of digital artwork—infinitely and immediately duplicable—has changed all that, and made the work-for-hire provision in a contract an increasingly ugly by-product of doing business.

What qualifies a commissioned freelance project as a work-for-hire? A surprisingly broad category of work:

- A contribution to a "collective work"—a large corporate website, a newspaper or magazine, or an encyclopedia.
- Something that's part of a motion picture or other audiovisual work—like contributions to an interactive CD or its storyboards.
- A translation, a test, or answer material for a test.
- Instructional text—a textbook or training package.
- A "supplementary work"—everything from maps and tables to indexes and bibliographies.
- A compilation—like a database or bookmark list.

If you've been looking for a common thread, you may have noticed that the law assumes that the work would not have been made without the larger project, and that the work would not necessarily stand on its own. On the other hand, both parties have to agree in writing that the project should be considered a "work made for hire." Any item that both parties put their names to that calls it such is considered a binding contract. The phrase has, therefore, been known to be tucked into a work contract and printed on the back of payment checks.

Assignment of rights

As a freelancer, try to avoid being pushed into work-for-hire. You are being asked to give up more than the time you spend creating the work, without any employee benefits and protections. At the very least, negotiate for rights to display the work in your portfolio when you and the client draw up a contract. The contract should state your intent to assign the rights to the client after the work has been completed and paid for in full. This differs from a work-for-hire because the two of you can write the specific provisions necessary to give your client the rights they need to use their material without denying you the right to claim your contribution.

Team work and individual rights

With the growing need for groups of people with different roles to work collaboratively, it becomes more important for the artist or designer to document such involvement. From the beginning, your contract should clarify the scope of your involvement. If you will be responsible for a project section, or a specific group of illustrations or layouts, keep copies of your process work. If, as sometimes happens, you are called upon to handle more material than was originally planned, make sure that the change is also documented, not just to make sure that you are appropriately paid, but so you can ask for rights to show the material.

PROTECTING YOUR WORK

Any time you provide an image at a resolution or in a format that would allow the work to be edited or printed, you could become the victim of art piracy. Besides threatening to sue, and then really doing it, what can you do to protect your work?

Copyrighting

In the U.S. and Europe, copyright is implied without the need for a symbol or any registration. However, you can't sue for copyright infringement without registering the work. In the U.S., you have five years after you create something to register. However, if you register before a copyright infringement—particularly if you did so within the first three months of the work's creation—your chances for winning a case are higher. It is possible to rush through a copyright registration, but it costs more than the basic $30—registration is $580 at press date. A high price to pay for procrastination.

For most art or graphic work, as well as architectural drawings and renderings, you need Form VA (for visual art). If you want to register an interactive or multimedia work, or your whole portfolio is a multimedia work, you will need Form PA instead. That makes protecting your digital portfolio very cost effective, because the $30 will cover everything. Both of these forms can be downloaded in PDF form from **www.lcweb.loc.gov/copyright**. You'll also need to send in a copy of the work itself. Read the government circular specific to your situation to determine what type of copy the government requires.

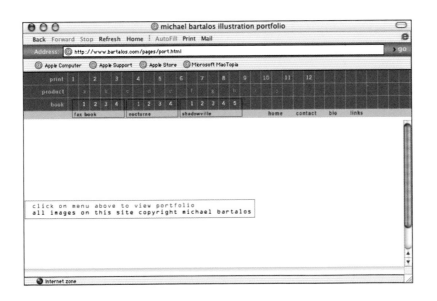

Michael Bartalos states his copyright before showing you any of his artwork.

A U.S. copyright is valid in most other countries, so you don't have to worry about taking out additional copyrights to show your work on the Web, or to send it to people in other countries. If you are in the U.K. and want to copyright your work, you can download a PDF of relevant information at **www.patent.gov.uk/copy/info/index.htm.**

Using the copyright symbol with your name can stop innocent appropriation. The proper form for doing this in the U.S. is:

Copyright © 2004 Your Name. All rights reserved.

However, any statement on your web portfolio that clearly states your copyright is considered valid.

PROTECTION TECHNOLOGIES

The most common way to claim copyright on a digital image is to simply overlay the copyright symbol and information directly onto it. Although more than adequate warning for the well-intentioned, this is not much protection against anyone with a good eye and a cloning tool, especially since you can't put the notice anywhere that is critical to viewing the work.

The most reasonable compromise between paranoia and laissez faire is to provide low-resolution images. An image large enough to represent your work onscreen but well below printable threshold prevents someone from easily "borrowing" your work. It doesn't prevent a determined or clueless violator from copying your image and using it in another, equally low-resolution medium, however.

If you stamp a big copyright C over the image, you are certainly safe, but you also degrade the quality of your work, often to the point that people fail to look at it carefully.

Because you're working with technology, you should make it work for you. There are several simple ways to help keep your work safe while still being able to display it:

- **Acrobat PDFs.** PDF files preserve font, format, and color decisions for artwork that combines type and image. (See Chapter 8, "Creating written content," for more about PDFs.) If they're not password-protected, anyone with the full Acrobat program can extract text and images from them. Fortunately, it's easy to lock your PDF. In Acrobat, go to File > Document Security, then select Standard Security from the drop-down menu. Check the second box in Specify Password (be careful not to check the first one, or no one will be able to open your file!) and type a password in the box. In Permissions, check the third box to prevent your work from being copied or extracted.
- **Player software.** Players make your work portable, while keeping it view-only. Although it is not impossible to extract material from a player file, it is very difficult, and far more work than it's worth.
- **Watermarking and digital "signatures."** Some programs allow you to imprint sound and image files with invisible digital watermarks—methods that hide identifying content inside the digital data of a file without changing the look or sound of the file. In theory, this embedded data makes it possible to prove ownership of an image, even if someone makes major alterations to the original.

Detailed copyright protection info

If you are hoping to use your portfolio to license your artwork, need to hire illustrators for your design projects, or are a freelancer hoping to protect your creative rights, check out Nolo Press' aptly named "Protect Your Artwork" (**www.nolo.com**). It includes detailed copyright information and several useful contracts and agreements.

DEALING WITH INFRINGEMENT

Anyone who has ever found their work passed off as someone else's, or has seen a portion of their art looking back at them from an unknown source, knows the feeling of personal violation. The reaction, after the shock passes, is to DO something about it. But what?

Your legal rights

Copyright law states that you are "entitled to recover the actual damages." This means that you can get the money you should have been paid, including any net profits that the infringer made through the use of your art. Though it may be tempting to overestimate the damage, assign a realistic dollar value to your artwork and the effect of its loss. If you have been getting a few hundred dollars an image, suddenly claiming $10,000 for one won't be believable.

If your work accounts for only a small portion of the piece (one design element in one screen of a CD, for example), the profits will be pro-rated accordingly. Even so, if the project was lucrative, you could be awarded statutory damages, as well as your legal fees. Statutory damages can punish a deliberate infringer more seriously than actual damages.

On the other hand, few infringers nowadays are major corporations. Large companies have departments responsible for tracking and getting releases for art, precisely to avoid this type of issue. Most likely, your infringer is not making any money from your work. If there is little or no financial impact and no damage to your reputation (particularly if the violator clearly thought they were operating under fair use), your time might better be spent educating the infringer.

Acting effectively

Unless you have a free lawyer, try to deal with the situation yourself first. The court can be unsympathetic to an action that should have been settled out of court. Send a certified, business-like letter (not a hot-tempered set of empty threats) to the infringer. Let them know that you've discovered that they are using your copyrighted artwork without your permission. Describe the work clearly and the date the violation was discovered. Then send them an invoice with a realistic usage fee, and a deadline before you take action. If the violation took place on a website, make it clear that they must stop displaying your work immediately. You may receive a shocked and contrite phone call, a request to work something out, or an apologetic note with a check attached.

While you're waiting for a response, search for a lawyer who knows intellectual property issues. If your infringer stonewalls, or you receive a corporate "up yours" letter—and if you've decided that the $1,000 or more cost is worthwhile—your lawyer will file a cease and desist order against them. Make sure your lawyer makes every effort to settle the case out of court. Even if you get less money than you think you deserve, anyone who has ever spent time in the court system will tell you that the wheels of justice turn slowly, when they turn at all.

You may decide that you can't afford to go to court. If the infringer is a professional, and they have chosen to stonewall rather than apologize or negotiate, call in your network of friends and associates. Speak to relevant professional guilds and associations. Some of them have funds set aside for copyright actions. If the work has been used to create a commercial product, contact the client directly. Send a cover letter with a clipping of your stolen artwork. Ask them to compare it to the non-original art and judge for themselves. If the work is on a website, contact the service provider. They may find it in their best interests to exert pressure on the violator. Sometimes public shame will do what good conscience will not.

PORTFOLIO HIGHLIGHT:
KEN LOH | ATTRIBUTION

kenloh.com

When you create a portfolio, you want to highlight your very best work. When someone sees your portfolio and likes it, they want to be able to share it. So this highlight is, at least in part, about what you can't see. Ken Loh, the creative director behind the current Sharpe Online site, goes out of his way to credit his collaborators. Even so, many of the pieces in his stylish portfolio won't be shown here.

Loh's portfolio is understated and focused, both in its color palette—grayscale with shades of tan—and its design. Its title, running across the page, is the first thing you see. But almost the first thing you read is an acknowledgment of his collaborators.

The creative process is often a collaborative one, where a lot of people bring their creative talents together to make something great. I always appreciate it when a photographer or illustrator credits me as AD or CD in their work, so I feel that I should do the same.

—Ken Loh

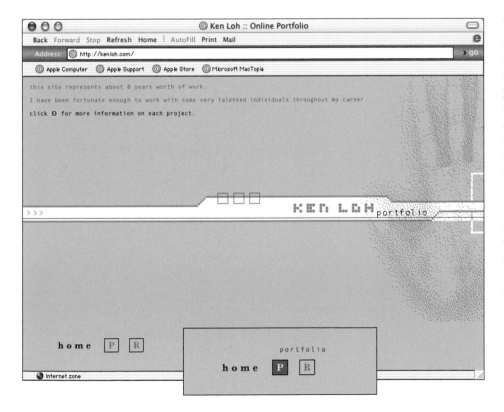

The lightly screened hand on the right both marks the page in a personal way and asks you to stop and look. Letters inside small squares on the bottom right fade in and out to indicate that they are interactive. Roll over a box and it reverses out. Choices are simple: the portfolio or a resume time line. Once you've selected the portfolio, its navigation persists at the bottom of the page.

Architecture and navigation

Loh knows why you're here—to see his work and check him out. This is clearly a job-seeker's portfolio. In fact, it's organized so you can approach the portfolio in two ways: by going into the portfolio and examining the work by category, and by using the résumé as a navigation tool.

If you start with the résumé, you are guided to project highlights throughout Loh's career. This avenue emphasizes his growth as a designer, both creatively and as a manager of others. It's such a clean, effective way of linking résumé text to portfolio work that you wonder why more people haven't explored this concept.

I make a distinction between my work as a Designer/Art Director and my work as a Creative Director. CDs are less hands-on and rely heavily on the talent of other designers and art directors. I wanted to make sure the right people got credit for the work.

—Ken Loh

Because the résumé is also a visual timeline, you can click on thumbnails to see how Loh's work has evolved. Although very small, the thumbnails are impressively legible. Click on a thumbnail, and the project's portfolio page appears.

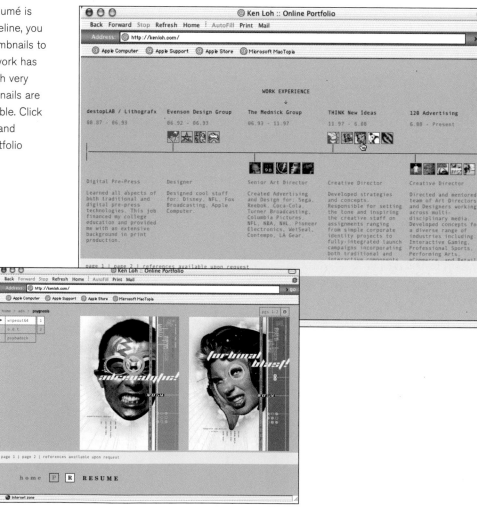

Choose the standard portfolio route, and you have three distinct ways of moving forward. You can click on a thumbnail, select a category from the nav bar at the bottom, or select a client.

Wayfinding issues are very well-handled here. There are breadcrumbs that tell you what category you're in and a grid that tells you how many projects are in each category. When a project is highlighted, a column of numbers to its right tells you how many pages of each project there are.

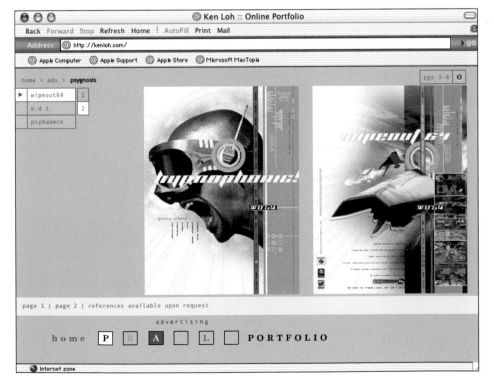

Click the Info icon in the upper right, and a window rises from the navigation area. It contains the design brief or other relevant information on the project on the left. On the right, Loh specifies his role and credits the agency and designer. He also makes it clear that the image was purchased from stock photography.

Content

Loh's site has plenty of finished projects, but is also well-stocked with comps. Some projects were never produced; others were started but never came to completion. In some cases, client changes made the finished art less interesting than the comps, and less an indication of Loh's creativity. Because the art was based on low-resolution stock, a website is the best place to show it.

> A lot of creative energy goes into creating comps. Generally, the best ideas never get produced, or at least get "watered-down" to the point that they're not as good as the original idea. So, for me, the website is a great place to showcase some of my favorite work that never got approved.
>
> —Ken Loh

Loh has been scrupulous in crediting and attributing for all of his projects, including orphan pieces. Taking this step, especially for a creative director, should be a no-brainer, but it is still the exception in a portfolio, not the rule. But Loh knows that taking credit for work that isn't solely yours, even if it is only by omission, comes back to haunt you. On the other hand, giving credit makes people want to return the favor, in the form of putting your name on their portfolios, or passing your name along to placement agencies.

Future plans

Ken Loh's site was extremely successful in its mission—it landed him a job that keeps him very, very busy. Future plans may wait awhile, but eventually he plans to enlarge the site and attach it to a database—a great way to archive projects and keep the site fresh as well.

CHAPTER 13

Presenting your portfolio

Planning, design, and production are the major stages in digital portfolio development, and certainly the ones that take the most energy and time. But uploading or burning doesn't mean your work is done. In creative endeavors, the details that surround your portfolio can shine a light or cast a shadow on your work. Exquisite presentation is not a bonus—it's the required last step in designing and producing a portfolio. It matters tremendously how you present your portfolio to others, both when you are physically present and when the portfolio must speak for you.

This final chapter considers the presentation as part of your portfolio design. When your artwork, your product, and your presentation are in harmony, you make a powerful statement to a prospective client or employer: "This person loves and cares about their work." That's exactly the type of person anyone would want to have on their team.

A good portfolio is going to get you in the door, but it's how a person talks about their work and how they express their ideas that's a large part of it. I remember hiring someone who had only one piece to show me, but she had such energy, and the piece that she showed me was good. I hired her on the spot.

—Bill Cahan

TESTING YOUR WORK

When you discover a bug while you're using a program, you get irritated and angry. Well, digital portfolios are software, too. It is much better to find a problem before it reflects badly on you and your work.

You may not think you need to test your work if you haven't made an interactive portfolio, but sometimes the simplest projects are the ones where something silly slips through. If you've made PDFs, or created a simple slideshow, or even used a template on a sourcebook site, you should still spend the time to verify that everything works, looks good, and reads well.

How to test

If you don't have one already, make a list of each page (Excel, or something like it, is the best place for this). Compared with most commercial websites, your portfolio is a small project and testing every page should be possible. As you test, check off the page.

A successful test is thorough and complete, and includes the following:

- **Test against your site map.** If you made a website, CD, or DVD, you should have a good site map to refer to. (See Chapter 11, "Designing a portfolio interface.") Are the pages linked from the places you planned, and are the links from those pages correct?

- **Test on different computers.** Open your project on a different computer. You may have browser default settings on your working machine that you take for granted, or discover errors in a style sheet or a font. You may also notice that some animations move too slowly or are much faster than you thought that they would be on a more or less powerful computer.

- **Test on different platforms.** If you designed your work on a Mac, test it on a Windows computer, and vice versa. Fonts, colors, and browser elements may look different or not work properly.

- **Test at random places.** Unless your work is in a Flash window, people could access your site from a page in the middle, not from the home page. Does all your navigation still work?

- **Test with guinea pigs.** Watch someone else look at your portfolio. Do they click in places that you never intended? If they do, does anything unexpected happen? If your guinea pig seems confused by your interface or slow to understand your environment, rework the difficult sections.

- **Test your media.** Particularly if you have created a DVD, you must verify that your disk will work, not just in your own computer or player, but in many player and platform combinations. Use brand-name DVD-R disks: Generic brands are often incompatible. A visit to an electronics megastore provides a great opportunity to pop your disk into a wide range of players.

What to test

Test everything, really—every page, every image, every interactive state. In particular, watch for the following:

- **Fonts.** Bugs may cause some fonts to be replaced with incorrect ones, or ones with incorrect weights.
- **Links.** When you update, links can break, especially if you retype file names. If you have links to launch an email program, or links that open new windows, make sure they all work. Use *absolute links*—ones that contain the entire URL (such as **http://www.out-sidelink.com/folder/mywork.html**)—for all external links.
- **Images.** Images should all be in one image folder, and accessed through a relative link (such as "images/mypix.jpg"), so they won't generate broken links when you upload your files to a server.
- **Downloads.** When you download a video clip, does it play on both platforms? How long does it take to start? Does it play correctly?
- **Platform issues.** Different versions of browsers, and browsers on different platforms, can read your code in a variety of ways. Layers, for example, don't always work on older browsers. You may need to change your code so it works in more browser versions.
- **Speed.** How long does it take your home page or Flash preloader to finish? How long does it take each of your artwork images to show up? Are these acceptable times for your target audience?

GETTING FEEDBACK

Once you're confident that your portfolio is in good shape technically, get some feedback. The more interviews and reviews you can get, the better. Even an accomplished professional can miss things that a fresh eye will notice. Trusted, discriminating friends are a valuable source. But sometimes, especially when you have created something in a new format, objectivity is very valuable.

It's easiest to get feedback if you're a student. In fact, taking a professional development or certificate program at an art and design school can give an older professional access to many of the school's faculty and placement services—and their portfolio reviews. Don't be shy about asking a favorite professor for an appointment to discuss your portfolio. How well you do reflects on them, and the school.

Local professional organizations also sponsor portfolio reviews, often in the spring. They offer the opportunity to get feedback from faculty and professionals from different schools or companies—offering a new perspective on your work.

No matter what your position, look for opportunities for informational interviews. Many design studios, for example, offer a specific process on their website for portfolio feedback. Another great place for feedback is a placement agency. You'll get unvarnished reaction from a place that sees hundreds of portfolios in your area.

www.bu.edu/prc/portfolio.htm

Boston University's Photographic Resource Center offers free monthly portfolio reviews to its members. It also provides a fee-for-service portfolio review for the entire photographic community.

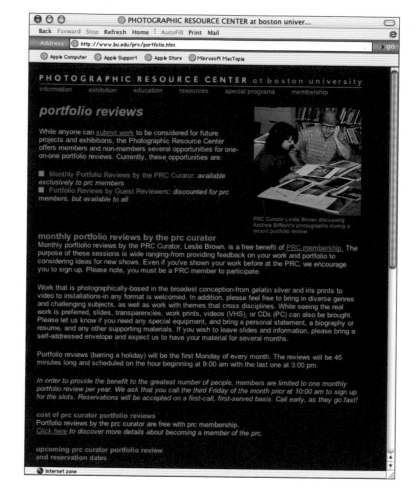

The online community offers endless feedback. Too endless—there are lots of critique sites. Unfortunately, I can't recommend one that gives good creative advice, although some offer good software tips and feedback on site function. To figure out if the site will be useful to you, look for three warning signs:

- **The site's design.** Even blogs and forums can be designed with taste or without.
- **Anonymous posters.** Do you really need a critique from someone named "stinkyfoot"?
- **Rated reviewers.** Except on purely technical advice sites, high-rated reviewers get there by being supportive, not by being effectively critical.

You might have better luck joining—or starting—a local community of creatives who critique each other's work. Again, professional organizations can be good sources for such a network.

	Critiques and reviews needed.pls	3DeSiGnZ	7	84	July 23 '03 11:22 PM by **3DeSiGnZ**
	Please critique	lmarshall	1	37	July 23 '03 04:14 PM by **buntine**
	What do you think?	thuffner	10	153	July 23 '03 11:29 AM by **buntine**
	New Person Site Layout! Thoughts?	MACORA	8	118	July 23 '03 03:23 AM by **MACORA**
	what do u think?	fuzaboy	11	109	July 23 '03 01:50 AM by **splufdaddy**
	Very basic layout	Brak	8	100	July 22 '03 06:01 PM by **Brak**
	please review my site	Nickhead	8	113	July 22 '03 05:16 PM by **nickc**
	New sites, feedback please...	Sajata	4	74	July 22 '03 02:36 PM by **nickc**
	Looking for some feedback on my new site design.	DiZASTiX	11	90	July 21 '03 05:59 PM by **JR**

Forum sites like this one may sometimes provide good feedback, but it's hard to separate the knowledgeable posters from the poseurs.

One last consideration about critiquing: You may not always like what you hear. Any professional who is offering feedback should be polite and offer constructive criticism—you shouldn't have to take tantrums and abuse. But they are doing you a favor if they honestly point out that a project doesn't belong in your book, tell you that it needs work, or give suggestions on improving your presentation. Even if you disagree, don't argue. If you really think that they are wrong, ask someone else. Second opinions can be as useful for portfolios as they are for medical decisions.

I'm much less inclined to be opinionated about a portfolio now in front of a student. Because when, in the past, somebody asked for my honest feedback, I would actually give it to them.

—Bill Cahan

PACKAGING A PORTABLE PORTFOLIO

If you've designed and produced a DVD or CD portfolio, you'll certainly be sending it out for review. Almost any place you target probably gets dozens of other portfolios in a month. You want your work to stand out from that crowd. Generic-looking material could easily be tossed in the trash in a fit of end-of-project house cleaning.

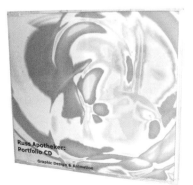 

To raise the odds that your work will be viewed and retained, your digital portfolio should be attractively packaged. At the least, you should design a disk label. Even better is to add a matching sleeve or case and a mailer insert.

Disk labeling do's and don'ts

It's important to label your work, but not all labeling is equally good:

- **Don't use standard pre-stick labels.** Most labels, including many laser-safe brands, are made with an adhesive that eats away at the disk coating.

- **Don't tape or glue a label.** Anything that isn't absolutely flat can ruin a CD player if it gets caught inside.

- **Don't send a disk without a sleeve or case.** CDs and DVDs may be long-lasting media, but if you scratch them, they may not play.

- **For single disks, consider using a kit.** Kits come with printable labels precut to the right sizes. Most come with a holder to help you position the printed label (very important—a CD with an unbalanced label may not play), as well as either labeling software or templates for standard applications, like Quark, Photoshop, or Illustrator.

- **For short multiples of disks, check your local service bureau.** Many now have printers that can print directly onto CDs at cost-effective prices.

- **Burn your CDs before you label them.** Chances are that the disk will not burn properly after the label is on.

Designing a CD or DVD package

There is a difference between adequate and excellent portfolio packaging. Design creativity is of course critical, but good process will help you maintain quality and produce a better package.

> At the Art Academy, for instance, every student has put together a really well-crafted book of their work. The presentation is really exceptional. The person that told the students what to do did them a favor, because they would never have even have gotten in the door had they not presented their work in a very strong way.
>
> —Bill Cahan

Consider these issues as you develop your design:

- **Maintain design consistency.** You might be surprised by how many people begin their package design from scratch. Packaging, like your portfolio, is part of a self-branding process. You should reinforce that branding whenever you can.

- **Aim for legibility.** You want your package to be distinctive, but your design should never sacrifice legibility for effect. Make sure your name, and the word "portfolio" figure prominently.

- **Design all elements.** If you are using a jewel case for your CD, make sure to design all surfaces: front, back, and the side. The side is particularly important, since disks are often stored standing up on their sides.

- **Design a leave-behind.** Despite having a digital portfolio, it's always a nice touch to have another form of portfolio leave-behind to accompany it. It offers a way to show your work in tangible form, and can double as a great way to advertise your site. (See "Mailings," later in the chapter.)
- **Design your print portfolio.** You may still be maintaining a print portfolio for pieces that can't be shown or don't work well digitally. It should be organized and designed to match your digital presentation.

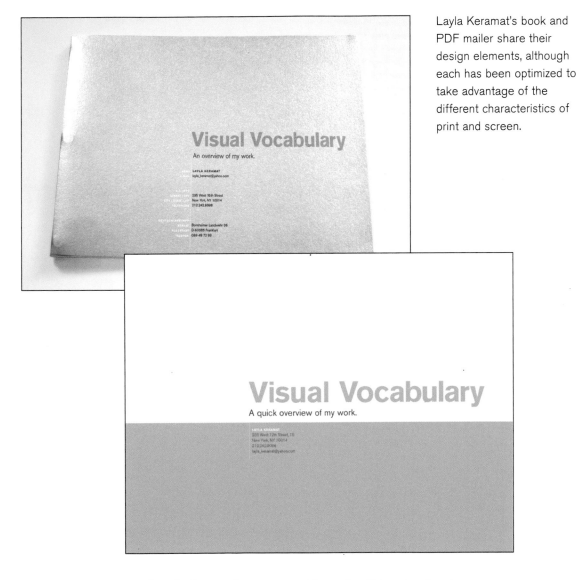

Layla Keramat's book and PDF mailer share their design elements, although each has been optimized to take advantage of the different characteristics of print and screen.

- **Print on stiff stock.** Your jewel case cover and insert should be printed on (or constructed with) heavy paper. If you're lucky, it will be opened and closed multiple times as people pass your disk around. You don't want the design to look shop-worn after a few people have handled it.

GETTING THE WORD OUT

Promotion is not a dirty word. True, there are people whose tireless and egotistical self-flogging give the practice a bad name. But if you believe in your work, you should be prepared to be your own advocate.

Advertising your portfolio

Publicizing your portfolio is the other side of researching your audience. All the connections you made in lists, forums, and other groups are places to let people know that your portfolio is ready. In particular, be sure to contact everyone who critiqued your portfolio and send them a personal thank-you. If someone was particularly helpful, you might even add a line of thanks or credit in your online portfolio. It may prompt them to send people to see your site, but even if it doesn't, they'll appreciate the public thanks.

If your portfolio is a website, add its address to your email signature, along with one or two lines about its content. Be descriptive, short, and subtle. If you're good with words, try to include a teaser to draw people in.

Gabe Rubin uses the main graphic device from his portfolio on his html signature file. He also includes a link to his most recent project—an easy way for a prospective client to check him out immediately.

Redo your business card and put your URL on it. Never leave the house without carrying a few business cards with you. Go to art and design events, and offer your card when you can. Contacts in the community can lead to recommendations and referrals later.

List yourself at the basic level at sourcebook sites. Most of them allow you to post another Web address besides their own as part of your contact information.

Send out postcards (see the section, "Mailings," later in the chapter) to all your targeted prospects. Each time you update your site with new work, mail postcards again. That way, people know that you are still around and available.

CONTACTING INDIVIDUALS

You spent a lot of time researching target audience possibilities. Now is the time to pull that material out. You know who you'd like to work with and for, and now that you have a portfolio, it's time to let them know about you.

Email

If you found the name of a specific person, email is probably the best way to contact them. Even if their email address isn't on their website (although probably it is), it's usually pretty easy to figure it out. Look at the email addresses for other site contacts. Chances are they're all in one of these forms:

j.jones@firm.com	jjones@firm.com	Janine_j@firm.com
JanineJ@firm.com	Janine@firm.com	Jones@firm.com

Try them all, one at a time. The incorrect ones will bounce back to you, and the contact person will never know that you tried them. The correct version will hit their inbox.

Be sure to have a subject in the email that describes what you want. Good possibilities are "informational interview request" or "interested in your studio." Don't use subjects like "Hi!" or "want a job." Besides being unclear, they are headings that spam software reads as junk mail. The body of your email should also be clear and direct. Look at Chapter 9, "Creating written content," for suggestions on how to compose an appropriate email cover letter.

If the contact person doesn't reply, don't give up. Wait a few days, then politely acknowledge that they might be very busy, and ask if there is someone else at the firm to whom you might direct your email. You want to strike a balance between showing your interest and being too persistent.

Cold-calling

If you don't have the name of a person to speak with, call the company. Be straightforward about what you want, don't make them guess why you're calling, and above all, be polite. Ask if you can send your résumé and a PDF, or your portfolio URL. Describe succinctly and clearly the kind of work you do and why you think you might be a good fit with their firm.

Even if your contact says that there are no positions available, or that they're happy with their current suppliers, send a short follow-up note thanking them for giving you their time, and enclose your resume and URL. Situations can change quickly, and your information could arrive just as an employee unexpectedly leaves.

Mailings

If you are trying to get as much coverage as possible, one of the best ways to do that is through the mail. Do not send a copy of your portfolio…send a printed example of your work. Postcards are the best way to do that. They're inexpensive to send, and you can produce them yourself. Many studios keep a file of prospective freelancers and collaborators. When a new project comes in that requires a new hire or outside help, that file is one of the first places they look.

If something catches my eye, I put it in a file for future reference, to show to one of my designers, or to show to a client. In every case, it's easier to do this with a hard copy than a digital file. I recommend that photographers and illustrators use the tried-and-true postcard method. Every art director I know has a box or folder of work, filled with tearsheets, postcards, pages from magazines.

—Alex Isley

Your postcard should be extremely simple: an example of your work on one side, and your name, contact info, URL, and what you do (illustrator, interface designer, photographer, and so on) on the other. Check out **www.modernpostcard.com** for good-quality, reasonably priced custom postcards.

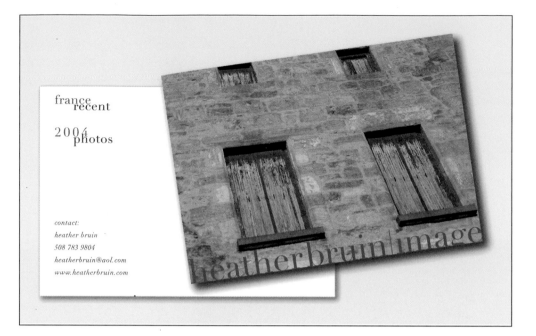

france recent

2004 photos

contact:
heather bruin
508 783 9804
heatherbruin@aol.com
www.heatherbruin.com

THE PERSONAL PRESENTATION

With any luck, between advertising, job listings, and your network, you'll get the chance to present your work—and yourself. You want to bolster the positive impression you've given by how you look and act in person. There are too many books and job sites that offer hints on interviewing well to list them here. One whose style and approach I like is *The Interview Rehearsal Book*, by Deb Gottesman.

> I want people to be fashionable. But I don't care whether or not they're wearing a suit.
>
> —Cynthia Rabun

Dress code

Even if you have very strong opinions about style and dress, avoid extreme clothing, and cover your tattoos. Being unwilling to adapt your style implies that you are inflexible, as well as being someone who would have to be insulated from most clients. Your work had better be astoundingly good to balance these negatives.

Dressing appropriately doesn't mean that you should show up clad in a corporate uniform. Clients expect a creative person to "look" creative. Sharp, good-quality clothes that telegraph a personal style are very acceptable for professionals in the arts.

Rehearsal

After you set up a date for a personal presentation, go through your portfolio and rehearse what you are going to say about each piece, and about your work in general. Rehearsal doesn't mean memorization, which leaves no room for personality or spontaneity. Nor does it mean developing a sales pitch. That turns other creative people off. It does mean having a sequence and feeling prepared, which should make you feel more confident.

How to rehearse

Don't just rehearse in your head—speak out loud and act the process out. If you are bringing a traditional portfolio with you, go through the physical act of presentation to make sure that it's easy to pull out mounted boards from a case, and that you can access each individual element without rummaging around for it.

Ask in advance if you'll be projecting your work. Most projectors are a generation behind desktops in screen resolution. Make a special version of your presentation to run at 800x600 resolution so you'll still be able to access your interface if the projector is an older one.

> People were never prepared to talk about their work with me, because I'm a recruiter. They were sometimes a little taken aback when I want to rip apart the portfolio and talk about their design approach.
>
> —Cynthia Rabun

Be prepared

You can't know in advance exactly who will be present at your interview, and how much knowledge they have. Even if it's "just" a screening meeting at a placement agency, bring your portfolio materials.

You'll want to clarify your role in creating the work, especially if you have done more than the design. Did you also create the illustrations or write the copy? Was the work completed in a very tight timeframe? Remember issues of attribution and honesty in Chapter 12, "Copyright & portfolio," and claim only your fair share of the work you present.

Know why you made your creative decisions, and find words to describe them. "It just came to me," will sound as weak as it is. How can you be hired as a client problem-solver if you can't describe the problem? If appropriate, bring process materials that aren't part of your regular portfolio to help you describe how you think.

Talking about your work can also involve listening. I once attended a presentation by a mid-career design professional who turned every query about how he approached a specific client problem into a lecture about how good he was at addressing client problems. Despite his reputation, this introduced doubts in his audience about whether they could work with him. He, too, clearly projected his own agenda.

> We don't ever hire anybody without an interview, and I interview all of the creatives that join us. I want to be sure that they're people who will fit well in this culture. I've always figured that if I like everybody who works here, they will like each other.
>
> —Stan Richards

Think about your personal assessment in Chapter 3, "Audience," and allow yourself to be who you really are. Your chemistry with the interviewers is something you can't control—either it's there or it isn't. But if you're prepared to field questions about how you deal with deadlines and your experiences in collaborative situations, it will be easier for you to loosen up and let your personality come through.

Presentation do's

These basic hints will help you enhance your portfolio with the presentation it deserves.

There's so much more that you need to evaluate. If you're hiring someone, you're looking at their personality and their demeanor—even their vocabulary in some cases. Are they going to be nice to be around? Are they going to take direction? And are they going to be capable of handling a client relationship or directing other people eventually?

—Nancy Hoefig

- **Face your audience.** Be familiar enough with your material that you can concentrate on the people you'll be presenting to, not your screen. Avoid turning your back while you present.
- **Speak up.** If people ask you to repeat what you've said, you are probably talking too softly or quickly.
- **Make eye contact.** If you want to know whether you can work with them—as well as whether they can work with you—try to catch your interviewers' eyes occasionally as you speak.
- **Show interest and enthusiasm.** Energy and good humor can be infectious. So can whining. Don't complain about your previous job, or introduce any negative topics about your past work experience.
- **Be proud of your portfolio.** Above all, never apologize for your work. You can discuss design constraints, your client's specific requirements, or problems and solutions, but never point out what's wrong with a piece or with your skills. That isn't perfectionism—it's suicide. By this time, you should have eliminated from your portfolio anything that doesn't reflect well on you.

FOLLOWING UP

If you are interested in the assignment or position, you should make that clear. The form you use will depend on the nature of the interaction and the position. For job or informational interviews, a thank-you note, particularly on your own letterhead or a nicely designed card, can make a big difference. But if time is important, it's better to send an email than to take the chance that they will decide before the snail mail arrives. It's also legitimate to make one follow-up phone call before you have to move on.

Finally, don't get discouraged if the presentation doesn't result in a job or assignment initially. Your style may not fit their current concept, or they may have found someone with more experience. Stay in touch. If you have a new collection of work in a few months, send if off to your contacts with a cover letter reminding them of who you are. Make phone calls on a regular cycle (once every six weeks is reasonable) to see if there's something new available, or if they'd like to see more work. Keep the conversations short and upbeat. If you had a PDF and add a website, or significantly update the website they saw originally, send a note to announce the URL and invite your contacts to visit it. If your work is good, persistence will be rewarded.

> People shouldn't take it personally when someone doesn't follow up. Just because someone doesn't call you back after they said that they're interested in talking to you, it doesn't mean that they're not interested. It just means that they haven't had the time.
>
> —Bill Cahan

Thank-you note

The text for a thank-you should be professional, short, and warm, but not effusive. It should be sent to the person who conducted the interview. Make sure you spell their name right, proof your work for spelling and grammatical errors, and don't refer to other people in the interview by name unless you are very certain of who they are. Do mention something specific about the interview, so they know your note isn't generic. Such a note could go something like this:

Dear Scott,

Thank you for the opportunity to present my portfolio to your group yesterday. I really appreciated the give and take, and hope we'll have the chance to continue the process in the future.

Hope to hear from you soon,

Linda Jones

STAYING RELEVANT

It's so tempting, once you finally have a portfolio in place, to treat it as a complete. Many people who use their portfolio as a tool to find a new job throw it on their mental shelf once they start the new position. But very few jobs are permanent. You should clean house and freshen your portfolio on a regular cycle. If you ignore it and let it become stale, you hasten the day when your portfolio can no longer be presented. It becomes a major project once again.

The simplest chore is to check your links, if you have any. One typical boo-boo is to fail to update your mail-to link when your provider email address changes. If you link to any sites outside your own (friends, Web-based projects you contributed to or designed) check every one to make sure that they haven't changed as well. Link-checking should go on your calendar as a monthly housecleaning task.

> Very often, a couple of years later, we'll take a look at a person's book, if he or she volunteers it to us. There may have been enough growth by that time that we have a serious interest.
>
> —Stan Richards

Of course, as you accumulate new projects, you should add them to your site, or replace some older ones. If you have created a modular design, inserting a new project should take very little time. The energy you invest in scanning or repurposing is small compared to the benefits of a lively, current site.

Many artists and designers include a résumé, vita, or biographical timeline as part of their portfolio. Every six months at least, you should look at these items again. Have you changed jobs, added a new, noteworthy client, or taken part in a group show? It's much easier to add new things while they are still fresh in your mind.

In general, pay close attention to places on your site that include specific dates. When you first put them up, they can be useful markers, and in some cases, as with annual reports, listing the year is almost obligatory. But as your site grows older, the lack of anything with the current year stands out as a signpost of a dead site.

AND, THE END. MAYBE.

With luck and perseverance, your digital portfolio will do its job and get you the recognition and clients you deserve. Once it does, celebrate! You've worked hard, and smart. Start your new job, or your new projects. But don't forget the portfolio that got you there. If you've chosen to make creativity your life's work, you owe it to yourself to continue to show the world your best efforts—your latest concepts. Your portfolio is never really finished until you stop creating. It's merely a stage in your constant journey to better work and more satisfaction.

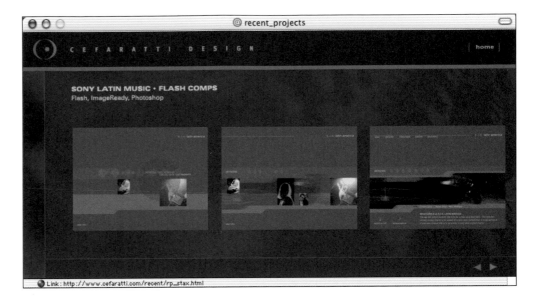

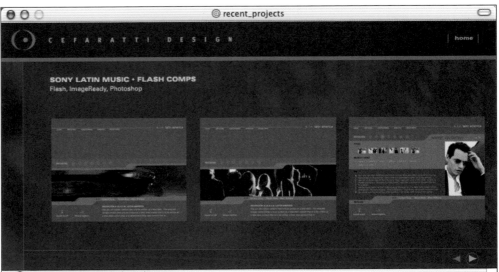

www.cefaratti.com

Mike Cefaratti's Recent Projects section is one way to add legs to an existing portfolio site. The original design remains intact, but a new section allows him to advertise his latest and greatest.

PORTFOLIO HIGHLIGHT:
IVAN TORRES | THE NEVERENDING STORY

www.meshsmith.com

One of the big challenges of having a personal portfolio is that as an artist, you are in motion. I needed more than a static site. I needed a tool that can go dynamically with me. And I need that expandability.

—Ivan Torres

For most people, having a portfolio that had gained national recognition—and still looks great—would be a justifiable excuse to relax. Update an occasional project, add a little news, or work on a tutorial to show your expertise, and you can just watch the work roll in. Many people do precisely that, and there's nothing wrong as long as your site continues to perform for you. But others can always see a way to improve on what they've done before, or have new ambitions for their portfolio or their career that they'd like to realize. For them, illustrator and designer Ivan Torres should stand as a role model.

By any standards, Meshsmith is a commendable portfolio, hard-working and effective. The work is up to date, and all links are functional. However, it's like a too-tight shoe for Ivan Torres. The site's architecture gives no space for new ideas or projects, and its navigation bar is already full. Adding more links would break the design integrity of the page. Beautiful as it is, Torres finds it cramps his need for growth and is deeply engaged in an ambitious rethinking and redesign. His new site will retain his current projects as one small segment of a geometrically larger environment.

Navigation and architecture

In Chapter 11, I said that all good sites—portfolio or otherwise—require a good site map. Without spending the time to organize your content, you'll inevitably be condemned to radical revision and projects that drag late into the night. Torres not only knows this lesson, he can recite chapter and verse. Although the look and feel is still a work in progress, the complex site architecture is fully formed, and easy to follow with the site map.

The way I am building this site is similar to building a house. First I am setting the base structure, which in this case can be a frame layout, Flash-based, etc. When the structure feels comfortable on the ground (the format, or the relation of the monitor sizes to the actual content) and all adjustments are done, I will begin to bring in the other components. I want to make the entire site very modular, so components can be easily expanded or dynamically updated.

—Ivan Torres

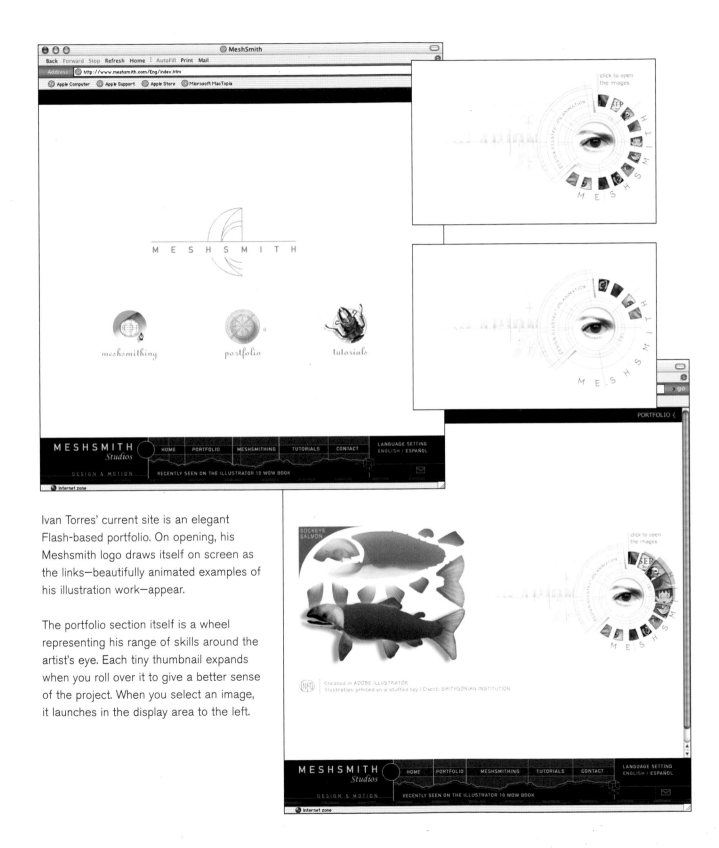

Ivan Torres' current site is an elegant Flash-based portfolio. On opening, his Meshsmith logo draws itself on screen as the links—beautifully animated examples of his illustration work—appear.

The portfolio section itself is a wheel representing his range of skills around the artist's eye. Each tiny thumbnail expands when you roll over it to give a better sense of the project. When you select an image, it launches in the display area to the left.

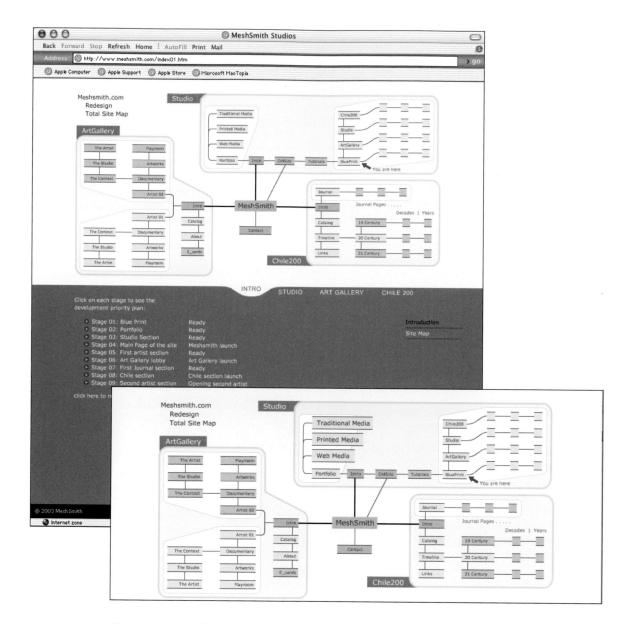

The new Meshsmith site map is an interactive space inside the Blueprint section. Like a real map, it has a "you are here" to orient you. Using it, it's easy to visualize the site's different areas and levels.

Roll over different areas of the site, and they enlarge to be more legible, an effective device that Torres uses in his current portfolio. Here, the considerably expanded portfolio section of the Studio is being explored.

The site map will remain in the redesigned site—an archive of the creative process behind the site's design and development.

The building metaphor is very appropriate for Ivan Torres' new site. He envisions three separate, but linked, spaces, each of which contains rooms of its own. A gateway Intro page like a lobby will provide access to three discrete areas: Studio, Art Gallery, and Chile 200—an historical-cultural site celebrating Torres' home country of Chile in its bicentennial year. Each of these areas will have its own introductory page and its own interface design, and will function like a separate site.

Elements of the old site are visible in the new one, not as interface graphics, but as ways of thinking about an interface. For example, the site will continue to have a navigation bar at the bottom of the page, and the window will likely maintain the same overall dimensions.

I've been always a big fan of the proportions of Le Corbusier and the modernist movement. But I'm extracting the thought process more than the look. I want my eyes to breathe on the website.

—Ivan Torres

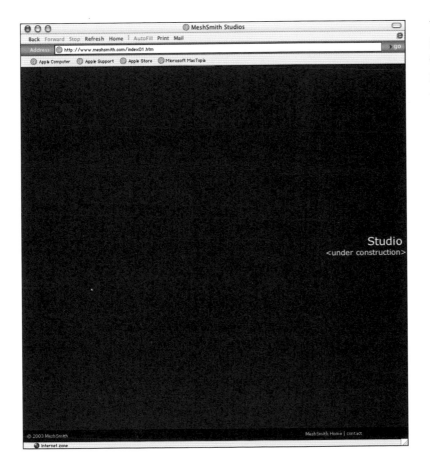

The structural metaphor Torres is using for his portfolio site takes more concrete form in his renderings of virtual spaces for the gallery section.

These placeholder pages are the skeleton of the site to come. The Studio intro page is still in development. The contents page, however, already has the beginnings of a layout. A space is blocked out for the portfolio image, and a navigation device is planned as a grid below the image area. Creating such outline pages helps Torres, his collaborators in Chile, and interested colleagues visualize and give feedback on his plans.

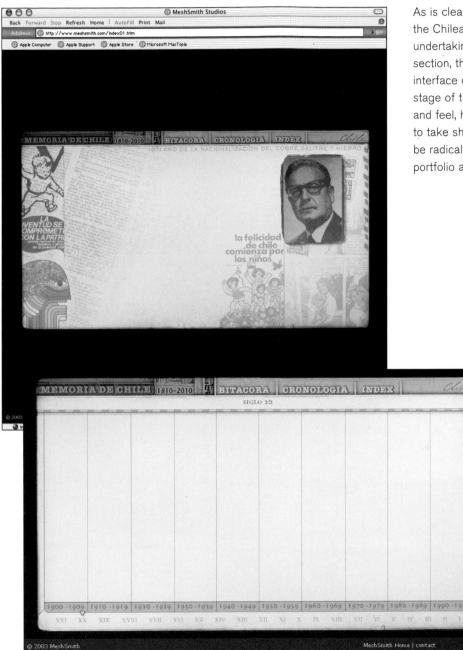

As is clear from the site map, the Chilean site is a major undertaking. Like the studio section, the introductory page's interface design will be the last stage of the process. The look and feel, however, is beginning to take shape, and will clearly be radically different from other portfolio areas.

The gallery and history project are two big works where I have artistic freedom. They are outside the main portfolio. When customers or clients want to know all of the things I do, I'm going to send them to the lobby area so they can see these three sections. But I'll send the targeted audiences directly to each area, I'll send them directly to each one, because each section will have a very different look.

—Ivan Torres

Content

Although all the spaces are related to his work, only one part is a traditional portfolio, in the sense that Torres shows a sampling of a variety of projects. This content, however, will be expanded to include not just his computer-based illustration, but scans of his traditional art and examples of his web design.

Although the other two sections of the site will not be called "portfolio," they are as much a part of his work as the studio section. In effect, they are similar in concept to the portfolio that includes links to live websites. The gallery is a professional experiment in a new model for web-based galleries where Torres will host other artists. The Chilean site is a research project and journal created in collaboration with others, but hosted on Meshsmith. In both, he has clients, but a great deal of creative control.

Working process

Unlike other portfolio sites profiled in this book, Torres' current plans are his future ones. The site has been moving forward through its stages for several months of preparation. Torres is closing in on designing the actual interfaces for the discrete sections, and expects to have the site go live in stages. The first may be ready as you read this.

Ivan Torres combines meticulous planning with elegant presentation. He treats his portfolio as his most important project—a way to enlarge his client base, share his work with friends and collaborators, and provide an important creative outlet. Hopefully, he can inspire you to do the same.

I'm having fun. It's like I'm moving with the project. It's not like I know all the answers down the road. Like, I'm going in the jungle, trying to open my way in.

—Ivan Torres

PART V

Appendixes

Resources

A bountiful collection of portfolio resources is just a few mouse clicks away. Although I've been forced to group these sites under headings for ease of use, you'll find that some sites, particularly those for associations, actually offer listings or information in other categories.

Copyright and legal issues

These sites address intellectual property and the law. They're good places to check in for help in registering your portfolio content and keeping your nose clean when you're not sure what you can, and can't, legally do.

Art Law Center

www.artlaws.com

The Art Law Center offers intellectual property and other legal services to creatives. The site has a collection of standard legal forms, useful articles, and links.

Copyright Website

www.benedict.com

This site is dedicated to intellectual property issues of all sorts. It has a copyright wizard that painlessly and quickly walks you through the process of filing a copyright on your work.

Digimarc

www.digimarc.com

Digimarc is the developer of the best-known method of embedding watermarks in digital images. The site explains how the technology works, and allows you to enable the service plug-in.

United States Copyright Office

lcweb.loc.gov/copyright/

This is the site for the U.S. government's copyright office. It's a well-written, easy-to-navigate site for downloading relevant publications and registering your work.

Group sites and forums

This group of sites is particularly handy for posting your portfolio for feedback (taken with a grain of salt, I hope), or for marketing to potential clients or employers. Some are specific to one or two disciplines; others are open to all creatives.

Animation and modeling

CG Channel

www.cgchannel.com/forum/

This glossy site is dedicated to all forms of computer graphics. Besides providing news and interviews, it boasts a large and vital community that revolves around their forums. The Cool Links forum allows registered users to post links to their own sites or others of interest, and then open them to critique and discussion. In addition, there is a formal portfolio area called CG Art divided by type of work, and a recruitment section with job listings.

Gallery of 3D.com
www.galleryof3d.com

Less glossy than some of the other sites devoted to the 3D community, this site is exactly what its name implies. It displays member animations and 3D renderings. Anyone can become a member and post their work, but the site also profiles some members and places a few in the Cream Gallery. Among the forums is one (3Dartwork>Critique) dedicated to peer critiques.

InsideCG.com
www.insidecg.com   www.cgchat.com/forum/

The computer graphics community is full of enthusiasts, which may be why there are so many good sites and forums for them. Industry focused, this site has a large community following, in part because of a good jobs listing and a great sub-site forum that includes separate posting/critiquing areas for 2D and 3D work.

Flay.com
flay.com

Flay has been around for what is, in Internet terms, a long time—since 1996. Similar to other forum-based CG sites in format, Flay offers a particularly strong Jobs section with postings sorted with the most recent (and most likely to still be unfilled) at the top. Newly posted links are advertised in the navigation area, but the links and galleries are sorted alphabetically—making it harder for someone late in the alphabet to be found by chance.

Fine arts

Absolutearts.com and World Wide Arts Resources
www.absolutearts.com   wwar.com

This is a marketplace and portfolio site for fine artists. It offers a mailing list of dealers and galleries for the artist trying to get a show or representation, and has a large gallery and portfolio database. The basic portfolio of four images is free. As of this printing, a 40-image portfolio is $36 per year, and the premiere version—a mind-boggling 1,000 images—is $75.

ArtistsRegister.com
artistsregister.com

This site, run by WESTAF (Western States Arts Federation), positions itself as a marketing tool to connect artists with both art buyers and galleries, non-profit organizations, and participating state agencies. Membership is by application, and requires a membership fee.

Artvitae.com
www.artvitae.com

A multi-lingual portfolio site used by artists in both the U.S. and Europe, the site boasts a substantial database of artists' curriculum vitae and their portfolios. For an annual fee, you can use their template to quickly get your information and a sampling of your work online, or you can design, create, and manage your own portfolio but use the site as a home address. One nice touch: Their ArtPostcards service allows both visitors and artists to email postcards of work—a nice way to do a cold-call email.

Art in Context Center for Communications
www.artincontext.org

This is a non-profit site that creates a library of artists and organizations. They will put you into their searchable database for a small registration fee, which is renewable for a small discount annually. Because it's part of the art community and not a commercial venture, it attracts many academics and museum curators. Posting an image along with your vitae information will incur an additional cost per image.

Graphic arts and design

Communication Arts
www.commarts.com

Communication Arts is a magazine whose site includes one of the very best job and portfolio listings for the design professions. Jobs can be viewed by location, title, or discipline. In addition, using their template, you can create a portfolio and profile and post for free in their Creative HotLists section. The site also provides occasional articles of great value on career and other professional topics.

Coroflot
www.coroflot.com

Coroflot is a cross-disciplinary professional development site for creatives, although it is most frequently used by people in the related areas of graphic design, interaction, and industrial design. It provides a comprehensive listing of design firms and organizations, a very good job board, and a portfolio site used by professionals around the world. The posting rules are generous: Posting of five images, including animations, is free. You create a portfolio by uploading your work into their template, which includes a link to your own portfolio site if you have one. The site also has forums devoted to design careers and practice.

Graphic Artists Guild Portfolios
portfolios.gag.org

The Graphic Artists Guild offers a portfolio site for its members only. Areas range from cartooning to graphic design to video/broadcast design. There are two options: a free link from your own site to the guild one, or a guild-hosted page for someone who doesn't yet have their own site.

Portfolios.com
www.portfolios.com

Along with the California site, this is the best sourcebook site for most creatives—from ID specialists to photographers—to post a basic portfolio and market their work. It has a good and efficient search engine, so if you are specific with your keywords, your name should come up when people look for your specialty. Portfolios come in several levels, with the basic portfolio—the best level if you have your own, dedicated site—allowing the free posting of five static images. The next larger site supports QuickTime, Flash, and PDFs, but costs $21.95 a month.

PROFESSIONAL ORGANIZATIONS

Not at all comprehensive, this group of associations represents the best-known and most useful organizations for creatives. Most offer a variety of member benefits, including career help and job listings. See the Directories section later in this appendix for links to an encyclopedic catalog of organizations.

ACM (Association for Computing Machinery)
www.acm.org

Far more than its name might suggest, the ACM is the home of the special interest group (SIG) SIGGRAPH. This group can be an extremely valuable networking resource for creatives in animation, modeling, and interactivity. Another good group for Web professionals is SIGCHI, which covers areas of human-computer interaction and usability.

AIA (American Institute of Architects)
www2.aia.org

The defining organization for architecture, this site offers extensive career and job search support. Their "Find and Architect" database allows potential clients to search the member listing with very specific criteria. Architects looking for a firm can post a résumé on the site. In addition, there are several articles and links for professional development.

AIGA (American Institute for Graphic Arts)
www.aiga.org

AIGA partners with Aquent to provide an excellent job posting area for graphic design and related positions in the U.S. Although anyone can search the listings, you must be an AIGA member to post a job-seeker profile. The AIGA site also hosts a lively collection of forums and sponsors discussion lists on design theory and practice.

American Society of Media Photographers
www.asmp.org

Professional photographers, particularly those who shoot for advertising and editorial clients, will find help with business issues, a listing of local chapters, and a friendly network of people like you at this site. They have a gallery where they feature members' work, and a good database for photo buyers.

Broadcast Designers of America (BDA)
www.bda.tv

This site is the resource for creatives in broadcast design to connect with others through the message boards, create a link to your portfolio site, or search for posted jobs. You must register to be able to post, but the registration is free.

Graphic Artists Guild
www.gag.org

A multi-discipline organization for industry creatives, particularly designers (graphic, web, and so on) and illustrators. This site is particularly useful for freelancers and small studios, with chapters in many cities in the U.S.

Industrial Designers Society of America
www.idsa.org

The IDSA is to industrial designers what the AIGA is for graphic designers. It covers a variety of related disciplines with ID: from furniture to consumer electronics to usability design. Included on the site is a listing of employment opportunities, as well as ID firms. The site offers links to each of the local chapters.

National Portfolio Day Association
www.npda.org

The National Portfolio Day Association is an invaluable clearinghouse for portfolio days for all disciplines that take place throughout the U.S. and Canada. It offers a month-by-month calendar of portfolio events, with links to the sponsoring organizations' email contacts and websites.

Rhode Island School of Design
intranet.risd.edu/alumni/weblink/

Most art and design schools have websites, and offer services to their students. I single out RISD's site, however, because it is particularly full and rich. It provides a comprehensive list of extremely useful links on topics ranging from a listing of job banks to company profiles, ostensibly for alumni, but available to anyone. For RISD students and alumni, the school sponsors a special subsite on portfolios.com, and provides an excellent online database for jobs.

Society for Environmental Graphic Design
www.segd.org

If your interests lie in the real world of three-dimensional environments—from exhibit design to architecture to ID—this site is what you need. It has a job bank with very detailed postings and a new referrals section where SEGD members can provide profiles for potential clients.

Art Directors Clubs

In addition, there are Art Directors Clubs in several major cities, including, of course, the flagship Art Directors Club in New York City (**www.adcny.org**).

Other club links are as follows:

Cincinnati	**www.adcc.org**
Denver	**www.adcd.com**
Houston	**www.carlberg.com/adch/main.html**
Washington, DC	**www.adcmw.org**

DIRECTORIES

It's impossible to list in this short appendix all the directories for researching companies, studios, or business opportunities. They could be gathered into their own short book. The best places to start are links from organizations in your specific area of specialization. After that, searches in the Open Directory project (**dmoz.org**), Yahoo (**yahoo.com**), and in Google's Directory tab (**google.com**) are extremely useful. To search all these sites at once (and more), visit **www.thrall.org/proteus.html**.

In addition, this small sampling of resource sites are essential to creatives:

Bogieland Information Design and Architecture
www.bogieland.com/infodesign/resources/

This international listing zeroes in on resources for information designers. It has live links to an alphabetical listing of firms from the U.S. to Japan, links to information designers and information architects, and the jobs section.

Business to Business Resources
www.business-to-business-resources.com

This site is perfect for researching potential clients, or for local design or advertising firms.

creativepro
www.creativepro.com/directory/home

This is the mother of all directories for creatives. You can find every creative association in the U.S., as well as a comprehensive listing of agencies, firms, publishers, and suppliers.

The Designers Network
designers-network.com

This is an international blog-based directory of firms and advertising agencies, with short descriptions of each one. It also offers a listing of freelance artists and illustrators. The Designers Network is invaluable for locating small local possibilities, particularly when you're contemplating relocation.

The Firm List
us.firmlist.com

Looking for a web-design firm who might be looking for someone like you? If so, this is a good first stop. Listings are sorted by state, then by city/town.

CAREER SITES

Like directories and associations, there are dozens of career sites. Some are very local; others are truly enormous. Rather than try to cover every permutation, I've provided three very different ways to approach a job search: a large, extremely rich general site, a creatives-only company, and a targeted creative recruitment firm.

Vault
www.vault.com

All careers, all jobs, all the time. The Vault is not a creative's site, but it has research on over 3,000 companies (great for targeting an audience) and a daunting collection of message boards where you can read what people who are (or were) working at these companies have to say about the experience.

The Creative Group
www.creativegroup.com

The Creative Group is a staffing firm for marketing and advertising creatives. It has placement offices in a variety of cities around the U.S. The website allows you to search for opportunities by geographical local and job description, as well as by keyword. Each local area posts a small portfolio for their featured artists on the main website.

Roz Goldfarb Associates
www.rga-joblink.com

Roz Goldfarb Associates is a recruitment firm in NYC specializing in creatives of all sorts. Most of the jobs listed there are for established professionals, not entry-level positions. They are broken down into job categories, and the number of postings in each area are listed—a fast way to see what types of positions are generating traffic.

SOFTWARE HELP BOOKS

You'll need to master at least one software program in making your digital portfolio. You may need more than one. There are many excellent books to choose from as companions in your learning process—usually more than one covers its topic effectively. The ones that follow are simply my personal pick of books that I think cover their topics well.

Create Your Own DVDs
By Brian Underdahl

This is an unusual book, because it covers not one, but several applications, while also explaining the basics of preparing and making a good DVD. Really good for Windows users.

DVD Studio Pro
By Martin Sitter

For Macintosh creative professionals, I recommend *DVD Studio Pro* over *iDVD*, even though it is not as blindingly easy to understand. Sitter's book eases the transition and handles the application well.

Eric Meyer on CSS: Mastering the Language of Web Design
By Eric Meyer

A truly well-designed website needs formats and good typography. With style sheets, you can attain these goals. With this book, you'll actually know what you're doing, and why.

JavaScript for the World Wide Web
By Tom Negrino and Dori Smith

I'm prejudiced, because the authors are good friends. But I thought the book covered the subject beautifully even before I knew them. If you need a little website scripting, this is the book for you.

Web Design in a Nutshell
By Jennifer Niederst

A clear and concise explanation of how to make a website, from soup to nuts.

Macromedia Dreamweaver MX 2004 Hands-On Training
By Garo Green

Lynda Weinman (**lynda.com**) really knows how to do effective training, and she has a designer's touch as well. If you need to use Dreamweaver, this book by Garo Green, lynda.com's Director of Publications, is required reading. *Macromedia Flash MX 2004 Hands-On Training*, by Rosanna Yeung, is an equally good resource.

Visual QuickStart Series
By Peachpit Press

In addition, almost all the Peachpit *Visual QuickStart* series will help you master the software they cover. They are inexpensive, well-organized, and easy-to-follow references.

Contributors

This book would have been far less rich, attractive, and exciting without the words and images of this international group of professionals, who so graciously allowed me to showcase their talents and ply them with questions. Some are at the beginning of their careers, and are certain to surprise and delight with their future great work and terrific portfolios. Others are well-respected professionals at the top of their game, who were generous enough to donate their time and thoughts to this project. My only regret is that I couldn't show more of their work, and include all of their insights.

MICHAEL BARTALOS

Illustrator   www.bartalos.com

Michael Bartalos was born in Germany and grew up in the New York metropolitan area. He studied at the Art Institute of Chicago and Pratt Institute, where he earned a BFA degree. He has worked extensively in the graphic arts in the U.S. and Japan, creating works both digitally and by hand. He also produces limited edition letter-pressed artist's books, postcards, and assemblages using unconventional printing materials. He lives and works in San Francisco with his wife, Lili, and their son, André.

MICHAEL BOROSKY

Creative Director, Eleven, Inc.   www.eleveninc.com

Michael Borosky spent the first 15 years of his career working in the traditional (offline) side of the design business for a variety of firms, including the San Francisco office of Pentagram. He started specializing in online media after joining CKS Partners (which then became USWeb/CKS and later still, MarchFirst). As Creative Director, he led interactive projects for clients ranging from MCI to General Motors, Visa, and Levi Strauss. As partner and Creative Director at Eleven, Michael oversees the online brand integration for a wide range of clients, including Kodak, Microsoft, and Williams-Sonoma.

RICK BRAITHWAITE

President, Sandstrom Design   www.sandstromdesign.com

Rick Braithwaite co-founded Sandstrom Design in 1990 after 16 years in the advertising industry. He has three children, two grandchildren, and is an avid golfer, hiker, and reader. He grew up in Los Angeles, spent three years as an officer in the Marines, and has been married for 34 years. He is a former President of APDF (Association of Professional Design Firms), loves the theater and long walks on the beach, and is the only male in America who has not appeared on a reality TV show.

BILL CAHAN

Founder and Creative Director, Cahan & Associates
www.cahanassociates.com

Widely praised for its evocative annual reports, packaging, corporate branding, advertising, and web design, San Francisco-based Cahan & Associates has a diverse clientele ranging from Fortune 500 companies to consumer, high-tech, and biotech leaders to emerging growth companies. The company has won over 2000 awards and garnered write-ups in hundreds of periodicals and books. The Princeton Architectural Press book, *I Am Almost Always Hungry*, chronicles the agency's culture, process, and portfolio. Most recently, Cahan's penchant for refreshing the stodgy world of annual reports has been chronicled in "Cahan & Associates on Annual Reports."

MIKE CEFARATTI

Principal, Cefaratti Design   cefaratti.com

In his eight years in new media and broadcast design, Mike has created Web-based solutions for agencies like Think New Ideas, Nicholson NY/IconMedialab, DePlano Group, Atmosphere, and Plural. He has played a critical role in the strategic development and execution of branded internet solutions, CD-ROMs, television commercials, and music compositions. Most notably, he has created award-winning sites for both Avon and Rockport, and developed websites and banner campaigns for clients including AIG, Chase, Marriott, and Frito-Lay. Mike holds degrees in both marketing and graphic design. He currently works in New York City as a freelance designer.

CHRIS DAVIS

Partner | Designer, Horsepower Design   www.horsepowerdesign.net

Chris Davis is a partner in the Seattle-based design firm Horsepower Design. He graduated from the School of Visual Communications at California State University, Chico, and then started his career at Landor Associates, London. Moving back to the states in 1996, he settled into Seattle and co-founded Horsepower Design with another designer from his alma mater, Jeff Rodriguez. Their firm's unique solutions help to forge a deeper connection between clients and their customers.

BRITT FUNDERBURK

Principal, Dialogbox   dialogbox.com

Britt Funderburk has specialized in interactive design since 1995, and has extensive experience in creative direction, branding, and information architecture. Britt has led the design of websites for Discovery Online, Icon | Nicholson, Children's Television Workshop, Oxygen Media, Inc., and AOL/Time Warner, among many others. He has worked on a wide range of interactive projects, from information kiosks and interactive features to web advertising, e-commerce, entertainment, and corporate branding sites. His work has been internationally recognized by *ID Magazine*, *Print* magazine, the AIGA, MILIA, and more.

CHRIS GRIMLEY

Senior Designer | Architect
Machado and Silvetti Associates, Boston   file-cabinet.org

After receiving a MArch (Honors) from the University of British Columbia, Grimley has worked both in Canada and the United States. His areas of research include the relationship between architecture and interior design; how digital tools can be used in the development of an architectural language; and the ways in which criticism and architectural journalism can aid in public debates about architecture. Chris is the founder of file-cabinet.org, an interdisciplinary group of artists and architects who publish work and criticism on the Internet, and an editor of the architectural magazine, *loudpaper*.

NANCY HOEFIG

Principal, Hoefig Design   hoefigdesign.com

Nancy Hoefig brings more than twenty years experience in brand image campaigns and design systems to Fortune 500 clients, including BP, Charles Schwab, Ford Motor Company, and Visa. Before founding Hoefig Design, Nancy served as Creative Director at Landor Associates, an Associate Partner at Pentagram in New York, Executive Art Director at CBS in New York, Deputy Art Director at the *New York Times Magazine*, and as a Principal with The Richards Group in Dallas. Nancy holds a BFA in Graphic Design from Syracuse University and served as an instructor at The School of Visual Arts in New York. She has received numerous awards from AIGA, CA, Cleo, Graphis, Mead Show, Potlatch Annual Report Show, NY Art Directors Club, Society of Illustrators, Society of Publication Designers, and Type Directors Club.

ALEXANDER ISLEY

Principal, Alexander Isley Inc.   www.alexanderisley.com

Alexander Isley heads Alexander Isley Inc., a nine-person design firm with offices in Connecticut and NYC. He is also a partner in The Dave and Alex Show, an advertising and marketing communications agency. Alex is a graduate of The Cooper Union and the N.C. State University College of Design. He is a visiting critic at the Yale Graduate School of Art.

JEFF KAPHINGST

Graphic Designer   www.jeffthedesigner.com

Jeff Kaphingst is a graphic designer working in the Minneapolis, Minnesota area. Jeff attended Northeastern University's Graphic Design program in the early stages of its development, receiving his design education in an environment where experimentation with a wide range of media was encouraged. Jeff continues to use his interests in illustration, photography, and animation to create primary elements for his work both in print and interactive media.

MARY ANN KEARNS

Curator, 911 Gallery   911gallery.org

Mary Ann Kearns has an M.A. in art history, but believes that "art history" is in the making. Her exhibits have been reviewed in *Art New England*, *The Boston Globe*, *ARTnews*, and *The New York Times*. In 1992, Kearns co-founded 911 Gallery, which specializes exclusively in digital media. In 1994, it became one of the first galleries to exhibit on the Internet. Kearns is a major organizer of the Boston Cyberarts Festival, co-organizing seven events in 1999 and 2001. In 2003, she curated two exhibits for the third biennial Boston Cyberarts Festival, at the new Art Interactive Gallery in Cambridge, and at the Brush Gallery in Lowell. Both shows featured pioneering video artists and art.

LAYLA KERAMAT

Senior Designer, frog design, inc.   layla_keramat@yahoo.com

After attending the State University of New York in Binghamton, Layla Keramat began her design career at Sony Music Entertainment GmbH in her hometown of Frankfurt, Germany. There she designed branding, packaging, and advertising for a multitude of international artists, such as Bruce Springsteen and Mariah Carey. After 10 years, she moved to New York to lead a team developing direct mail components for The Columbia House Company. In 1999, Layla transitioned to design consultancy for a variety of user interface and brand projects. Layla's work has been published in Europe and in the U.S. She is an Adjunct Professor in typography in the Graphic Design Department at the School of Visual Arts.

YANG KIM

Principal and Creative Director, BBK Studio   bbkstudio.com

Yang Kim's fruitful client collaborations include efficient communications management for Southern California-based SitOnIt Seating, edgy retail brochures for Jaguar Cars, and landmark annual reports for Herman Miller. Yang's work has been recognized by major design competitions including the New York Art Directors Club, the Type Directors Club of New York, *Communication Arts* magazine, *Critique* magazine, the American Institute of Graphic Art, *Graphis*, *How* magazine, *ID* (International Design) *Magazine*, the Mead Annual Report Show, *Print* magazine, *AR100*, and *Creativity*. Yang has served as a judge in many international design shows and conferences. She has a BFA in Graphic Design from Carnegie Mellon University.

KEN LOH

Creative Director, Overture Services, Inc.   kenloh.com

Ken Loh has created materials for a wide range of clients including Sega, Reebok, Pioneer Electronics, the NFL, NBA, and NHL. His primary interest is in creating brands and fully integrated campaigns that span traditional and interactive media. He strives for work that communicates its intended message while maintaining a high level of execution and creativity. At Overture Services, Inc., his in-house group is responsible for developing Overture's brand, communications, and user experience, from strategy to concept to final implementation. Mr. Loh is a graduate of the Visual Communications program at California State University, Long Beach.

PATRICK MARCKESANO

Architect, Donovan Hill Architects   marckesano.com

Patrick Marckesano graduated from UC Berkeley in 2001 with a bachelor's degree in architecture. He currently resides in Brisbane, Australia, where he works for Donovan Hill Architects. In the interval between his education and current career, he lived and worked in Scandinavia—a region and culture that he credits as the source for much of his own design sensibility. In addition to architecture, Patrick has worked variously in web, print, and fashion design.

Lili Ong

Graphic Designer   lili@bartalos.com

Lili Ong was born in Singapore and holds a BS degree in Computer Science from the University of Hawaii and a BA in Graphic Design from the Academy of Art, San Francisco. Her design experience has taken her from editorial work in Singapore to Yomiko Advertising in Tokyo, followed by positions with Pentagram Design, Jacqueline Jones Design, and the Burdick Group in San Francisco. She currently designs on a freelance basis.

Cemre Ozkurt

Animator, Blur Studios   cemre@3dluvr.com

Cemre Ozkurt was born and was educated in Istanbul, including studying at the Carsaf Caricature School for seven years. He started animating on his brother's Amiga when he was 7 years old, creating short animations and educational multimedia games. At 13, he displayed his drawings as the youngest caricaturist in Turkey. His work was published in many magazines, and won several awards in international competitions. He entered the Graphic Design Academy at Mimar Sinan University, creating 2D and 3D illustrations and animations. Currently, Cemre lives in Hollywood and works at Blur Studios.

Cynthia Rabun

Staffing Director, Dolby, Inc.

Cynthia Rabun has over 15 years experience recruiting creative and marketing professionals for companies as diverse as Sony Music Entertainment Inc., Levi Strauss, and Landor Associates. Currently, she heads up the recruitment function for Dolby in San Francisco, CA. Cynthia has a bachelor's degree from U.C. Berkeley's Business Administration, where she studied marketing.

Stan Richards

Principal, The Richards Group   Richards.com

Stan Richards founded The Richards Group, now one of the nation's premier creative resources, after graduating from New York's Pratt Institute. His work has received awards in virtually every major competition in the world. The company was named ADWEEK's Agency of the Year five times between 1988 and 2002. In 1997, *Graphis* magazine named The Richards Group one of the 10 best agencies in the world. Stan received the AIGA Gold Medal for career achievement in design in 1996, and in 1999, he received the highest honor available to a creative with his election to the Art Directors Hall of Fame, joining such luminaries as Walt Disney, Norman Rockwell, and Andy Warhol.

GABE RUBIN

Graphic Designer, 65 Media   wrecked.nu

By the time Gabe Rubin was 9, he had already lived in three countries and three states. The last place his father was stationed before he retired from the military was Charleston, SC, where he spent the majority of his childhood growing up, and one day plans to return. He had always loved the arts and being creative, so it was only a matter of time until he stumbled upon graphic design as a hobby and later on as a profession. Having just turned 21, he is off to 65Media in the whimsical yet gratuitous City of Angels to embark upon his career (and raise a little hell while he's at it).

JON SANTOS

Principal, Common Space   commonspace.fm

Jon Santos received his BFA in graphic design at CCAC in 2000. As an artist who works in print and digital media, Jon considers Common Space, a multidisciplinary design studio based in New York, NY, to be an exploration into the universal nature of communication, by studying the structural relationships between audio and visual media. In addition, Jon designs graphics for varied musical projects. He is a DJ himself and regularly collaborates with emerging electronic musicians, allowing him to apply theory into practice. As a student, Jon was nominated one of the top forty designers under thirty by *ID Magazine*, and he received the AIGA medal of distinction.

JOHN SHARPE

Principal, Sharpe & Associates, Inc.   www.sharpeonline.com

Sharpe & Associates, Inc. is a Los Angeles-based national creative repping agency specializing in style-driven commercial photographers. John Sharpe began his career on the agency side of the advertising business as an account executive, where he learned the value of having a point of difference versus the competition—a lesson he's used ever since. While beginning his business career as a suit, he quickly realized he enjoyed the creative side of advertising more. Recognizing his own limitations in creating and executing commercial art, he decided to apply his agency experience to marketing photographers. In his spare time, John fancies himself a sculptor in the lost art of papier-mâché.

ROBERT SHEARING

Industrial Designer   rob.id.au

Robert Shearing was born in London in 1976. When he was 16, he moved with his parents and brothers to Australia. He first studied electronic and computer engineering, but switched to product design when he realized that this would best suit his interests and abilities. Robert graduated with an industrial design degree from the University of Technology Sydney, where he is currently lecturing part-time in digital portfolio design. He also has his own product and web design consultancy in Sydney. Robert has designed websites for a range of clients, including product designers, engineering and exhibition display companies, and a recording studio.

JAMEY STILLINGS

Photographer   www.jameystillings.com

Jamey Stillings' work spans advertising, documentary, and fine art photography. A passionate interest in people, world cultures, and travel are guiding forces in his photography and life. Personal and assignment work are approached with similar sensitivities: to celebrate the human spirit and seek magic moments of light and expression within each image. For over twenty years, Stillings has traveled throughout the world for a wide range of international clients, enjoying assignments that bring unique challenges and experiences. Find more of his work at **jameystillings.com**.

GUNNAR SWANSON

Principal, Gunnar Swanson Design Office   gunnarswanson.com

Gunnar Swanson's design has won over fifty awards and publications for trademark, publication, type, packaging, and graphic design from the AIGA, *Print*, *Graphis*, *How*, the American Corporate Identity series, and other graphic design organizations, books, and magazines. His articles have appeared in many periodicals, been included in three major graphic design anthologies, and been published internationally. He is the editor and designer of the Allworth Press book, *Graphic Design & Reading*. He has taught at the Otis College of Art and Design and the University of California Davis, headed the graphic design program at the University of Minnesota Duluth, and directed the multimedia program at California Lutheran University.

SO TAKAHASHI

Principal, Heads, inc.   www.headsinc.com

So Takahashi, born in Japan, moved to New York in 1992 to study graphic design at the School of Visual Arts. After graduating, he started his career as a graphic designer and opened his studio 1998. So has had a varied design career. His assignments are mainly concerned with art direction and design for the cosmetics industry, but he is also involved in other fields. He has released three albums of electronic music on the New York label, Carpark Records, and is also involved in product design. So has won several awards, including from The Art Directors Club New York, The Tokyo Art Directors Club, and SPD, and he was also featured in the Young Guns Show Exhibit and book, published by The Art Directors Club New York.

IVAN TORRES

Illustrator and Web Designer   www.meshsmith.com

Ivan Torres began his career as a fine artist in Patagonia, Chile, where he worked on such diverse projects as mural painting, stage design, and theatrical production. His arrival in the United States marked the beginning of his interest in computer graphics. His work has been featured in several respected computer illustration books. Ivan resides in Southern California with his wife, Jessica, where he works a senior web designer for an advertising agency, as well as a freelance interactive designer.

Index

Symbols

2D graphics (category of creative professionals), 11
    graphic artist portfolios, 12
    photographer portfolios, 11
3D materials, photographing, 104
    camera selection, 104
    lighting, 107
    stage setup, 105-107

A

absolute links, 257
Absolutearts.com website, 283
ACM (Association for Computing Machinery) website, 285
Acrobat PDFs. *See* PDFs
adapting artwork. *See* repurposing artwork
adjusting. *See* editing
admission portfolios, 9
advertising finished portfolio, 262
AIA (American Institute of Architects) website, 285
AIGA (American Institute for Graphic Arts) website, 285
alumni associations as research tools, 48-49
American Society of Media Photographers website, 286
analog video formats, resolution of, 111
animation forum websites, 282-283
animator portfolios, 17-18
architect portfolios, 13
architecture
    BBK Studios case study, 54-57
    Britt Funderburk case study, 228-231

Eleven, Inc. case study, 134-135
    Gabe Rubin case study, 95-96
    Horsepower Design (HPD) case study, 36-37
    Ivan Torres case study, 270-274
    Jon Santos case study, 206-207
    Ken Loh case study, 249-251
    Michael Cefaratti case study, 157-158
    Sandstrom Design case study, 181-182
    So Takahashi case study, 202
archiving. *See* backup files; cataloging
art (category of creative professionals), 8
    fine artist portfolios, 10-11
    student portfolios, 9
Art Directors Club websites, 287
Art in Context Center for Communications website, 284
Art Law Center website, 282
artifacts, 124
ArtistsRegister.com website, 283
Artvitae.com website, 284
artwork. *See also* original artwork; samples; traditional materials
    line art, editing, 127-128
    organizing, 86-87
    photographing, 85
    repurposing
        Michael Cefaratti case study, 155-160
        with PDFs, 141-143
        tips for, 140-141
    storing original artwork, 85
        digital output, 86
        traditional materials, 85
aspect ratio, 150
assessment. *See* self-evaluation
assignment of rights, 244

Q-R

Visit Peachpit on the Web at www.peachpit.com

- Read the latest articles and download timesaving tipsheets from best-selling authors such as Scott Kelby, Robin Williams, Lynda Weinman, Ted Landau, and more!

- Join the Peachpit Club and save 25% off all your online purchases at peachpit.com every time you shop—plus enjoy free UPS ground shipping within the United States.

- Search through our entire collection of new and upcoming titles by author, ISBN, title, or topic. There's no easier way to find just the book you need.

- Sign up for newsletters offering special Peachpit savings and new book announcements so you're always the first to know about our newest books and killer deals.

- Did you know that Peachpit also publishes books by Apple, New Riders, Adobe Press, Macromedia Press, palmOne Press, and TechTV press? Swing by the Peachpit family section of the site and learn about all our partners and series.

- Got a great idea for a book? Check out our About section to find out how to submit a proposal. You could write our next best-seller!

You'll find all this and more at www.peachpit.com. Stop by and take a look today!

VOICES THAT MATTER

VISIT OUR WEB SITE

WWW.NEWRIDERS.COM

On our web site, you'll find information about our other books, authors, tables of contents, and book errata. You will also find information about book registration and how to purchase our books, both domestically and internationally.

EMAIL US

Contact us at: **nrfeedback@newriders.com**

- If you have comments or questions about this book
- To report errors that you have found in this book
- If you have a book proposal to submit or are interested in writing for New Riders
- If you are an expert in a computer topic or technology and are interested in being a technical editor who reviews manuscripts for technical accuracy

Contact us at: **nreducation@newriders.com**

- If you are an instructor from an educational institution who wants to preview New Riders books for classroom use. Email should include your name, title, school, department, address, phone number, office days/hours, text in use, and enrollment, along with your request for desk/examination copies and/or additional information.

Contact us at: **nrmedia@newriders.com**

- If you are a member of the media who is interested in reviewing copies of New Riders books. Send your name, mailing address, and email address, along with the name of the publication or web site you work for.

BULK PURCHASES/CORPORATE SALES

The publisher offers discounts on this book when ordered in quantity for bulk purchases and special sales. For sales within the U.S., please contact: Corporate and Government Sales (800) 382-3419 or **corpsales@pearsontechgroup.com**. Outside of the U.S., please contact: International Sales (317) 428-3341 or **international@pearsontechgroup.com**.

WRITE TO US

New Riders
1249 Eighth Street
Berkeley, California 94710

CALL US

Toll-free (800) 571-5840
If outside U.S. (317) 428-3000
Ask for New Riders

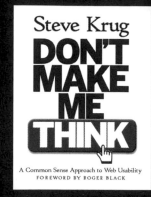

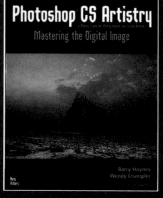